LIVING CHRISTIANLY

SYLVIA WALSH

Living
CHRISTIANLY

KIERKEGAARD'S DIALECTIC OF CHRISTIAN EXISTENCE

THE PENNSYLVANIA STATE UNIVERSITY PRESS
UNIVERSITY PARK, PENNSYLVANIA

Library of Congress Cataloging-in-Publication Data

Walsh, Sylvia, 1937–
Living Christianly : Kierkegaard's dialectic of Christian existence / Sylvia Walsh.
p. cm.
Includes bibliographical references and index.
ISBN 0-271-02764-9 (alk. paper)
1. Kierkegaard, Søren, 1813–1855.
2. Christianity—Philosophy.
I. Title.

B4378.C5W35   2006
230'.044'092—dc22
2004028712

*Dedicated in memory
of
Julia Watkin*

CONTENTS

ACKNOWLEDGMENTS ix

SIGLA xi

INTRODUCTION 1

1

The Consciousness of Sin / Faith and Forgiveness 17

2

The Possibility of Offense / Faith 51

3

Dying to the World and Self-Denial / New Life, Love, and
Hope in the Spirit 79

4

Suffering / Joy and Consolation 113

5

Christian Existence Within the Broader Dialectic of Christianity 149

NOTES 165

WORKS CONSULTED 183

INDEX 193

ACKNOWLEDGMENTS

Special thanks go to Dr. H. Douglas Lee, president of Stetson University, and Dr. Grady Ballenger, dean of the College of Arts and Sciences, for university support toward the publication of this volume.

Permission from the copyright holders to use materials from the following articles of mine is gratefully acknowledged: "Standing at the Crossroads: The Invitation of Christ to a Life of Suffering," in *International Kierkegaard Commentary: "Practice in Christianity,"* vol. 20, ed. Robert L. Perkins (Macon: Mercer University Press, 2004), 125–60; "Dying to the World and Self-Denial in Kierkegaard's Religious Thought," in *International Kierkegaard Commentary: "For Self-Examination" and "Judge for Yourself!"* vol. 21, ed. Robert L. Perkins (Macon: Mercer University Press, 2002), 169–97; "Echoes of Absurdity: The Offended Consciousness and the Absolute Paradox in Kierkegaard's *Philosophical Fragments,"* in *International Kierkegaard Commentary: "Philosophical Fragments" and "Johannes Climacus,"* vol. 7, ed. Robert L. Perkins (Macon: Mercer University Press, 1994), 33–46; "Kierkegaard's Philosophy of Love," in *The Nature and Pursuit of Love: The Philosophy of Irving Singer,* ed. David Goicoechea (Amherst, N.Y.: Prometheus Books, 1995), 167–79; and "Kierkegaard's Inverse Dialectic," *Kierkegaardiana* 11 (1980): 34–54.

Permission to quote from the following texts is also gratefully acknowledged: *Søren Kierkegaard's Journals and Papers,* 7 vols., ed. and trans. Howard V. Hong and Edna H. Hong (Bloomington: Indiana University Press, 1967–78); Søren Kierkegaard, *Practice in Christianity,* ed. and trans. Howard V. Hong and Edna H. Hong (Princeton: Princeton University Press, 1991); Søren Kierkegaard, *For Self-Examination* and *Judge for Yourself!* ed. and trans. Howard V. Hong and Edna H. Hong (Princeton: Princeton University Press, 1990).

Finally, I wish to thank my husband, Robert L. Perkins, for his constant encouragement, love, and support in the preparation of this volume for publication. Without him, I doubt that it would ever have come to fruition.

SIGLA

BA   *The Book on Adler.* Edited and translated by Howard V. Hong and Edna H. Hong. Princeton: Princeton University Press, 1995.

C   *The Crisis and a Crisis in the Life of an Actress.* See *Christian Discourses.*

CA   *The Concept of Anxiety.* Edited and translated by Reidar Thomte in collaboration with Albert B. Anderson. Princeton: Princeton University Press, 1980.

CD   *Christian Discourses* and *The Crisis and a Crisis in the Life of an Actress.* Edited and translated by Howard V. Hong and Edna H. Hong. Princeton: Princeton University Press, 1997.

CI   *The Concept of Irony with Continual Reference to Socrates.* Edited and translated by Howard V. Hong and Edna H. Hong. Princeton: Princeton University Press, 1989.

COR   *The Corsair Affair and Articles Related to the Writings.* Edited and translated by Howard V. Hong and Edna H. Hong. Princeton: Princeton University Press, 1982.

CUP   *Concluding Unscientific Postscript to "Philosophical Fragments."* 2 vols. Edited and translated by Howard V. Hong and Edna H. Hong. Princeton: Princeton University Press, 1992.

EO   *Either/Or.* 2 vols. Edited and translated by Howard V. Hong and Edna H. Hong. Princeton: Princeton University Press, 1987.

EUD   *Eighteen Upbuilding Discourses.* Edited and translated by Howard V. Hong and Edna H. Hong. Princeton: Princeton University Press, 1990.

FSE   *For Self-Examination* and *Judge for Yourself!* Edited and translated by Howard V. Hong and Edna H. Hong. Princeton: Princeton University Press, 1990.

FT   *Fear and Trembling* and *Repetition.* Edited and translated by Howard V. Hong and Edna H. Hong. Princeton: Princeton University Press, 1983.

JC   *Johannes Climacus.* See *Philosophical Fragments.*

JFY   *Judge for Yourself!* See *For Self-Examination.*

JP   *Søren Kierkegaard's Journals and Papers.* 7 vols. Edited and translated by Howard V. Hong and Edna H. Hong, assisted by Gregor Malantschuk. Bloomington: Indiana University Press, 1967–78.

PC   *Practice in Christianity.* Edited and translated by Howard V. Hong and Edna H. Hong. Princeton: Princeton University Press, 1991.

PF   *Philosophical Fragments* and *Johannes Climacus.* Edited and translated by Howard V. Hong and Edna H. Hong. Princeton: Princeton University Press, 1985.

PV   *The Point of View: On My Work as an Author; The Point of View for My Work as an Author; Armed Neutrality.* Edited and translated by Howard V. Hong and Edna H. Hong. Princeton: Princeton University Press, 1998.

R   *Repetition.* See *Fear and Trembling.*

SKP   *Søren Kierkegaards Papirer.* 16 vols. Second enlarged edition. Edited by Niels Thulstrup. Index (vols. 14–16) by Niels Jørgen Cappelørn. Copenhagen: Gyldendal, 1968–78.

SUD   *The Sickness unto Death.* Edited and translated by Howard V. Hong and Edna H. Hong. Princeton: Princeton University Press, 1980.

SV1   *Søren Kierkegaards Samlede Værker.* 14 vols. First edition. Edited by A. B. Drachmann, J. L. Heiberg, and H. O. Lange. Copenhagen: Gyldendalske Boghandels Forlag, 1901–6.

TDIO *Three Discourses on Imagined Occasions.* Edited and translated by Howard V. Hong and Edna H. Hong. Princeton: Princeton University Press, 1993.

TM   *"The Moment" and Late Writings.* Edited and translated by Howard V. Hong and Edna H. Hong. Princeton: Princeton University Press, 1998.

UDVS *Upbuilding Discourses in Various Spirits.* Edited and translated by Howard V. Hong and Edna H. Hong. Princeton: Princeton University Press, 1993.

WA   *Without Authority.* Edited and translated by Howard V. Hong and Edna H. Hong. Princeton: Princeton University Press, 1997.

WL   *Works of Love.* Edited and translated by Howard V. Hong and Edna H. Hong. Princeton: Princeton University Press, 1995.

INTRODUCTION

Kierkegaard has been interpreted for the most part on the basis of his writings up to and through *Concluding Unscientific Postscript* and in terms of his differentiation between the aesthetic, ethical, and religious spheres of existence. This study, by contrast, places its focus primarily on Kierkegaard's writings after the early pseudonymous literature and concentrates on his understanding of Christian existence as distinct from aesthetic and ethical-religious forms of life. It thus supports and amplifies the view advanced by others that Kierkegaard should be regarded primarily as a Christian thinker and writer.[1] Modern and postmodern emphases upon his early pseudonymous works have tended to obscure the importance of his later religious and specifically Christian writings and to project an image of Kierkegaard as being primarily a philosophical, aesthetic, or general ethical-religious author.[2] But the thrust of Kierkegaard's labors and the deepest significance and consequences of them go beyond his early authorship and its broader philosophical, literary, and religious significance. Kierkegaard's foremost concern as a writer was to delineate how to become a Christian and what the existential qualifications of Christianity are. Consequently, a more critical distinction concerning the nature and purpose of Kierkegaard's writings and a shift in focus of attention on them are in order.

To find the heart of Kierkegaard's thought and to see him as he most desired and deserves to be remembered, one must turn to the second period of his literary activity, to the remarkable quantity of writings produced during the years 1847–51.[3] In the course of these five years Kierkegaard completed nineteen works as well as a number of diverse articles and sketches for projects left undeveloped or unfinished. Most of these writings were published under Kierkegaard's own name as author or editor and thus undoubtedly represent his own views and/or existential positions. Others were withheld, for various reasons, and appeared in print only posthumously. The writings of this period generally fall into two categories: (1) those designed as "upbuilding," instructive or polemical works for the purpose of elucidating, wholly or in part, the distinguishing characteristics of Christian existence; and (2) those directly or indirectly providing or supporting Kierkegaard's own explanation of the nature and purpose of his authorship and his personal relation to it. The works comprising the first group include *Upbuilding Discourses in Various Spirits* (1847), *Works of Love* (1847), *Christian Discourses* (1848), *The Lily in the Field and the Bird of the Air: Three Devotional Discourses* (1849), *Two Ethical-Religious Essays* (1849), *Three Discourses at the Communion on Fridays* (1849), *The Sickness unto Death* (1849), *Practice in Christianity* (1850), *An Upbuilding Discourse* (1850), *For Self-Examination* (1851), *Judge for Yourself!* (1851), *The Changelessness of God* (1851), and *Two Discourses at the Communion on Fridays* (1851).[4] Those making up the second group are *The Crisis and a Crisis in the Life of an Actress* (1848),[5] *The Point of View for My Work as an Author* (1848), *On My Work as an Author* (1851), *Armed Neutrality* (1849), *"The Single Individual": Two "Notes" Concerning My Work as an Author* (partly drafted in 1846–49), and *An Open Letter* (1851).

Since Kierkegaard neither wrote nor published any major works after 1851, the writings from 1847 through 1851 form a clearly distinguishable unit. Consequently, Kierkegaard's final writings, consisting of some newspaper articles and a series of polemical pamphlets called *The Moment*, which were published in 1854–55, will be excluded from consideration here. These writings deserve careful consideration in their own right, especially since Kierkegaard's full-blown attack upon Christendom is articulated in them. With respect to this study, however, they are primarily important for determining whether Kierkegaard was consistent in the understanding of Christian existence developed in the second period of his authorship, that is, whether they represent the logical conclusion of certain tendencies in his thought or a significant departure from his central perspective. That is an important issue to determine but cannot be adequately addressed and decided until Kierkegaard's central position has been established.

Among the large body of writings from 1847 through 1851, it is the more substantive works of the first group that will be the primary focus of attention in this investigation. These works contain the most developed and most balanced statement of Kierkegaard's understanding of Christian existence and establish him as a Christian author whose ultimate purpose was to cast Christianity into reflection in such a way as to lead the reader to the decisive categories of Christian thought, and then out of reflection to the task of becoming a Christian and the simplicity of living Christianly. For as Kierkegaard saw it, "Christianly, one does not proceed from the simple in order then to become interesting, witty, profound, a poet, a philosopher, etc. No, it is just the opposite; *here* one begins and then becomes more and more simple, arrives at the simple. This, in 'Christendom,' is *Christianly* the movement of reflection; one does not reflect oneself into Christianity but reflects oneself out of something else and becomes more and more simple, a Christian" (*PV* 7).

Kierkegaard claimed that his entire authorship was designed to serve his function as a Christian author.[6] According to his explanation of the authorship, the aesthetic and philosophical writings from 1843 through 1846 were preparatory for the central task that lay ahead. The early aesthetic works were intended to establish communication with the public, to define where they were, and to begin there, talking about aesthetic existence in order to get to religious themes. Thus people would not immediately be put off by the author and his earnestness, and when they suddenly found themselves in the midst of the distinctive categories of Christianity, they would at least be compelled to take notice. Kierkegaard regarded *Concluding Unscientific Postscript* as the turning point in this endeavor inasmuch as it stated the problem of the whole authorship, which was how to become a Christian. One way had already been indicated by the aesthetic works—by movement away from the aesthetic. The *Postscript* posed the problem explicitly and described the other mode of movement—away from speculation. Having used the aesthetic literature to dispel the illusion that those who live under aesthetic categories are Christian and the philosophical discourse to show that one cannot reflect oneself into Christianity, Kierkegaard assumed that those who had benefited from the early works would be, "like the empty jar that is to be filled," in a condition of receptivity, ready for an introduction to the decisive Christian categories (*PV* 8). Toward the end of 1846, after the publication of the *Postscript*, he remarked in his journal: "The whole pseudonymous production and my life in relation to it was in the Greek mode. Now I must find the characteristic Christian life-form" (*JP* 5:5942).

This search informed the second period of Kierkegaard's authorship. As an artist transfers a vision to canvas, so Kierkegaard sought in casting Christianity into reflection to depict in language, the medium of reflection, the ideality of Christianity—its distinctive conceptual categories, its absolute character, and its ethical requirements—in terms of Christian existence. He maintained that Christianity is not a doctrine (although it has doctrines) but an "existence-communication," that its truth consists not in dogmatic propositions but in the realization of a spiritual qualification of existence exemplified and ultimately conferred by Jesus Christ. Thus Kierkegaard's literary task, as he saw it, was "to present in every way—dialectical, pathos-filled (in the various forms of pathos), psychological, modernized by continual reference to modern Christendom and the fallacies of scientific scholarship [*Videnskabens Vildfarelser*]—the ideal picture [*Billede*] of being a Christian" (*PV* 131, translation amended slightly). Kierkegaard's aim was not to construct or systematize the qualifications of Christian existence, but simply to describe (*at fremstille*) them. This was something which he, possessing a touch of the poet intensified by the passion of his own personal striving toward the ideal, was uniquely qualified to do.[7] Indeed, in *Armed Neutrality* he asserted of himself: "I know with uncommon clarity and definiteness what Christianity is, what can be required of the Christian, what it means to be a Christian. To an unusual degree I have, I think, the qualifications to be able to present this" (*PV* 138).

Kierkegaard's hope was to distinguish Christian existence from a background in which the qualities and levels of existence are generally confused and undifferentiated. He thought that most Christians of his day lived out their lives in categories entirely foreign to Christianity and that Christendom had

> made the finite and the infinite, the eternal and the temporal, the highest and the lowest, blend in such a way that it is impossible to say which is which, or the situation is an impenetrable ambiguity. It is not as difficult to chop a vista through the most tangled jungle as it is to make ideals shine into this ambiguity, where everything is murky, where we live protected against ideals, also by means of shoving a sensible point of view between them and us so that we understand one another in any striving for something higher—that brings some advantage—but would look upon an authentic higher striving that renounces advantages as being utterly ridiculous, the most ridiculous "exaggeration." (*JFY* 123)

In Kierkegaard's estimation, Christendom had allowed itself to conceive of that which is Christian as the superlative degree or the fulfillment of that which is purely finite, human, natural, and worldly. Kierkegaard thought this had produced "the greatest possible corruption of Christianity" (*SKP* X[4] A 460). In his view Christianity is indeed the highest, but only in the eternal sense of what is highest; it is not the highest degree of the temporal or earthly but its opposite.

If Christian existence is distinct from, even opposed to, other forms of existence and their conceptual categories, the possibility of anyone becoming committed to Christianity in a decisive and appropriate manner is not a viable option until those qualifications have been set forth clearly and precisely.[8] Kierkegaard claimed that knowing what Christianity *is* (knowing the truth objectively) is not synonymous with knowing what it means to *be* a Christian (knowing the truth subjectively or inwardly). Being a Christian requires the application of one's knowledge of Christianity to one's existence, *becoming* the truth rather than just *knowing* the truth. Thus Christianity is actually known and represented only by existing in it. But the ideal form or definition of the qualifications for this actuality can be cast in reflective form. In electing to describe this ideality, Kierkegaard sought to interest persons in learning what Christianity is in order that Christian existence might become an existential possibility for their lives. He hoped that all individuals would make it the standard and goal for their lives and assume the task of becoming a Christian.

Kierkegaard's purpose in depicting the existential qualifications of Christianity was therefore more evangelical than theological. Kierkegaard did not consider himself to be a theologian, although this does not prevent others from applying his depictions and clarifications of Christian existence and its distinctive categories to the theological enterprise. Certainly his thought is not without theological content and significance.[9] Nevertheless, Kierkegaard regarded his task as descriptive rather than constructive, systematic, or speculative in the traditional theological manner. In fact, he hoped to delineate the qualifications of Christian existence so adequately that no further objective reflection on them would be necessary. In a journal entry of 1850 he states:

> My activity with regard to the essentially Christian.
> It is to nail down the Christian qualifications in such a way that no doubt, no reflection, shall be able to get hold of them. It is like locking the door and throwing away the key; thus the Christian qualifications are made inaccessible to reflection. Only the choice remains: will you believe or will you not believe, but the chatter of reflection cannot get hold of it. (*JP* 1:522)

Kierkegaard's portrayal of Christian existence is given its distinctive character by the *dialectical* manner in which he conceives and correlates the qualifications for living Christianly. Indeed, Kierkegaard understands dialectic to be so intimately related to the Christian life that it is appropriate to speak of "the dialectic of Christian existence" and to regard the elucidation of this dialectic as the central achievement of his thought. In *Armed Neutrality* he states: "Every decisive qualification in being a Christian is according to a dialectic or is on the other side of a dialectic" (*PV* 130). Consequently he maintained that "only a dialectician can portray Christianity" (*JP* 1:761). In assuming the task of presenting the Christian ideals he aimed to "jack up the price" of becoming a Christian "by bringing a dialectic to bear" (*JP* 6:6464). He often chided Luther for being undialectical while claiming without modesty of himself: "My service through literature is and will always be that I have set forth the decisive qualifications of the whole existential arena with a dialectical acuteness and a primitivity not to be found in any other literature, as far as I know" (*JP* 5:5914; cf. 3:2467, 2474, 2521, 2541, 2556).

The term "dialectic," then, is not an alien epithet imposed on Kierkegaard's thought but indicates how he understood his own procedure and the qualifications he sought to describe. An awareness of his conception and use of dialectic is thus essential to an accurate assessment of his writings and the content of his thought.[10] But since "dialectic" is a philosophical term that is generally understood in terms of its Socratic, Platonic, and Hegelian conceptions, it requires some redefinition and explanation when used with reference to Kierkegaard's existential and religious thought.[11] Kierkegaard basically identifies and distinguishes between two kinds of dialectic: conceptual or quantitative dialectic and existential or qualitative dialectic (*JP* 1:759). Conceptual dialectic refers to the logical method of bringing opposite concepts together in the realm of thought and generally has as its goal an "objective knowledge containing a greater or lesser degree of probability."[12] In Kierkegaard's view the dialectical task is to sustain a dual or paradoxical perspective that emphasizes the opposition, duplicity, and tension between concepts rather than a synthesis and mediation of them as in Hegelian dialectic. Opposites, however, do not always contradict each other; sometimes they are complements, and as the reader will see in the following chapters, this is especially true of the dialectical concepts and categories of Christianity as Kierkegaard understands them.[13]

But for Kierkegaard dialectic is never simply a dialectic of concepts; rather, it involves the interpenetration of thought and existence. Existence itself is dialectical, but in a qualitative rather than a logical sense (*JP* 1:637). The perception of this second kind of dialectic, the dialectic of inwardness or the ethical in human existence, is one of Kierkegaard's most notable achievements. Existential dialectic comes to expression both in terms of the qualitative contradiction between one's present condition and one's ethical or ethical-religious *telos,* and in terms of the potential qualities, capacities, or conditions that may be realized in human existence. Even the aesthete in *Either/Or* expresses an awareness of existential dialectic: "Ordinarily, dialectic is thought to be rather abstract—one thinks almost solely of logical operations. But life will quickly teach a person that there are many kinds of dialectic, that almost every passion has its own" (*EO* 1:159). The terms of qualitative dialectic vary according to each individual's apprehension and appropriation of inwardness, and they change with the movement from one existence sphere to another. What is regarded as the highest or the *telos* at one level is negated as an absolute and relativized in the next.

This poses a problem of communication in ethical and ethical-religious teaching, for what it primarily seeks to communicate is a capability (*Kunnens Meddelelse*) rather than knowledge (*Videns Meddelelse*) (*JP* 1:651). Thus communication of the ethical and the ethical-religious must be indirect and dialectical in form and content. Kierkegaard paid close attention to the dialectic of communication appropriate to the qualitative dialectic of existence.[14] In turning to the depiction of the ideal Christian, however, he assumed a direct method of communication, although he considered that he was abandoning only the deceptiveness of indirect communication, not its basic principle that ethical capability cannot be communicated directly. Thus Kierkegaard preferred to characterize Christian communication as "direct-indirect" (*JP* 1:657). Initially it supplies an element of knowledge, but it still affirms that a direct relation to Christianity is not Christianity and that the essentially Christian is the rigor of existentially actualizing the qualifications of Christian existence (*JP* 1:518). Kierkegaard conceded that "a knowledge about Christianity must certainly be communicated in advance," but he maintained that "it is only a preliminary" (*JP* 1:653). As in indirect communication, "the communication is not in the direction of knowledge but of capability" (*JP* 1:657). Thus his direct description and clarification of the existential qualifications or determinants of Christianity must be viewed in this light as the provision of a preliminary knowledge of what Christianity is so that it may be inwardly appropriated by interested persons.

There is another feature of Kierkegaard's understanding and use of dialectic that is of central importance in his perception and presentation of Christianity and Christian existence. The existential dialectic appropriate to Christianity is informed by a peculiar dialectical method and character which Kierkegaard identifies as "inverse dialectic" (*omvendt Dialektik*) or "the dialectic of inversion" (*Omvendthedens Dialektik*).[15] Briefly stated, in inverse dialectic the positive is known and expressed through the negative, what appears to be negative may be indirectly positive (and vice versa), and the positive and the negative, Christianly understood, are always the inverse of the natural, human, worldly, and pagan understandings of these terms.[16]

Although not yet labeled as such, this dialectic of inversion first receives explicit formulation in *Concluding Unscientific Postscript*, where it is seen as applying not only to Christianity but also to the religious sphere in general. As Johannes Climacus, the pseudonymous author of that book, states the formula: "The sign of the religious sphere is . . . that the positive is distinguished by the negative" and "the religious continually uses the negative as the essential form" (*CUP* 1:432, 524; see also 240, 455, 532). Climacus goes on to point out that "the negative is not once and for all and then the positive, but the positive is continually in the negative, and the negative is the distinctive mark" (524). In the *Postscript* this inverted or positive-negative dialectic is conceived even more broadly as informing the very structure of human existence. Climacus points out that in relation to truth the existing subjective thinker, who is a synthesis of the temporal and the eternal, is just as negative as he or she is positive, since certainty can be had only in the infinite or eternal, which is illusively or deceptively present in human existence; that is, it is never fully realized and thus requires continuous striving through the increase and deepening of subjectivity or inwardness in the human subject (80–85). Inwardness in turn is precisely the medium through which the subjective thinker becomes conscious of the negativity or illusiveness of the infinite or eternal. The more subjective one becomes, the more one becomes aware of one's distance from the eternal.

As Climacus sees it, this negative relation to the eternal is intensified in Religiousness A or immanent religiosity through the expression of existential pathos in the forms of resignation, suffering, and the consciousness of guilt, and in Religiousness B or Christianity through the consciousness of sin and the possibility of offense.[17] At the same time, however, these negative expressions of religious pathos are indirect signs of a positive relation to the eternal or God. Climacus understands Christianity to consist essentially in inwardness or subjectivity, but it is not just any and every type of inwardness or pathos.[18] In his view, Christian subjectivity is conditioned in such a way that it is made specifically different from all other forms of inwardness by the introduction of dialectical factors that serve to intensify its pathos to the highest pitch. These include, first of all, a negation of the individual's essential continuity with the eternal in the counter-recognition that subjectivity is untruth or in a state of sin,[19] and second, an affirmation of the com-

8

ing into existence of the absolute paradox or the eternal in time, in relation to which the individual lays hold of the truth in existence through faith defined as "this absurdity, held fast in the passion of inwardness" (210).

In the religious writings and journals of the second period of his authorship, Kierkegaard associates the dialectic of inversion even more specifically with Christianity and regards it as the form by which every qualification of Christian existence should be understood and distinguished even though the basic formula applies to the ethical-religious sphere as well. In his journals Kierkegaard states that "the formula for essential Christianity is: the essentially Christian is always the positive which is recognizable by the negative," and he points out that "the apostle always speaks out of this inverted dialectic" (JP 4:4680; see also 4:4682, 4696). It is in this period that Kierkegaard begins to refer to this positive-negative dialectic as "inverse dialectic," and he views it as applying to the Christian's relation to God as well as to the world. The Christian's inverted relation to God is expressed in various ways. For example, progress toward the eternal is indicated by retrogression (JP 1:77; 2:1425). The heightening of the God-relation is achieved by lowering oneself and becoming as nothing before God. One draws closer to God as one acquires a sense of one's distance from the divine. In a communion discourse from 1848 Kierkegaard states that "God and the human being resemble each other only inversely. You do not reach the possibility of comparison by the ladder of direct likeness: great, greater, greatest; it is possible only inversely. Neither does a human being come closer and closer to God by lifting up his head higher and higher, but inversely by casting himself down ever more deeply in worship" (CD 292). In other discourses Kierkegaard uses the lilies of the field and the birds of the air and the parable of the Pharisee and the tax collector to illustrate the Christian's inverted relation to God. The lilies and the birds teach one to keep silent in order to become nothing before God, for in becoming silent and making oneself nothing one begins to seek first the kingdom of God: "Thus in a certain sense one devoutly comes backward to the beginning. The beginning is not that with which one begins but that to which one comes, and one comes to it backward" (WA 11). Similarly, the tax collector who stood by himself far off from the altar feeling unworthy before God was nearer to the divine than the Pharisee, who also stood alone, but only presumptuously to exalt what he imagined to be his own greater righteousness (WA 127–34; see also JP 4:3933).

While Christians stand in an indirectly positive relation to God through negative qualifications, their relation to the world is directly negative because Christianity is diametrically opposed to the world's presuppositions, values, and goals. In *Judge for Yourself!* Kierkegaard maintains that "the world and Christianity have completely opposite conceptions. . . . The difference between secularity and Christianity is not that the one has one view and the other another—no, the difference is always that they have the very opposite views, that what the one calls good the other calls evil, what the one calls love the other calls selfishness, what the one calls piety the other calls impiety, what the one calls being drunk the other calls being sober" (*JFY* 96). The Christian striver needs, therefore, to be "torn out of his conceptual setting and his world of ideas" in order to acquire the Christian point of view (*JP* 2:1409). The world's procedure is to understand everything in a direct manner, while Christianity views everything inversely and indirectly. In Christianity the positive is not immediately, simply, or directly what it is but appears in the first instance as its own opposite or has negative consequences.

The qualifications for living Christianly are actualized in existence through an inverted dialectical process Kierkegaard calls "reduplication" (*Reduplikation*). In general, reduplication means to exist in what one thinks, to express the content of one's understanding in one's actions in order to realize a fusion of thought and being in existence, not merely conceptually or abstractly but actually. Kierkegaard defines it this way in another passage from his journals: "When Christianity (precisely because it is not a doctrine) does not reduplicate itself in the one who presents it, he does not present Christianity; for Christianity is an existential-communication and can only be presented—by existing. Basically to exist therein [*at existere deri*], to express it in one's existence etc.—this is what it means to reduplicate" (*JP* 1:484). But Christian reduplication as Kierkegaard understands it refers more specifically to the dialectical manner in which the actualization of the Christian qualifications takes place in Christian striving. In his journals Kierkegaard says that

> every striving which does not apply one-forth, one-third, two-thirds, etc. of its power to systematically *working against* itself is essentially secular striving, in any case unconditionally not a *reforming* effort. Reduplication means to work against oneself while working; it is like the pressure on the plow-handles, which determines the depth of the furrow—whereas working which does not work against itself is merely a superficial smoothing over. . . . Again the difference between the direct and the inverted, which is the dia-

lectical. Working or striving directly is to work and strive. The inverted method is this: while working also to work against oneself. (*JP* 6:6593, translation amended slightly; see also 3:3661)

This passage, written in 1850, is strikingly similar to a note in *On My Work as an Author* (written in 1849 and published in 1851), where Kierkegaard writes with respect to the maieutical (as opposed to direct) movement of his authorship:

> This again is the dialectical movement . . . or it is the dialectical method: in *working* also to *work against oneself,* which is reduplication and the heterogeneity of all true godly endeavor to secular endeavor. To endeavor or to work *directly* is to work or to endeavor directly in immediate connection with a factually given state of things. The dialectical method is the *reverse:* in working also to work against oneself, a redoubling [*Fordoblelse*], which is "the earnestness," like the pressure on the plow that determines the depth of the furrow, whereas the direct endeavor is a glossing-over, which is finished more rapidly and also is much, much more rewarding— that is, it is worldliness and homogeneity. (*PV* 9n)[20]

In *For Self-Examination* Kierkegaard specifically identifies this inverted dialectical movement as the way of Christ, who "knows from the very beginning that his work is to work against himself" and whose narrow way is made even more difficult and absurd for his followers inasmuch as "when you must use your powers to work against yourself, then it seems infinitely too little to say that the way is narrow—it is, instead, impassable, blocked, impossible, insane! And yet it is this way of which it holds true that Christ is the way" (*FSE* 61).

Kierkegaard understands reduplication, therefore, as an inverted dialectical movement that is appropriate to existence, especially Christian existence. It is a dialectic that informs the Christian striver's action as well as thought, and it refers not only to the process of appropriating in one's finite, temporal, or natural life the inverted Christian concepts and existential qualifications but also indicates *how* this is to be done—not directly but indirectly and inversely. Humanly understood, Christian striving seems to produce the opposite of the effect or condition one expects or strives for, but Christianly understood, to work against oneself means to work against one's true condition or goal only in the sense that one goes about attaining and expressing it in an opposite manner from what the world would recommend or do. A corollary of this inverse procedure is that Christian strivers bring upon themselves opposition from the world as they succeed in actualizing the Christian qualifications in this indirect and inverted manner.

As inverse dialectic applies in the differentiation of Christian concepts and corresponding actions from their merely human, natural, or worldly correlates, it may be described as being *exclusive* in character, although Kierkegaard does not regard this exclusivity as signifying an unqualified negative relation of Christianity to the world. In spite of the fact that the Christian concepts and existential qualifications are diametrically opposed to merely human, natural, and worldly conceptions and incur opposition from the world as a result, what Christianity seeks, he claims, is to relativize, transform, and inform these views and actions, not simply set itself against them or maintain an attitude of indifference toward the world.

Initially, however, it would appear that Kierkegaard intended in his later religious writings to suggest a disjunction between the Christian concepts and method of reduplication and those concepts and methods which obtain in other existence-spheres, even the ethical-religious. He does not discuss this matter directly, and his failure to do so causes a certain amount of ambiguity concerning how he regards the ethical-religious once he begins to concentrate entirely on Christian existence. He tends to use the terms "natural," "immediate," "human," "pagan," "earthly," "temporal," and "worldly" almost interchangeably, implying that their common frame of reference is of greater relevance to his thought than any particular nuances in their meanings. Kierkegaard makes it quite clear that Christianity is opposed to aesthetic immediacy, and it is basically this aspect of existence toward which the exclusive dialectical relation is directed.[21] But in *Concluding Unscientific Postscript* the ethical-religious is portrayed as also being opposed to aesthetic immediacy and as beginning with a dying away from that stage of existence. In this respect, therefore, the ethical-religious stands in continuity with Christianity. Likewise, in "An Occasional Discourse" (more popularly known as "Purity of Heart") the ethical individual is characterized as one who recognizes the opposition between the temporal and the eternal and whose vision "is formed to see everything inverted," in accordance with "eternity's true thought—that everything in life appears inverted [omvendt]" (UDVS 135; translation amended slightly).

Inverse dialectic and opposition to aesthetic immediacy thus clearly apply in the broader dimension of the ethical and ethical-religious as well as in Christianity. But insofar as the ethical-religious does not envision an absolute discontinuity with and heterogeneity to the eternal, it remains along with aesthetic immediacy within the bounds of immanence or within the limits of a purely human conception of what is possible and true. The ethical-religious represents the highest potentiality of the purely human, and in comparison with the lower, entirely direct understanding of the immediate person it signifies the beginning of, and considerable growth in, the rejection of the unqualified immediate, natural, worldly values and goals that most people embrace in life. Thus, ethical-religious individuals feel themselves to be strangers in the world, although in Kierkegaard's view they may not exhibit any external sign of their opposition to the values and goals of the society in which they live. But such persons cannot succeed in transcending purely human expectation and understanding in order to embrace the kind and extent of inversion and contradiction that Christianity introduces into the world and requires of the Christian. Thus the inverted dialectic that applies in Christianity serves to distinguish it from the ethical-religious as well as from aesthetic immediacy and to provide the form by which this distinctiveness can be expressed.

In contrast to the exclusive dialectic that informs the Christian striver's relation to the world, the inverse dialectic operative in his or her relation to Christianity is *complementary* in character. Here the negative stands in a dialectical relation to the eternal or the positive, but both the negative and the positive are essential to the definition of a Christian. The negative qualifications must come to expression in Christian existence, since the positive is indirectly present in or known through the negative. Thus Kierkegaard defines and depicts Christian existence on two levels. *Ideally* it is conceived in terms of its positive characteristics: "The essentially Christian is always the positive" (*JP* 4:4680). But *in existence* these are always coupled with, and are only indirectly recognizable through, negative qualifications, so that existentially the essentially Christian must be defined to include the negative either as a simultaneous complement of the positive or as a temporal precondition for it. The negative qualifications are also presented as *ideal* requirements inasmuch as they define Christian existence in the strictest sense or in its highest expression in existence. Since Kierkegaard understands human existence as a process of becoming, the existing Christian is never a Christian in a directly positive or ideal sense but is always in the process of striving toward that ideal. Properly speaking, that person should always be referred to as a Christian *striver*.

There are essentially four basic and decisive negative qualifications of Christian existence that must be viewed and correlated in the dialectical manner just described. These are *the consciousness of sin, the possibility of offense, dying to the world or self-denial,* and *suffering.* Through these negative qualifications Christian strivers stand related to or bring to expression in their existence the positive qualifications of Christianity: *faith, forgiveness, new life, love, hope, joy,* and *consolation.* These qualifications constitute the complementary dialectical determinants of Christian existence to which Kierkegaard devoted most of his attention in the second period of his authorship. His task, as he conceived it, was to bring the negative qualifications, which he believed had been virtually eliminated in Christendom, once again into view, to provide them with conceptual clarity, and to show their essential relation to, and necessity in, securing a correct understanding and expression of the positive qualifications of Christian existence.

In the chapters that follow, these complementary dialectical qualifications for living Christianly will be placed in bold relief, and the ways in which they are correlated and informed by inverse dialectic will be shown in detail. The negative factors of the consciousness of sin and the possibility of offense will be correlated in separate chapters with the positive qualifications of faith and forgiveness. Dying to the world and self-denial will be shown in their inverted dialectical relation to the experience of new life, love, and hope in the Spirit. And suffering, the capstone of living Christianly as Kierkegaard understood it, will be delineated in its essential correlation to joy and consolation. Finally, Kierkegaard's portrayal of Christian existence will be situated within the broader complementary dialectical framework of Christianity as incorporating both gospel and law, grace and works, mildness and rigor, through a relation to Christ in his dual role as the Christian striver's redeemer and prototype for living Christianly.

There are of course other specific qualities, actions, and characteristics of Christian existence in addition to these basic qualifications. As Kierkegaard saw it, living Christianly cannot be tightly systematized and minutely pinned down, and even in relation to the basic qualifications there is no direct or unequivocal concrete expression of them that obtains in every situation in life or that unconditionally and concretely identifies them and their actualization in existence. It is precisely this ambiguity that makes living Christianly so difficult to define and to bear, for after all possible clarification has been applied to the basic qualifications, Christian strivers are still left with the responsibility—which they must exercise with a large dose of uncertainty, humility, fear, and trembling—of concretely reduplicating these qualifications in their lives. The inverse understanding of the qualifications and the inverse method of reduplicating them that Kierkegaard presents in his writings can serve as guides in this task, but they can never be a complete systematic formulation of what it means to be a Christian or to strive to become such. As noted earlier, Kierkegaard does not proceed in this way or with such a goal, although certain of his writings concentrate heavily on the elucidation of particular qualifications. But they are always treated in an unsystematic fashion and in an existential context in which the problem of becoming a Christian, rather than an objective concern about what Christianity is, informs his reflection on them.

Consequently, even the systematic way in which the basic qualifications are identified, correlated, and considered in the following chapters is to a degree arbitrary and a departure from Kierkegaard's own practice. For in the procedure to be followed, Kierkegaard's understanding of these qualifications will be abstracted to some degree from the contexts in which they are discussed in his writings and journals in order to encapsulate the conceptual clarifications and dialectical relations he proposes. To the extent that this procedure can contribute to the elucidation of Kierkegaard's achievements in this regard, it nevertheless seems justified for academic purposes, especially if Kierkegaard's continual reminders to his readers are heeded—that the correct objective understanding of Christianity does not make one a Christian and that once one properly understands what Christianity is, existentially the most essential and most difficult task still lies ahead in the actualization of these qualifications in one's own life.

No attempt will be made in this study to assess Kierkegaard's personal success or failure in reduplicating the qualifications of Christian existence in his own life or to interpret his understanding of this life-form by reference to his own existential situation. While Kierkegaard's understanding is undoubtedly conditioned by his relation to Christianity as well as by other experiences and individuals in his life, his description of Christian existence and the inverted dialectic that informs it is not merely the projection of, or a reaction to, his psychological state of being, social environment and encounters, and personal relationships. Rather, it a deeply reflected and original account that has an objective foundation in both scripture and Christian tradition. It is quite possible, therefore, to discuss Kierkegaard's understanding of Christian existence generally apart from his personal relation to it. Indeed, such a procedure is even necessary in order to permit his depiction to stand on its own for assessment of its adequacy as a description of Christianity and Christian existence and for reduplicating it in one's own life. But this does not mean that Kierkegaard was personally unrelated to the Christian ideals which he strove to depict. On the contrary, from his point of view it is essential that any person who undertakes to depict the qualifications for living Christianly stand related to this ideality as one engaged in striving to fulfill it; otherwise the whole project of "poet-communication," as he characterized his presentation of the Christian ideals, would become an intellectual enterprise and a failure (*JP* 6:6528).

Finally, no attempt will be made here to recast Kierkegaard's language into less patriarchal terms. Kierkegaard was a man of his time with respect to linguistic form and the use of sexual stereotypes. Thus it would seem artificial and untrue to present his views in linguistic terms uncommon to his age and his own practice, however inadequate, exclusive, or negative in connotation they may be. But Kierkegaard's language is not always as androcentric as his translators sometimes make him out to be. Where that is the case, I have taken the liberty to amend the standard translations of passages quoted in this study in order to render Kierkegaard's meaning and intent more accurately. In regard to discussion of his thought and its general application, however, gender inclusiveness or neutrality is entirely appropriate and will be maintained throughout the study. Although one can find ambivalent and negative attitudes toward women expressed throughout Kierkegaard's writings (some of which belong to the spokespersons for particular life-views rather than to Kierkegaard himself), the primary emphasis in his authorship is upon our common humanity and spiritual equality.[22]

1

THE CONSCIOUSNESS OF SIN / FAITH AND FORGIVENESS

The central dialectical relationship in Christian existence is between sin and faith, or more precisely, between the consciousness of sin and the forgiveness of sin in faith. This relationship constitutes a major topic of concern in the writings of the second period of Kierkegaard's authorship. Johannes Climacus, the pseudonymous author of the *Concluding Unscientific Postscript,* had already determined that sin is the "crucial point of departure" and "crucial expression" for religious existence and that it "is not a factor within something else, within another order of things, but is itself the beginning of the religious order of things" (*CUP* 1:267–68). In the *Postscript* sin is viewed as signifying an absolute breach of subjectivity with the eternal that posits a radical separation between human beings and God and results in the loss of their essential self-identity in relation to the divine. At the same time, however, sin functions dialectically in an inverse manner as the decisive expression *for* the religious mode of existence inasmuch as the consciousness of this condition serves as the basis for an individual's *relation to* God or the eternal. That is, in the consciousness of sin one is consciously related to the eternal, but one's relation to it is informed by a sense of *separation from* the eternal rather than by a positive continuity and unity with it. The consciousness of sin is at once a *direct* recognition of one's radical breach with, and qualitative difference from, the eternal and an *indirect* expression of faith or a passionate commitment to the eternal in time as the source of one's eternal happiness. Sin, the consciousness of sin, and faith are considered in the *Postscript* primarily in their functions as boundary categories that set Christian subjectivity off from other forms of subjectivity and provide the crucial expression of religious or Christian existence.[1] To this extent, then, Kierkegaard had already begun the conceptual clarification of these qualifications in his earlier pseudonymous literature. Over against the objectifying tendencies of the church, dogmatic theology, and speculative philosophy, Johannes Climacus makes the claim that Christianity is inwardness and then proceeds to show how Christian subjectivity is made qualitatively distinctive by these factors and must not be confused with or understood as the direct intensification of other forms of inwardness.

In the literature of the second period of his authorship, Kierkegaard approaches the category of sin, the consciousness of sin, and the forgiveness of sin maieutically and existentially. The problem of sin is initially referred to obliquely in the context of discussing other Christian qualifications and is explicitly taken up along with its dialectical correlates at a time when they were beginning to become crucial in his own life. A few days after completing the manuscript of *Works of Love* (1847), Kierkegaard made the following report in his journals: "From now on the thrust should be into the specifically Christian. . . . 'The forgiveness of sins' must be emphasized. Everything should concentrate on that point; it must be established again as a paradox before anything can be done. Christianity these days has become nonsense; that is why one is obliged to take on the double task of first of all making the matter beneficially difficult" (*JP* 5:6037). In subsequent journal entries during this period he exhibits an increasing preoccupation with the consciousness of sin, the atonement, and the forgiveness of sin.[2] But in the published literature the approach to the category of sin comes slowly and covertly through carefully planned steps of progression. Part 2 of *Christian Discourses* (1848) emphasizes the suffering that comes with being a Christian, but it also begins to hint at the fundamental problem of sin. At the end of every discourse except the first, Kierkegaard reiterates the phrase: "Only sin is a human being's corruption."[3] And in his journals he explains that

> these discourses are presented in such a way as to be continually tangential to the consciousness of sin and the suffering of sin—sin etc. are another matter: these discourses come to the subject of sin. Because the consolation lyrically rises as high as possible over all earthly need and misery, even the heaviest, the horror of sin is constantly banished. Thus another theme is cunningly concealed in these discourses: sin is a human being's corruption.
>
> In the ordinary sermon this is precisely the confusion: need and adversity are preached together—with sin.
>
> Thus the category for these discourses is different from "The Gospel of Sufferings," which leaves the suffering indefinite. Here the distinction is made: innocent suffering—in order to approach sin. (*JP* 5:6101, translation amended slightly)

As Kierkegaard progressed in the later literature and journals to a more specific determination of the categories of sin, the consciousness of sin, faith, and the relation of these factors to forgiveness, he focused primarily on conceptual confusions regarding the qualifications themselves as well as misunderstandings that obscure their proper position as the fundamental concern of the Christian gospel. Kierkegaard believed that people were ignorant of what sin is, or at most had only a confused, partial, and superficial notion of it. This condition was just as characteristic of the clergy and theologians of his day as it was of the common person. In fact, Kierkegaard blamed the former for fostering confusion in the latter. He attributed the clergy's misunderstanding and misrepresentation of sin in large part to the fact that it had confused the Christian conception of sin with pagan and speculative notions that were actually incommensurable with the Christian viewpoint on this category. What was requisite, therefore, was a clarification of the Christian understanding of sin in distinction from these other views and a reconstitution of people's understanding in regard to this Christian doctrine.

Part of this task of clarification consisted in elucidating the dialectical relation of sin to faith. Whereas the pagan understanding contrasted sin to virtue, Kierkegaard conceived sin to be the opposite of faith: "Very often . . . it is overlooked that the opposite of sin is by no means virtue. . . . No, *the opposite of sin is faith*. . . . And this is one of the most decisive definitions for all Christianity—that the opposite of sin is not virtue but faith" (*SUD* 82).[4] But sin may also figure in an indirect way as a negative factor *in* faith. Directly understood, sin leads a person away from faith, but indirectly it may function as a factor in the definition of and movement toward faith. Sin is thus both the dialectical counterpart and correlate of faith. The same may be said of a person's consciousness of sin. It too is dialectical in nature, for the consciousness of sin can precipitate the continuation and intensification of sin as well as figure importantly in its forgiveness and annihilation. In the latter instance, the consciousness of sin functions as an indirectly positive aid in the movement toward faith. It is in this capacity that it emerges as the decisive negative qualification of Christian existence and the inverse sign of a positive relation to God and Christ.

Kierkegaard couples with this clarification of sin and the consciousness of sin the correction of another and even more fundamental confusion concerning the main purpose and promise of the gospel. As indicated in the quotation from *Christian Discourses*, part of the problem of human beings is that they do not know wherein their true sickness, real misfortune, and greatest danger in life lies. They generally associate these situations with earthly afflictions, whereas the true Christian has come to recognize and fear sin as a far greater danger, in comparison to which the other misfortunes of finite existence count as nothing. Christianly understood, only sin is "the sickness unto death." Kierkegaard insists that the gospel is primarily directed toward the alleviation of this sickness, not external afflictions in life, and that the promise of Christianity is the forgiveness of sin, not the restoration of good fortune. But the common conception and application of Christianity are just the opposite. People turn to Christianity looking for solace and a reversal of their temporal misfortunes; Christian preaching presents the gospel to them precisely in this vein and reinforces their misconceptions; and the notion of the forgiveness of sin is superficially incorporated into this inverted framework and interpreted to include not only forgiveness but the memory of forgiveness. The result is that forgiveness too is misunderstood and taken in vain.

There are, then, basically three concerns that are addressed in the later literature relating to the dialectic of sin and faith and the consciousness of sin and forgiveness: (1) to provide a conceptual clarification of the Christian understanding of sin; (2) to indicate the indirectly positive role of the consciousness of sin in Christian existence; and (3) to clarify the role of the gospel in relation to the alleviation of sin and suffering.

The Definition of Sin

Clarification of the Christian understanding of sin is primarily undertaken in *The Sickness unto Death*. With the publication in 1849 of this important book under a new pseudonym, Anti-Climacus, with Kierkegaard's own name as editor, the authorship assumed a different character. This new pseudonym represented the Christian existential position to which Kierkegaard, no less than his readers, was related as a striver. Through the pseudonym Kierkegaard could depict the Christian qualifications according to the most ideal standard, although he regarded it as nevertheless essential that he be related to this ideality as one engaged in striving to fulfill it. In his view, "it is a terrible thing for the requirements of the ideal to be presented by persons who never give a thought to whether their lives express it or not" (*JP* 6:6528; translation amended slightly). The fact that "the speaker and author himself defines himself as striving in relation to what is being communicated" is precisely what, in Kierkegaard's estimation, distinguishes the religious poet from a typical poet and makes his communication authentic even though he does not fully embody the ideal described in it (*JP* 6:6528).

According to its subtitle, *The Sickness unto Death* is "A Christian Psychological Exposition for Upbuilding and Awakening" (*SUD* iii). These two terms project a didactic and authoritative connotation that Kierkegaard was reluctant to attach to the writings he claimed as his own. The third part of *Christian Discourses*, "Thoughts That Wound from Behind," had also been intended "for upbuilding" (*til Opbyggelse*), but when it came to assuming the authority to educate people in the strictest Christian categories, Kierkegaard demurred: "The upbuilding is mine, not the esthetic, not [the pseudonymous works] for upbuilding either, and even less those for awakening" (*JP* 6:6461). Anti-Climacus, therefore, could presume to do what Kierkegaard could not, which was to instruct people in the Christian understanding of sin and the consciousness of sin and to awaken them to an understanding of their essential nature as spirit or a self in relation to God and Christ.

Accordingly, in the first part of *The Sickness unto Death,* Anti-Climacus defines a human being as spirit or a self, identifies despair as the condition that results from a person's unwillingness to become a self, points out the universality of this "sickness," and analyzes the basic forms of despair (despair in weakness and despair in defiance) that reveal a misrelation to oneself as a self and to God or the eternal as the transcendent power that constitutes the self. His analysis of the forms of despair is carried out in terms of the constituents that serve as the basis for despair (finitude and infinitude, possibility and necessity) and in terms of the unconscious and conscious levels of despair that denote its intensification.[5] Anti-Climacus traces the forms of despair in order to display the heightening in conscious despair of three factors: (1) a true conception (*Forestilling*)[6] of what despair is; (2) the individual's consciousness of his or her own condition as despair; and (3) the consciousness of oneself as a self. Both *conceptual clarity* and *existential clarity* about oneself accrue in conscious despair and are the conditions requisite for the intensification of despair. The despair of the ethically conscious person culminates in a substantial realization of these conditions. But the determination of whether a person can have complete self-clarity and understanding and still remain in despair or whether knowledge and self-knowledge are in themselves sufficient to "wrench a person out of despair" is deferred to the second part. There "the whole deliberation . . . dialectically take[s] a new direction" and is viewed in a different way, from a Christian standpoint, in which despair is identified as sin (*SUD* 79).

In part 2, which is the section of the book most relevant to the present study, Anti-Climacus moves progressively in the delineation of a specifically Christian understanding of sin, which may be outlined in the following series of propositions:

1. *Sin is despair.* This statement does not mean that the foregoing stages of despair are simply redesignated as sin. Like subjectivity, sin is not any and every form of pathos but signifies a new level of despair. The despair that properly may be called sin presupposes, and represents a further intensification of, the factors that make up the two basic forms of conscious despair: despair in weakness and despair in defiance. Thus sin is the intensification of despair, either in the form of an intensification of weakness through not willing to be oneself, or an intensification of defiance in despairingly willing to be oneself. The lower forms of despair do not, in a strict sense, constitute sin, although ultimately all despair, when judged from the perspective of the higher viewpoint, may be seen as sin, since the misrelation in the self to whatever degree and in whatever respect is recognized as being grounded in a prior misrelation to God.

2. *Sin is despair before God.* The fact that sin is a form of despair establishes an element of continuity with the foregoing levels of despair and further heightens the factors that characterize conscious despair. Despair becomes even more intense, the individual in despair has a truer conception of what despair is, and he or she acquires a greater consciousness of having a self over and about which to despair. But the pathos of sin is not the result of a *direct* intensification of weakness or defiance, nor is the continuity that is preserved through intensification a direct continuity. This is entirely consistent with how Christian subjectivity is viewed in the *Postscript.* But in *The Sickness unto Death* the consciousness of the individual in sin is conditioned by the fact that, unlike the individual in the lower stages of despair, he or she exists "before God." It is specifically this factor that makes "qualified despair" or intensified despair synonymous with sin and which, in Anti-Climacus's opinion, radically distinguishes the sinner from other persons in despair. Sin is not merely despair or intensified despair, but is more closely defined as despair *before God.*

For Luther, to be "before God" or *coram Deo* meant in a general sense to be in the sight or presence of God in such a way that God becomes present to and exists for, or stands in relationship to, an individual. But according to the Luther scholar, Gerhard Ebeling, "the most important element in the situation that is implied by the preposition *coram* is not the way in which someone else is present before me, in my sight, but the way that I myself am before someone else and exist in the sight of someone else, so that my existential life is affected."[7] In like manner, for Anti-Climacus "before God" means to have a conception (*Forestilling*) of God that functions existentially as the criterion and goal of one's selfhood. The "criterion" of a person is that in the face of which one is a self or is that which determines in a qualitative sense what one's self essentially is or should be (*SUD* 79–80). Even when one is not that which is qualitatively one's criterion and goal, it still functions as one's criterion, manifesting "judgingly" that one is not what one should be (cf. 80 and *SVI* 11:192).

At the lower levels of despair the criterion of selfhood is the human itself, or the human being conceived in terms of its highest, humanly imaginable potentiality. By contrast, the person who has God for a criterion seeks to become not merely a human self, or the highest in terms of a merely human conception of the self, but a "theological self," that is, a human self who is like God or who exists before God with the quality of being or reality that God defines for a human being rather than that which one projects for oneself (*SUD* 79). This has the radical effect of altering the very conception of the self. For now the self acquires "a new quality and qualification," an infinite reality, that distinguishes it from the merely human conception of the self (79). Although the merely human conception of the self also includes the concept of infinity, it is envisioned according to a merely human criterion and in despair becomes fantastic, lacking any finite or limiting qualifications. It is only when "a self as this specific single individual is conscious of existing before God" that it becomes an infinite self (80). The consciousness or conception of oneself as a self or spirit is infinitely intensified by this transcendent (though not external) criterion, projecting for oneself a reality "so extraordinary that [one] cannot grasp the thought" (83).

Correspondingly, the despair that results in failing or refusing to achieve the quality of selfhood commensurate with the quality of divinity is infinitely intensified as well. Now despair is seen as being due not only to a misrelation to oneself but also to a misrelation to God, or more precisely, the misrelation to oneself is now seen to lie in and be due to a misrelation to God. Despair is sin because of a person's misrelation to God. The situation of the sinner is prodigiously dialectical in an inverse manner, for the conception of God functions for the individual in both a positive and a negative capacity. The introduction of God as the criterion of selfhood brings an awareness of and increase in one's *distance* from being a self at the same time that it infinitely qualifies and increases the conception and awareness of oneself as a self. In like manner, the addition of a conception of God brings one into relation to God and projects as one's goal the kind of self that can exist directly in the sight of God. But the effect of this change is to bring about a confirmation of one's distance from *God* as well as from selfhood. Consequently, the insight to be gained in relation to God is not of one's relative likeness to God but inversely of one's absolute *unlikeness* to the divine. Sin posits an infinite qualitative difference between the human being and God.

3. *Sin is conscious and willful despair before God.* The Christian definition of sin is formally completed with the addition of the qualification that sin, properly speaking, includes a knowledge of sin and is thus the expression of a person's willful disobedience of God. But the knowledge of sin is not something human beings can acquire by themselves. Strictly speaking, "sin is—after being taught by a revelation from God what sin is—before God in despair not to will to be oneself or in despair to will to be oneself" (96). The previous partial definitions have emphasized that sin includes a consciousness of despair and the true nature of despair, a consciousness of oneself as a self and its infinite potentiality, and a conception of God that transforms and further qualifies this consciousness. But sin in the strictest sense also includes the consciousness of what sin is. The effect of this qualification is threefold: (1) it confirms the act of despair before God to be an act of conscious disobedience; (2) it specifically correlates the definition of sin to the individual who has acquired a conception of God as his or her criterion and goal rather than to the pagan or natural human being; and (3) it establishes that sin lies in the *will* rather than the *intellect,* that is, in the fact that a person *will not* understand and do the good rather than, as Socrates thought, that he or she does not *know* what is good. Anti-Climacus charges that Socrates never really arrives at the category of sin, "which certainly is dubious for a definition of sin," inasmuch as his definition lacks any recognition of the power of the will in governing the transition from understanding to action (89–90, 93). A person may be conscious of right and wrong and still neither do the right nor eschew the wrong. However, Christianity views humanity as being so deeply in sin that people do not know what sin is or the extent of their condition as sin. In a certain sense, then, sin *is* ignorance—ignorance of what sin is. Christianity holds that the influence of the will is far more pervasive than is immediately evident and that the will was instrumental in a much earlier obscuring of human intelligence. Thus ignorance is an initial but not the original or primary condition with which Christianity must deal by means of a revelation before it gets to the real cause and determinant of sin.

4. *Sin is a position.* This statement is sometimes construed as referring to the condition in which humans find themselves in existence, namely, in the position or state of being in sin. Certainly Anti-Climacus views sin as being fundamentally an inward ontological condition of humanity rather than consisting in particular external immoral acts. Particular sins are merely an expression of the more fundamental state of being in sin. But the statement that sin is a position refers not so much to this condition or state as to the fact that sin is not a *given* condition or state in human beings, such as weakness, finitude, ignorance, or sensuality, nor is it, as in a Plotinian/Augustinian understanding of sin, a privation or lack, and thus a purely negative condition. Rather, sin is a condition that is *posited* by humans themselves. Anti-Climacus attributes so much importance to this determination of sin as something positive or posited that he declares (together with orthodoxy he believes) "the battle must be fought here . . . orthodoxy has correctly perceived that when sin is defined negatively, all Christianity is flabby and spineless" (96). Anti-Climacus brands all negative definitions of sin as pantheistic. Thus the qualitative distinction between humans and God is one crucial tenet of Christianity at stake here. Further, if sin is defined negatively, a danger arises that the understanding will usurp the role of faith, leading to a consideration of Christian determinants according to an abstract logical dialectic rather than the concrete qualitative dialectic to which they are subject in actuality.

The battle against these threatened compromises and substitutions is waged by Anti-Climacus particularly against the speculative dogmatic theology of Kierkegaard's Danish contemporary, Hans Lassen Martensen, who in company with other speculative theologians of that time is accused by Anti-Climacus of covertly transforming sin into a negation by presuming to comprehend (*begribe*) it as a position (97 and note 38).[8] For according to the rules of logic in speculative dogmatics as Anti-Climacus understands them, the "comprehending is itself higher than any position it posits; the concept establishes a position, but the comprehension of this is its very negation" (*SUD* 97). Consequently, in Anti-Climacus's estimation the speculative theologians conceive sin as a position only to a certain degree, that is, only to the point of its being comprehended, and they deal with it only within the medium of pure thought. In this medium God and humanity tend to coalesce into one, and there is no real difference between the positive and the negative, since the element of time is missing and no actual transition from one to the other can take place (97–98). The application of conceptual dialectic in an attempt to comprehend sin as a position is therefore in Anti-

Climacus's judgment both self-contradictory and invalid, since the act of comprehension negates the very thing it seeks to establish and abrogates the qualitative difference between the positive and the negative that obtains without mediation in the realm of actuality.

5. *Sin is a paradox.* In contrast to the speculative attempt to comprehend sin, Anti-Climacus insists that sin is a paradox that can only be believed and repented (98). In fact, he maintains that sin cannot, strictly speaking, be "thought" at all. Attempts to deal with it speculatively turn it into a negation. But even more important, sin cannot be thought because it is not a concept but rather a characteristic of the individual. Thought can think the concept of humanity or the concept of sin, but not the actual individual human being or individual sinner. Thought abstracts from the individual or particular and subsumes it under the universal. Thus it never gets to the *actuality* of sin, which resides in the individual. In Anti-Climacus's view, the actuality of sin is encountered only through qualitative dialectic by accentuation of the ethical, wherein one does not abstract *from* actuality but moves deeper into it by gaining the consciousness of sin in one's own existence. Reflection is thus to be carried out with an eye toward oneself. Sin can and should be conceptually defined in a way that directs the reader inward and aids one in this task, but this is quite different from conceptually comprehending sin. Even the proper understanding of what sin is cannot be ascertained without a revelation from God. Humans must either believe or be offended at this revelation. When this is the case, Anti-Climacus says it becomes neither meritorious nor admirable for a person to try to comprehend sin; one's ethical duty, on the contrary, is "to admit that one is neither able nor obliged to comprehend it" (99). This is the kind of Socratic ignorance that Anti-Climacus readily recommends, for it is an ignorance that "guards faith against speculation" rather than incites a person to it (99).

The paradox of sin, Anti-Climacus contends, "is the implicit consequence of the doctrine of the Atonement," inasmuch as Christianity at first "seems to be *working against itself* by establishing sin so securely as a position that now it seems to be utterly impossible to eliminate it again—and then . . . by means of the Atonement wants to eliminate sin as completely as if it were drowned in the sea" (100, emphasis added). In this way Christianity becomes "as paradoxical on this point as possible" (100).

6. *Remaining in sin constitutes the intensification of sin.* New sin is posited not by committing additional sinful acts but by the failure on the part of the individual in sin to repent (105–6). The state of remaining in sin further qualifies the definition of sin in that it constitutes sin in the deepest sense,

signifying the decision of individuals to maintain themselves in opposition to the good. Furthermore, Anti-Climacus suggests that sin has the power to sustain and intensify itself on its own: it grows every instant a person does not get out of it and gathers momentum in the process (106). Most people are so caught up in the power of sin that they sin daily almost as a matter of course and are not even conscious of the continuity or consistency of sin that dominates their lives. In fact, they live so haphazardly in the moment that they hardly have any idea of what "consistency" is. According to Anti-Climacus, only two kinds of persons are conscious of and strive for consistency: *believers,* who have a conception of themselves as spirit and seek to realize and sustain consistency in the eternal or the good; and *demonic individuals,* who also know themselves to be spirit but despairingly maintain the consistency of evil (107–8). Demonic individuals maintain consistency by hardening themselves in opposition to repentance and grace. They will have nothing to do with these possibilities and thus sink deeper into sin. The demonic person's despair thus represents not only sin but the intensification of sin into *despair over sin* (109–10). In this condition one cannot accept oneself in one's actuality as a sinner, much less humbly acknowledge and repent that one is less than one should be before God. Thus Anti-Climacus says of the demonic person: "His sorrow, his cares, his despair are selfish . . . because it is self-love that wants to be proud of itself, to be without sin" (112). Yet adherence to and persistence in this hidden pride and self-love are exactly what fixes the demonic person in sin.

7. *The intensification of sin in the form of despair of forgiveness constitutes offense.* The refusal to accept oneself *qua* sinner is the basis for the potentiation of sin to an even greater intensity and depth in the despairing individual whose relation to the eternal is further qualified by a knowledge of and relation to Christ, who offers the forgiveness of sin. But the forgiveness of sin presupposes and requires a consciousness of sin or the consciousness of oneself as a sinner. This means that a *double* consciousness of oneself is requisite in Christianity. First comes the consciousness of one's ideal or eternal self, the projected self positively defined in terms of what it is primitively intended to be before God. Both the conception of God and the knowledge of Christ intensify this ideal conception of the self. The conception of God makes the criterion and goal of the self infinite, transforming it into a theological self. But God *first* becomes the criterion and goal of a human being in and through Christ, who provides a confirmed expression of what a theological self is and of the "staggering reality" it possesses (114). At the same time, however, the determination of the self in its *ideality*

is the inverse criterion for the determination of a human being in his or her *actuality*, revealing that the actual or lower self is not what it should be, that in existence the human being is not qualitatively its own criterion and goal. While Christ further intensifies the ideal conception of the self and in his person gives humans a concrete expression of what a theological self is, he also provides by way of contrast a confirmation of the actual self's condition as sin. Consequently, one's task as an individual before Christ is not simply and directly to become oneself (the ideal self) but to will first of all to be oneself *qua* sinner, that is, to admit what one is in actuality before Christ. One must accept oneself "in the category of one's imperfection" and then believe in the possibility of the forgiveness of sin through Christ (113).

Individuals who will not admit their sinfulness are in despair over sin, but when one exists before Christ, one's despair is further intensified and qualified as despair of the forgiveness of sin. This is true also of persons who, conversely, possess such a demonic consciousness of their sinfulness that they think they are *beyond* forgiveness. Both types of individuals harbor a despair of forgiveness, although it appears in opposite forms, either as weakness or as defiance, only now these are conceived *inversely*: "Ordinarily weakness is: in despair not to will to be oneself. Here this is defiance, for here it is indeed the defiance of not willing to be oneself, what one is—a sinner—and for that reason wanting to dispense with the forgiveness of sins. Ordinarily, defiance is: in despair to will to be oneself. Here, this is weakness, in despair to will to be oneself—a sinner—in such a way that there is no forgiveness" (113). Whether one is unwilling to be characterized as a sinner (defiance) or whether one regards oneself irredeemably a sinner (weakness), the despair is essentially the same, only in the first instance the forgiveness of sin is resisted and deemed unnecessary, whereas in the second it is viewed as impossible. In both instances the despair of forgiveness is an expression of *offense,* inasmuch as they constitute a positive, though partly defensive, self-assertion of the individual before and against God. Anti-Climacus likens this situation to a "close combat" with God in which the individual walks right up to God and declares that the forgiveness of sins is impossible, asserting his or her own human understanding over against God's offer of reconciliation through the forgiveness of sin by Christ (114). Not only is it offensive to the human understanding that a human being offers forgiveness of sins to other humans, even the notion that sin can be forgiven is for the human understanding "most impossible" (116). The greatest possible intensification or positive assertion of sin occurs when the despairing individual becomes entirely offensive and aggressive, denying everything Christian and declaring it to be a falsehood. Anti-Climacus calls this "sin against the Holy Spirit" because it regards Christ as "an invention of the devil," just as in the Gospel of Matthew (12:24–32) the sin of the Jews who accused Jesus of exorcising demons by the help of Beelzebul, the prince of demons, is called sin against the Holy Spirit (131).

The characterization of sin as offense, or offense as the intensification of sin, makes the Christian conception of sin even more distinctive in that, according to Anti-Climacus, this form of sin did not and could not exist in paganism. The pagans lacked both the conception of God and a true conception of sin, but more than this, they lacked the relation to Christ that is the basis for the determination of sin as offense. Offense is the most critical form of sin, indicating that one has the highest consciousness of oneself as a self and stands in relation to that One who is able to help one become that self, yet rejects or refuses to believe in the only thing that can save or help one along the way.

8. *Sin is dialectical.* A final and very important point that emerges in *The Sickness unto Death* is that despair, sin, and the consciousness of sin are all dialectical in nature. That is, they may function either as negative factors or as indirectly positive ones, and they constitute both an advantage and a disadvantage to Christian strivers. Inasmuch as the consciousness of sin signifies an intense consciousness of despair, Christian strivers possess an advantage over the natural human being in being conscious of despair at a far deeper level and in understanding the nature of their sickness in a way unknown to the natural human being, grasping as they do that the misrelation to oneself is due to a misrelation to God, which is sin. Furthermore, Christian strivers possess the possibility of being cured from despair since they stand in relation to God and Christ. According to Anti-Climacus, the self is itself only when it is related in total dependency to the Power that establishes it, and the task to become oneself is one "which can be done only through the relationship to God" (30). The self cannot become itself or abolish despair by itself; indeed, the attempt to do this only lands one deeper in despair. But persons who are *aware* that they are in despair are "dialectically closer . . . to being cured than all those who are not regarded as such and who do not regard themselves as being in despair" (26). One becomes aware of oneself as spirit and as existing before God through despair and the consciousness of despair. Thus, "compared with the person who is conscious of his despair, the despairing individual who is ignorant of his despair is simply a negative step further away from the truth and deliverance" (44, translation amended slightly). When one is so spiritless that one does not

know what despair or sin is, one cannot be expected to have a consciousness of one's condition or a desire to be cured of it. Although the true (ideal) Christian is not in despair or has been cured of it, all Christian strivers must pass through despair and must have entered into its intensified forms in order to win themselves and to become transparently grounded in a relation to God (22, 26–27). The more a person is conscious of despair, the more that person is conscious of self and God. Since these positive results accrue from despair, it may function as the *first factor in faith* or that which, dialectically, leads one in the direction toward faith. It is because of this positive implication or possibility that Anti-Climacus says that despair is inversely the sickness of which it holds that "it is the worst misfortune never to have had" and "a true godsend to get it" (26).

Yet, if the possibility of despair is an advantage to humans and if having passed through it is requisite for sound health, Anti-Climacus says that it is dialectically also true that the actuality of despair is "perdition" and "the most dangerous of illnesses, if one does not want to be cured of it" (26). Every person who is in despair and knows it desires to be rid of despair, but often one thinks that the way to do this is to get rid of one's ideal self rather than to will to be oneself before God. But one cannot destroy the eternal potentiality in oneself that constitutes the self. The attempt to die from despair by destroying the self does not deliver one from despair but, on the contrary, lands one more deeply into it. In one sense, individuals who are unconscious of despair stand the greatest distance from salvation and being a self, since they are not even aware of themselves as spirit. But in another sense, individuals who are conscious of despair and remain in it stand even further from faith and selfhood. The more conscious of despair one becomes, the further from truth one moves. Although one is aware of the truth, one is infinitely remote from it. The consciousness of despair or sin constitutes for such a person only a form of awareness by which he or she moves further from faith rather than dialectically closer to it.

How, then, does one get on the right path or right direction to faith? The fact that sinners are fully conscious of their condition yet continue in sin suggests that *awareness* of self, despair, God, and sin is not in itself sufficient to tear a person out of despair, even though despair must become conscious before it can be dealt with and this consciousness forms the first factor in or prerequisite for faith. Along with, or more precisely, in and through this consciousness one must first acquire a genuine *will* to be healed in the way healing is possible. The increase in consciousness of oneself yields an increase in will as well; in fact, Anti-Climacus contends that the will bears the primary responsibility for sin and the intensification of sin (93, 95). What is needed, then, is an inversion of the will, an "about-face" (*Omvendelse*), "upheaval" (*Omvæltning*), or "metamorphosis" *(Metamorphose)* of the will on the part of the person in despair (60, 61n, 65).[9]

Faith comes to expression precisely in the *will to believe*.[10] But what one is asked to believe in Christianity is that with God all things are possible, and more specifically, that forgiveness of sin is possible, precisely at that moment when a person is brought to the utmost extremity where, humanly speaking, *no* possibility exists *(SUD* 38–40). In one sense, then, faith is the inverse of human understanding and expectation, but it also incorporates that understanding as a dialectical factor in itself. That is, faith is not merely to believe, but to believe against the understanding. It is to fight for possibility, to have the will to procure possibility or the will to believe even though salvation seems impossible. One does not believe rightly or have a grasp of what is implied in a belief in possibility unless a sense of the impossibility of possibility is contained in that belief.

This understanding of faith constitutes what one might call Anti-Climacus's *existential* definition of faith—faith as expressed in existence in the process of striving toward selfhood. *Ideally* defined, faith is the opposite of despair and sin and constitutes that condition of the self when despair is completely eradicated in a person's life. This positive or ideal conception of faith is expressed in Anti-Climacus's definition of faith: "Faith is: that the self in being itself and in willing to be itself rests transparently in God" (82; cf. also 49). But *in existence* faith is defined in relation to the negative and assumes a dialectical character, incorporating in its definition the element of negativity in the form of an antithesis to human understanding.

With respect to Anti-Climacus's existential understanding of faith, then, we are brought back to the question of the will, or the transformation of the will, so as to lead a person out of despair and onto the path toward faith ideally defined.[11] *The Sickness unto Death* indicates that such a transformation is needed, but it only indirectly indicates the way out of despair. It suggests that one must have experienced the intensified forms of despair, through which one gains a consciousness of oneself, the eternal, God, and one's own condition as despair and sin, as a *precondition* of faith. One must pass through despair in order to come to faith, and the hopelessness of despair even figures as a dialectical factor in the definition and apprehension of faith. Indirectly, then, despair and sin may become dialectical *correlates* of faith as well as dialectical *counterparts* or opposites of faith. In like manner, the consciousness of sin is that by which a person becomes aware of, and even increases his or her *distance from,* the truth; yet it may also aid in bringing that person *to* the truth. The Christian striver is a person who sustains a positive relation to Christ and believes in the possibility of forgiveness through him, but one becomes a Christian striver by recognizing and expressing one's need for forgiveness for being a sinner. Thus, in existence the believer or Christian striver is never *directly* what he or she is, but is that by being, or having been, precisely the opposite, only in such a way that his or her dialectical condition is no longer directly what it is either but constitutes an indirectly positive aid in becoming a self before God.

The fact that faith is defined in relation to the negative and that the negative (despair, sin, the consciousness of sin) may become an indirectly positive aid in the movement to and expression of faith indicates how Anti-Climacus's thought is informed by inverse dialectic. This dialectic is given even stronger expression in other writings of the period through the further qualification of the consciousness of sin in such a way as to transform the will of individuals and lead them to seek forgiveness in Christ. For Kierkegaard, faith comes to expression *in existence* first and foremost through the forming of a *contrite* consciousness of sin.

The Consciousness of Sin and Forgiveness

Kierkegaard takes up and states much more explicitly in the devotional writings of the second period of his authorship what *The Sickness unto Death* indirectly suggests or implies about the indirectly positive role of despair, sin, and the consciousness of sin in relation to faith and forgiveness. Thus these works stand in a kind of dialectical relation to one another, *The Sickness unto Death* primarily tracking the movement *away from faith* through sin and the intensification of sin, and the devotional writings indicating the movement *toward faith* through the consciousness of sin and forgiveness. They all must be taken into account if the dialectical nature and correlations of sin and the consciousness of sin, on the one hand, and faith and the consciousness of forgiveness, on the other, that Kierkegaard envisions are to be fully perceived. Of all the later literature, *The Sickness unto Death* has probably received the most critical attention, while the devotional writings of the period have been virtually ignored. But it is precisely in these works that one finds the heart of Kierkegaard's understanding of the consciousness of sin and its relation to the forgiveness of sin in living Christianly.

The Sickness unto Death presents the consciousness of sin primarily in its function as a form of *existential awareness,* but this constitutes only the *first form* of the consciousness of sin. Louis Dupré has stated that "while sin alienated us from God, consciousness of sin returns us to Him."[12] But this is not necessarily so, since the consciousness of sin may contribute to the intensification of sin as well as to its annihilation. Christianly understood, the consciousness of sin must be further qualified so that it functions solely as an indirectly positive aid in bringing a person to Christ, in forming the appropriate attitude toward oneself in relation to God, and in adopting the appropriate posture for the expression of faith. The consciousness of despair, the sense of hopelessness, the unwillingness to believe in the forgiveness of sin, and offense at Christ are stages of consciousness that every Christian striver has known, been tempted by, or passed through. In order for the consciousness of sin to become an indirectly positive factor in faith and to provide the negative expression for faith, however, it must become a *contrite* consciousness of sin, expressing a *sensitivity to* and *sorrow over* sin that humbles the individual before God and makes him or her feel the need for forgiveness. This *second form* of the consciousness of sin comes to the fore in the devotional literature of the period and is what, as Kierkegaard sees it, Christianity ultimately requires and seeks to form in a human being.

Adi Shmuëli has pointed out in his study of the structure of consciousness in Kierkegaard's thought that consciousness is a broader concept than the intellective character generally associated with it, inasmuch as it incorporates "feeling, passion, desire, and other facets of the subjective life."[13] This insight particularly applies to Kierkegaard's understanding of the consciousness of sin. The *second form* or final stage of this consciousness corresponds closely to what Kierkegaard, following Luther, calls the anguished conscience (*den ængstede Samvittighed*) (JP 3:2461; 4:4018; WL 193). Emanuel Skjoldager has noted the close connection between the two thinkers on this topic, but he interprets the anguished conscience more as a consequence of sin-consciousness than as a form of it.[14] The devotional writings reveal, however, that Kierkegaard understands the consciousness of sin essentially in terms of the anguished conscience and that a conscience qualified in this manner constitutes the negative expression for faith in Christian existence.

This view appears in preliminary form in the first work of the second period, *Upbuilding Discourses in Various Spirits* (1847).[15] In part 1, "An Occasional Discourse," Kierkegaard suggests that the way out of despair lies in the negative expressions of *repentance* and *confession* formed by the voice of conscience in a person.[16] In repentance one withdraws from one's other relations and activities in life in order to center upon oneself in one's relation to oneself as an individual, or what is the same thing, one's relation to the eternal, since the consciousness of being an individual is equivalent to a consciousness of the eternal. In general, to be an individual means simply to pay attention to oneself, to cultivate self-examination and earnestness, that is, to examine one's own life with an eye toward entering into whatever action or posture is required to posit the eternal in one's life. To be an individual is the ethical prerequisite of, and the broader expression for, that activity by which a person becomes a self. Ethically speaking, the possibility of realizing the eternal appears in the demand incumbent upon every person to will the good. Since the good is always one thing, a unity, and abiding, eternal, and immutable, the prerequisite for truthfully willing one thing or the good is that the striver must also be a *unity*. That which most fundamentally defines being an individual, therefore, is *being at one with oneself*.[17] "An Occasional Discourse" emphasizes that despair arises from *double-mindedness* or a *divided will* in a human being (*UDVS* 30). One may desire the good but not wholly will it, or one may be powerless to will the good or perhaps will it out of false motives (such as for a reward) or for the wrong reasons (such as fear of punishment or the loss of worldly goods and esteem) (37–60). Moreover, one may will a variety of things—pleasure, honor, wealth, power—with an apparent or delusory single-mindedness without willing the good, for none of these things constitute one thing but rather a multiplicity (26–27). Only when the will is united in a single and total commitment to the good does one truthfully will one thing and will it with a pure heart.

Conscience is that form of consciousness within oneself whereby one becomes aware of oneself as an individual and is strengthened in the task of willing the good. Eternity takes hold of persons "with the strong arms of conscience" and sets each one apart from the crowd, positing an eternal vocation for each individual and calling that person forward to fulfill it (133).[18] This is the directly positive role of conscience. But it is also through the conscience that the eternal exacts an accounting within oneself of whether one has become what one should be and has willed the good in truth. In its negative or indirectly positive function, conscience forms a *sense of shame* in a person and an expression of *sorrow* over the fact that one has not allowed the eternal to rule in one's life, that one has not been related to oneself as an individual or truly willed the good. Repentance and confession thus form the negative or indirectly positive expressions by which one's conscience brings the consciousness of oneself as an individual once again to the fore and reestablishes it as one's task in life. They mark the reappearance of the eternal "under another name" or in a negative form that calls one back from evil and places one once again in contact with the demand to will the good, which one can do only as an individual (*UDVS* 151).

In order to be led to the act of repentance one must to a certain extent have already come to view one's life in the context of the eternal and through its inverted dialectic recognized that repentance is due. Individuals who are conscious of themselves as individuals have had their vision transformed "to see everything inverted" so that "everything in life appears inverted" (*omvendt*) (135, translation amended slightly). Thus all the things that seemed profitable at moments in the past and which one elected to do in preference to willing the good now in the moment of remembrance appear loathsome and prompt one to repentance.

This *inversion of vision* also conditions one's expression of repentance. The temporal conception of repentance is the *opposite* of the eternal conception of it and does not constitute *true* repentance in Kierkegaard's view. False or worldly repentance is momentary, selfish, sensuous, and impatient, seeking "to collect the bitterness of sorrow in one draft—and then be off" (*UDVS* 17). It wants to get away from guilt and banish all recollection of it through repentance, while true repentance is a "quiet daily concern" over one's guilt that, far from being forgotten, is felt deeper and stronger as time passes (18). In a temporal sense guilt is left behind by doing the good, but eternally guilt remains. In the truly penitent person even progress in doing the good produces an opposite effect from what one would expect—a greater intensity of repentance or sorrow over guilt rather than the termination of repentance and the forgetting of past guilt. From the eternal point of view, to forget is not a gain but a loss. Gain is found precisely in gaining the "inwardness to regret the guilt more and more fervently" (18).

Although "An Occasional Discourse" identifies sin as that which keeps one from willing one thing and virtually identifies repentance and confession with the consciousness and confession of sin, it is composed in an ethical mode that does not distinguish the ethical-religious from the Christian but incorporates both under a broader sense of the ethical as a person's inner concern with and for his or her consciousness of the eternal. Part 3 of *Upbuilding Discourses in Various Spirits,* "The Gospel of Sufferings," bears the important subtitle "Christian Discourses." This is the first of any of Kierkegaard's published writings to be designated "Christian."[19] In these discourses Kierkegaard correlates the negative expression of guilt and sorrow specifically with the Christian consciousness of sin and introduces its dialectical relation to the consciousness of forgiveness in Christian existence. From a Christian standpoint, one is not simply guilty in this or that act for which one must repent; rather, one is essentially and unconditionally guilty through being a sinner, and one is related to God *as* a sinner. Christian strivers are distinguished from other persons by the fact that they bear, in addition to the other burdens or sufferings of life, the burden of the consciousness of sin. This consciousness constitutes the heaviest of all burdens in life and is what sets for the Christian striver the tasks of contrition and repentance.

However, this burden is made light for Christian strivers through the forgiveness of sin by Christ. In forgiveness, *the consciousness of sin is taken away and replaced by its opposite, the consciousness of forgiveness* (246). This expresses the central dialectic of Christian existence.[20] The consciousness of sin, remorse, contrition, repentance, and the confession of sin form only one side of the dialectic. Christian strivers are characterized not only by the fact that they bear a contrite consciousness of sin but also by the fact that they believe in and are conscious of the forgiveness of their sin. "An Occasional Discourse" stresses that the anxiety or expression of sorrow in repentance, when it is true repentance, is something that remains and increases in the individual and that this is, from the eternal point of view, a desirable and positive thing, since it is precisely what helps a person to become an individual and to will the good. But "An Occasional Discourse" says nothing about the alleviation of conscience and rest for the soul that Christ provides through the forgiveness of sin. The consciousness of forgiveness is just as essential in Christian existence as a contrite consciousness of sin. Whereas the consciousness of sin is, in the moment of forgiveness, ultimately erased, the consciousness of forgiveness *must not be lost* or else forgiveness is taken in vain and faith is not really present in a person (247). For faith depends precisely on how forgiveness is borne. If one receives it with "heavy-mindedness" or melancholy, as something hard to bear, this means that one has refused to really believe in forgiveness and will not forget one's sinfulness. If it is borne thoughtlessly or with "light-mindedness," so that one forgets not only one's sinfulness but the fact that one has been forgiven as well, then forgiveness is taken in vain (246–47). In genuine faith everything in the past is forgotten, but the fact that it has been forgiven is constantly remembered. In fact, the past is forgotten only through the remembrance of forgiveness, for "when you forget the forgiveness, it [sin] is not forgotten, and then the forgiveness is wasted" (247).

For Kierkegaard the place where the consciousness of sin and forgiveness come together is in the service of Holy Communion at the altar. There private confession is made and the pledge of reconciliation with God is received. Kierkegaard's "Discourses at the Communion on Fridays," of which there are twelve in all bearing this title,[21] command a central place among the writings of the second period inasmuch as they describe and prepare one for this dialectical moment.[22] Thus they bring the authorship to its point of concentration and culmination in the assurance of the forgiveness of sin in and through the confession of sin. Seven of these discourses make up part 4 of *Christian Discourses* (1848). Five more appeared in sets of three (1849) and two (1851) discourses published in close company to *The Sickness unto Death* and *For Self-Examination* respectively. In a very real sense, the culmination and limit of Kierkegaard's own existential position was also reached and expressed in the communion discourses. In the preface to the last two he states:

> An authorship that began with *Either/Or* and advanced step by step seeks here its decisive place of rest, at the foot of the altar, where the author, personally most aware of his own imperfection and guilt, certainly does not call himself a truth-witness but only a singular kind of poet and thinker who, *without authority,* has had nothing new to bring but "has wanted once again to read through, if possible in a more inward way, the original text of individual human existence-relationships, the old familiar text handed down from the fathers." (*WA* 165)

When this passage was written, Kierkegaard thought that he had reached the conclusion of his authorship, but his comment also signifies that the communion discourses provide the resting point for that portion of the authorship which he claimed as his own, that is, the upbuilding works. The early pseudonyms were used to bring the upbuilding to the foreground, but they represented lower existential positions than his own. Yet Kierkegaard consistently regarded himself as "a penitent" who fell short of the Christian ideal and was constantly in need of grace and forgiveness (*JP* 6:6195, 6206, 6261, 6317, 6325, 6327, 6364).[23]

The communion discourses express precisely this situation of confession and forgiveness to which every Christian striver must continually return. They are "confessional addresses" (*skriftetaler*), or more accurately, "communion addresses" (*altergangstaler*) designed to give one "pause" on the way to the altar, so that through them one may "privately and secretly before God" make one's confession of sin and receive Christ's forgiveness by partaking of the Eucharist (CD 270–71).[24] Kierkegaard distinguishes them from sermons, inasmuch as they are without authority and do not seek to instruct the reader on what it means to confess or to impress upon him or her "the old familiar doctrines"; rather, they are intended to serve as a means through which the reader may make private confession before God and renew his or her pledge of faithfulness to God (CD 270–71; 286–87).[25] They do not seek to burden the reader "with the guilt of faithlessness," of which, in Kierkegaard's view, all human beings are *"fundamentally"* guilty, but rather to relieve or unburden them of that guilt through confession, which is itself an expression of faith (CD 286–87).

One finds in these discourses, first of all, a closer description of the quality or kind of sin-consciousness that brings one to the altar and constitutes the negative expression for faith, and second, an indication of how sin and the consciousness of sin are taken away by Christ's forgiveness and atonement. It becomes crystal clear in these discourses that the consciousness of sin in its deepest and most upbuilding sense is not merely an objective knowledge or understanding of what sin is, nor does it consist finally in a subjective awareness of one's own sinfulness, although both of these are essential components of that consciousness. The kind of sin-consciousness that brings a person to the altar in search of forgiveness is that which has become a quiet, humble, heartfelt sorrow over one's guilt and sin—that quality of inward consciousness which earlier in "An Occasional Discourse" was identified as constituting repentance. Although persons may be heavy laden in many different ways, those who sigh penitently over their sin in relation to God are heavy laden in a Christian sense or in the manner that is required by the gospel. Sorrow over one's sin, or penitence, is the *requirement* of the gospel; forgiveness is the *promise* of the gospel (CD 264–65). The two go hand in hand, each requiring the other. Penitence is the prerequisite for forgiveness, but forgiveness is the only thing that can give relief and rest to the anguished and penitent soul.

As Kierkegaard sees it, this dialectic of penitence and forgiveness is characterized by several *inversions*. The appropriate posture of penitence is that of a contrite or "broken" heart that condemns itself (CD 292). The more individuals condemn themselves before God, the greater God's mercy shows itself to be in forgiving their sin. God's mercy and forgiveness may be measured inversely in direct proportion to one's self-condemnation. Conversely, the better one makes oneself out to be, the more one ends in diminishing God's greatness in forgiving, for the more like God one claims to be, the less there seems to be for God to forgive in oneself. Kierkegaard therefore rejects any *direct* analogy of being or the use of a person's directly positive features, such as the capacity to love, to establish a *direct resemblance* between a human being and God. The true greatness of a person lies in the greatness of that person's heart, but this consists precisely in being a contrite heart that condemns itself, not one that elevates itself in direct comparison with God or which, conversely, measures the greatness of God on a scale with one's positive view of oneself. Only *inversely* in the *posture of penitence* does one resemble God. One should not say, therefore, that God is greater than the most loving person, for "all human purity, all human mercy is not good enough for comparison" (*CD* 292). Rather, God is greater than the heart that condemns itself: "As deep as this heart can lower itself, and yet never itself deep enough, so infinitely elevated, or infinitely more elevated, is God's greatness in showing mercy!" (292).

In like manner, Kierkegaard states: "Neither does a human being come closer and closer to God by lifting up his head higher and higher, but inversely by casting himself down ever more deeply in worship" (292). It is precisely in recognizing how *far away* from God one stands and in being *humbled by it* that one comes *near* to God. Kierkegaard observes that "hypocrisy and pride and conceit and the worldly mind may want to reverse the relation," which converts Christian humility into hypocrisy and Christian lowliness into pride and conceit (*WA* 127–28). From his point of view, therefore, it is not so much Kierkegaard or Christianity that inverts the Christian demand to make it appear negative and unattractive to human beings as it is, conversely, the worldly mind that has turned the Christian requirements around to make them conform to its nature and conceptions.

The paradigm for the implementation of this requirement of humility, as Kierkegaard sees it, is not the Pharisee or model churchgoer in Christendom who exudes a sense of righteousness by his or her piety, but rather the tax collector or sinner in the gospel who stands by himself, alone before God, with downcast eyes, feeling far away from God's holiness in his guilt and sin (*WA* 128). In Kierkegaard's view, the tax collector corresponds to the person who sincerely goes to confession. Kneeling at the altar corresponds to, and forms an even stronger expression than, the tax collector's downcast eyes. Making confession is equivalent to the tax collector's smiting himself upon the breast and crying for mercy. At the altar one is, like the tax collector, far off from God in the recognition of one's own sinfulness; yet through sorrow, humility, and confession one is brought near to God.

This means that, Christianly understood, *nearness* to God is not direct but indirect, determined not by the apparent forms of closeness but by a sense of, and appropriate attitude toward, one's *distance* from God. This *sense of distance* is inversely *a sign of closeness* to God (WA 131, 133). Being at the altar is not in itself an expression of closeness to God but becomes such only as one truly fulfills the conditions of confession. Second, Christianly understood, *humility* before God is really a form of exaltation or *uplifting* (132). A person becomes lifted up to God precisely by kneeling down before the divine in adoration and self-accusation. Humility and self-accusation are what secure the possibility of forgiveness and justification, whereas self-praise results in just the opposite, being accused by God. Humility and self-accusation are therefore indirectly positive expressions in Christian existence, not negative or demeaning ones.

One other factor figures in the consciousness and confession of sin as Kierkegaard understands it: the admission that one can do *nothing* of oneself to secure forgiveness. The consciousness of sin does not in itself procure forgiveness but is characterized quite conversely by a sense of one's *inability* to do anything that can of itself obtain it. Kierkegaard applies this assertion of human impotence not only to the attainment of forgiveness but to all human activities in life: "Whatever a person is going to undertake, whether the work is great and significant or lowly and insignificant, he is able to do nothing if God does not give his blessing" (CD 297). The more one becomes concerned with God or with assuring that one's actions have God's sanction and thereby constitute a "godly undertaking," the more one's own impotence becomes clear to one and the more one feels the need of God's blessing (298). But if in one's ordinary undertakings in life one is nothing or can do nothing without God, when one stands before God at the altar as a sinner it is even more emphatically true that one can do "less than nothing" as regards one's redemption and reconciliation with God (299).

Ironically, just at the point where it would appear to be most imperative that one be able to do *something* in order to make satisfaction for one's sin, the clearer it becomes that one can do nothing whatsoever and that, conversely, Christ must do absolutely everything. The admission of impotence is the only positive act that one can make toward one's own salvation. But Kierkegaard interprets the experience of nothingness at the altar as being so devastating that it is impossible even to "hold fast the thought of your unworthiness and in this make yourself receptive to the blessing" (CD 299). Conversely, however, the admission that one can do nothing of oneself is precisely what constitutes love of Christ (WA 139–40). Only Christ can accomplish a human being's redemption, but it is also true that this becomes so only by being *made true* in each person's own life through forgetting one-self completely in love of Christ (*WA* 140). To illustrate this complex situa-tion Kierkegaard offers the gospel example of the woman who was a sinner (Luke 7:36–50). This woman hated herself, but precisely in this negative feeling toward herself she also gave the strongest indirectly positive expres-sion to the fact that she loved Christ much. It was precisely because she hated herself and loved Christ much, forgetting herself completely in her love for him, that her sins were forgiven and forgotten.

This would seem to put Kierkegaard in the contradictory position of hav-ing claimed first that one can do nothing to secure forgiveness and then of immediately rescinding it by saying that forgiveness is determined by how much one loves Christ. Anticipating precisely this criticism, Kierkegaard de-nies that he has made love into a kind of work whereby forgiveness is meri-ted. This is prevented by the law of "the blessed recurrence of salvation [*Frelsens Tilbagevenden*] in love" that governs the relation of love and for-giveness: "First you love much, and much is then forgiven you—and see, then love increases even more. This, that you have been forgiven so much, loves forth love once again, and you love much because you were forgiven much" (*WA* 176). Love is like faith in this respect: "In order to be healed, the person must believe—now he believes and is healed. Now he is healed—and now that he is saved, his faith is twice as strong" (176). Faith elicits salvation, which in turn doubles faith. In like manner, forgiveness elicits more love, just as love in the first instance elicits forgiveness. The two go hand in hand, each evoking the other. But their relation is not to be con-strued as one in which one loves God simply as a means of obtaining for-giveness, for in such a case one's love would not be genuine and everything would revert back to the sphere of meritoriousness. Forgiveness is the pre-rogative of God, whether a person loves little or much, and it is given in response to, as well as in proportion to, a person's love of God. The differ-ence between meritoriousness and a relation of love is determined by how one views the relationship of love and forgiveness, that is, whether forgive-ness is seen as the *consequence* of love or as God's *response* to love. In the latter instance, which is the proper Christian understanding, it would not be correct to say that love begets forgiveness, but rather that when one loves much, much is forgiven one. This results in the inversion that forgiveness begets love, rather than *vice versa*.

Kierkegaard suggests further that the test of love lies not in one's willing-ness to love Christ more than mother, father, gold, honor, and so on, but in whether one loves him more than one's sin (*WA* 143). Since "there is nothing to which a human being so desperately firmly clings as to his sin," one may be willing to give up all else for Christ but not one's sin (143). One may even want to give that up, but as long as one is not willing to *confess* one's sin, one maintains a love for it that is stronger than one's love for Christ. Thus Kierkegaard says that "a perfectly honest, deep, completely true, completely unsparing confession of sin is the perfect love" and "such a confession of sins is to love much" (143). This turns the expression of love back to its negative correlative. The love that elicits forgiveness is not a *direct* expression of love on the part of a person, but consists in the degree to which one is willing to confess one's sin before God and to admit one's utter dependence upon God's love and forgiveness.

The relation of love and forgiveness reveals another complexity in that it forms the basis for a distinction between, and an inverse identification of, *love and justice* as these apply to the offer and denial of forgiveness. When one considers what is so often the case, that many people leave the altar without finding the relief of forgiveness promised them, one is naturally inclined to ask why this occurs. Kierkegaard remarks that "it is also difficult to receive aright the forgiveness of sins at the Communion table" and to do what is required (*WA* 169). But the real reason is that if one is forgiven little, it is because one has loved little (169). Thus anyone who is not sensible of forgiveness at the altar or who departs from it feeling not entirely lightened of one's burden has no one but oneself to blame. The invitation to the altar is given to all, but if one does not come expressing true sorrow before God, one will not find God or the forgiveness that God offers. It is when one hears at the altar that one's sins are forgiven but knows within oneself that it is not so that the word of love becomes the inverse, a word of judgment rather than a word of comfort (*WA* 171–73). This means that love has a *severe* side as well as a gentle one and that it may show itself conversely as *justice* and *judgment* when forgiveness is not rightly apprehended and received at the altar. The judgment of love is in a way more severe than that of justice because it begins with the declaration of forgiveness, making one all the more conscious that the fault lies within oneself and not in God's mercy or sense of justice when forgiveness is not received. Love therefore has the effect of revealing one's sin even more clearly than does justice. The sin it reveals is the lack of love. For when pardon and forgiveness are not forthcoming, it is not because, according to the annals of justice, one has *sinned too much* to warrant pardon, but because one has *loved too little* (*WA* 173). One is self-condemned not by one's former sins but by a new one, one's lack of love for Christ, who offers forgiveness of one's sins.

The transformation or qualification of the consciousness of sin into that which leads one *to* God rather than merely to accentuate and increase one's distance *from* the divine is initiated by God, but it comes to expression inwardly in one's sense of *need* for forgiveness. As one becomes increasingly sensible of one's sin, the temptation is to flee from God and confession as long as possible. Since the confession of sin entails, in a sense, the "annihilation" of oneself before God, it may appear as an even more frightening prospect than the continued hiding of sin in oneself. This is counteracted by the voice of *conscience* and by the development of a *longing* for the renewal of fellowship with Christ and a sense of one's *need* for forgiveness and reconciliation with God. These forces are what finally and truly bring one to the altar. Conscience acts in league with the divine by preventing one from hiding one's sin from oneself. One cannot escape one's conscience—it is with us everywhere. But it is just this desire to flee one's conscience, to find a hiding place where one is hidden from the consciousness of sin or to obtain a pardon that takes one's sin and the consciousness of sin away, that leads a person to Christ (*WA* 182–84). Ultimately the longing for communion comes *from* God or is the effect of the Spirit of God working in one (*CD* 253–54). It is that by which God draws one to the divine, although in another sense it is that which is required of *oneself* if one is to receive the longing as a gift from God and let it become a blessing. It is within a person's power to ignore the longing for communion with Christ, to resist it, to prevent it from taking hold. Therefore Kierkegaard says that one should not let the longing depart in vain but rather allow it to grow within one and employ it for one's own good. Only the person who has a hearty longing for this fellowship goes *worthily* to the altar (*CD* 251). Moreover, no one should come to the altar who does not feel the *need* to seek the forgiveness of sin and reconciliation with God. No external summons brings the true confessor to the altar, only a need within. One must have resolved inwardly, of one's own free will, to come, not because one is made to do so or because others do it (270). Kierkegaard prepared his confessional discourses for the communion on Fridays precisely with this point in mind, for in those days in Denmark Friday communion was not obligatory, or even customary, since on Fridays most people were busy in the fields or shops with their daily work (269–70).[26]

When one has become thoroughly sensible of and sensitive to one's sin— meaning that one is acutely aware of it, feels remorse over it, is humbled by it, has acquired a condemnatory attitude toward oneself and one's inabilities because of it, and is willing to make confession to find relief from it—one will at last truly fly to Christ. Christ awaits one at the altar and stretches out his arms precisely to the fugitive who would flee from the consciousness of sin and the gnawing remorse that person suffers over it (WA 184).[27] Kierkegaard adopts a substitutionary theory of atonement to explain how Christ is able to bring relief from the consciousness of sin: Christ brings consolation to human beings by putting himself in their place (WA 116). He is the only person who is able entirely and truly to do this because he offers "true sympathy" in contrast to the merely human sympathy human beings extend to one another. Although the compassionate person may be willing "to suffer almost as much as the sufferer," Christ not only suffers *as much* but *infinitely more* than the sufferer (116–17). J. Preston Cole has credited Kierkegaard with attempting to "historicize" the classical substitutionary theory of atonement inasmuch as he "struggles to understand how such a substitution could truly minister to the suffering of despair."[28] However, Cole thinks Kierkegaard's interpretation is inadequate because "it does not triumph over suffering, but worships him who is able to console us. . . . If Christ is to be an atonement he must do more than excite our admiration and console us in our misery."[29] But Kierkegaard claims that Christ *does* do more than that. Christ literally becomes the satisfaction for human sin, putting himself completely into our place and suffering the punishment for our sin and guilt in order that we may be redeemed (WA 123). "As (or yet infinitely more than) the hen in concern covers her chicks," he literally hides our sin by covering it with his death (185–86). This has the effect of transforming sin into purity and the sinful person into one who is justified and pure. The service of communion reenacts Christ's act of atonement by presenting the sacraments as an "eternal pledge" that Christ by his death has put himself in one's place in order that one may have life (124). But Kierkegaard warns that this remains the case only so long as one remains in communion with Christ. Communion at the altar *is itself* communion with Christ, but one should endeavor to maintain this communion in one's daily life as well by living more and more *out* of oneself and *into* Christ's love (188). Thus when one leaves the communion table, one must, as it were, "remain at the Communion table," that is, take it with one, making every day an act of worship by keeping Christ present and living in oneself (CD 273–74).

Thus the person who sincerely comes to and remains at the altar is quite different from the sinner who, as portrayed in *The Sickness unto Death*, is offended by Christ and denies him. Both are sinners, both have a knowledge of and a relation to Christ. But Kierkegaard draws a sharp distinction between those who through sin fall away and deny Christ and those who are merely unfaithful to him (*CD* 282). The first are also, in a sense, unfaithful in that no one can deny Christ unless in a stricter sense one had first belonged to him. But the latter, unlike the first, do not deny him. On the contrary, at communion they come to confess him. Nevertheless, they come with penitence and a feeling of their own unfaithfulness, for which they seek pardon through Christ's perfect and abiding faithfulness. By coming to the altar, therefore, one expresses that one reckons oneself as being among those who would belong to Christ. To be sure, one belongs to Christ as one who is guilty, but by abiding in Christ the multitude of one's sins are hidden or covered by Christ, and one is able to find rest in God through a contrite consciousness of sin and the forgiveness of sin.

Kierkegaard's concern with this dialectic of the consciousness of sin and forgiveness in Christian existence is a constant one in the literature of the second period. Unlike his understanding of some of the other qualifications of Christian existence, there is no real change or development in his thought on this matter, just a process of refinement and closer definition of it. This begins with the *Upbuilding Discourses in Various Spirits* in 1847 and continues in every publication through 1851, particularly the confessional or communion discourses. In 1850 Kierkegaard published along with *Practice in Christianity* another upbuilding discourse in which he returns to the gospel example of the woman who was a sinner, presenting her this time as the "prototype of piety" (*WA* 149). "Piety or godliness," he says, "is fundamentally womanliness" (*WA* 149). Consequently he suggests that one should learn from *a woman* what "the proper sorrow over one's sin" is (149).[30] This consists foremost in becoming *indifferent* to everything except one's sorrow over sin and in letting this become an "unconditional sorrow" in the sense that finding forgiveness for it becomes the one thing absolutely important in one's life (150). Indifference, then, is "only the negative expression of the confirmation that one thing is unconditionally important" (152). It extends not only to temporal suffering and the experience of hostility, opposition, and derision from others in life but to "everything temporal, earthly, and worldly, honors, esteem, prosperity, the future, relatives, friends, people's opinion" (153). This kind of sickness does not signify despair or a sickness unto death but rather "unto life" because "the life is in this, that one thing is unconditionally important to him [or her]: to find forgiveness" (152). The woman who was a sinner possessed the courage and energy of despair, but Kierkegaard says that "truly she is far from being a despairing person" for "she, who has this energy, is not in despair, she is a believer"

(154). The expression of an unconditional sorrow over sin is therefore the inverse sign of faith or forms the negative expression for faith in Christian existence.

In *Practice in Christianity* Kierkegaard via his pseudonym Anti-Climacus again stresses the vital role of the consciousness of sin in bringing one to Christianity, but here it is viewed in relation to the other Christian requirements of facing the possibility of offense, self-denial, suffering, and opposition from the world that these qualifications ignite. From a merely human point of view this form of existence appears to be entirely negative, unhappy, contradictory, and utterly undesirable. Thus the likelihood of anyone choosing it becomes almost more improbable than the entry of the eternal in time! Anti-Climacus himself poses the question: "But if the essentially Christian is something so terrifying and appalling, how in the world can anyone think of accepting Christianity?" (PC 67). His answer, "very simply" and "very Lutheranly" put, is "Only the consciousness of sin can force one, if I dare to put it that way (from the other side grace is the force), into this horror" (67). Posing virtually the same question in his journals, Kierkegaard agrees with Anti-Climacus but elaborates a bit more:

> The first answer might be: Hold your tongue; Christianity is the absolute, you shall. But another answer may also be given: Because the consciousness of sin within him allows him no rest anywhere; its grief strengthens him to endure everything else if he can only find reconciliation.
>
> This means the grief of sin must be very deep within a person, and therefore Christianity must be presented as the difficult thing it is, so that it may become entirely clear that Christianity only is related to the consciousness of sin. To want to be involved in becoming a Christian for any other reason is literally foolishness—and so it must be. (JP 1:493)

And in another journal passage he states further:

> If you are not conscious of being a sinner to the degree that in the anxiety of the anguished conscience you do not dare anything other than to commit yourself to Christ—then you never will become a Christian. Only the agony of the consciousness of sin can explain the fact that a person will submit to this radical cure. To become a Christian is the most fearful operation of all. Just as unlikely as it

is for a person who merely feels a little indisposed to think of submitting to the most painful operation, just as unlikely is it for a person to think of getting involved with Christianity if sin did not pain him inordinately—if, note well, he then knows what Christianity is and has not been talked into some nonsense about Christianity's gentle, life-beautifying, and ennobling ground of comfort. (*JP* 1:496)

These statements provide the clearest evidence that for Kierkegaard the consciousness of sin must take the form of an anguished conscience, expressing deep grief and agony over sin before it can drive a person to Christ. Yet the ultimate inversion of Christian existence also obtains in the insight that this is precisely the way one finally comes to see the truly positive, gentle, loving, and compassionate nature of Christianity. Anti-Climacus best describes this moment of inversion in "The Moral" of *Practice in Christianity:*

And at that very same moment the essentially Christian transforms itself into and is sheer leniency, grace, love, mercy. Considered in any other way Christianity is and must be a kind of madness or the greatest horror. Admittance is only through the consciousness of sin; to want to enter by any other road is high treason against Christianity. . . . Only the consciousness of sin is absolute respect. And just because Christianity insists on having absolute respect, from any other perspective Christianity must and will appear as madness and horror simply in order that the qualitative infinite emphasis can fall upon the fact that the consciousness of sin is the only admittance, is the view that, by being absolute respect, is able to see the gentleness and love and compassion of Christianity. (*PC* 67–68)

The Alleviation of Sin and the Possibility of Faith

As the foregoing statements show, for all Kierkegaard's emphasis upon the negative and demanding nature of Christian existence, he holds a very positive view of Christianity. The distinctive feature of his understanding is that this vision is obtained through, or comes to expression in, the negative, that is to say, his thought is informed by inverse dialectic. The central dialectic in Christian existence is between the consciousness of sin and forgiveness, and this dialectic is characterized by several inversions whereby one's likeness and nearness to God and one's expression of faith in God are brought to expression through self-condemnation, humility, a sense of distance from God, the recognition of human impotence apart from God, and the need and desire to confess one's sinfulness before God. Forgiveness requires a contrite consciousness of sin, not merely an awareness of one's sin, and such a consciousness in turn is what drives a person to seek forgiveness in Christ. Consequently, both terms must be affirmed, making the dialectic complementary rather than exclusive in character, although Christ's act of atonement ultimately covers one's sin and transforms it into purity, so that in this instance the consciousness of forgiveness replaces the consciousness of sin as the *temporal precondition* of forgiveness rather than as its simultaneous negative expression. If one is to relate oneself to Christianity in the proper manner, therefore, one must come to understand that Christianity has to do primarily with sin and the forgiveness of sin, that it makes sin the most terrifying thing in life and then proposes to do away with sin through forgiveness.

However, Kierkegaard believes most people turn to Christianity for quite different reasons. They are Christians because in Christendom it pays to be one; or if they have experienced a degree of adversity in life, they look to Christianity as a source of comfort and alleviation for their temporal suffering and worldly misfortunes in hopes that in the future their lot in life will be happier and more successful. They come to Christianity, therefore, for quite selfish reasons, not from remorse over sin or for the forgiveness of sin, and they confuse the truly gentle, loving, and compassionate nature of Christianity with the alleviation of their earthly distress and the promise of good fortune. This misconception and misuse of Christianity is reinforced by the clergy in that sin, faith, grace, and forgiveness are often preached in the same breath with reassurances about temporal misfortune and good fortune, as if Christianity were primarily concerned with these matters in life.

For this reason Kierkegaard makes a sharp distinction between *sorrow over sin* and *earthly sorrow* in his *Christian Discourses* and seeks to impress upon his readers that the misery with which Christianity is primarily concerned is sin and that this misery is far worse than any earthly distress (*CD* 172–73). True Christians, in fact, live without the ordinary human anxieties over wealth and station in life because their understanding of poverty, riches, lowliness, and highness are the opposite of the merely human, pagan, or natural understanding of them. One is able essentially to conquer temporal losses and misfortunes by inverting one's understanding of them.[31] But even more important, the reminder is constantly given that none of these temporal situations or adversities is the ruin of human beings. Over against sin they are as nothing. It is sin and sin alone that constitutes a human being's destruction. People commonly think that the church is a place of security where one can get away from the "terrors of existence" and the "storms of life," away from all the dreadful events that have happened or which they fear will happen (CD 163). But Kierkegaard says that one does not hear, at least *not at first,* anything about illness and adversity, earthly needs and misery, in the house of God. On the contrary, instead of coming to a place where one can find comfort and sympathy about these matters, one learns there something even more dreadful and heavy to bear—that one is a sinner (172). Concern over this state is enough to make one forget one's earthly troubles. One is enabled not merely to accept one's temporal adversities but to become *indifferent* toward them. One has come so far out that one has only one fear and one sorrow, which is sin, and it is this that Christianity proposes to alleviate through the forgiveness of sin (JP 4:4012).

The forgiveness of sin does constitute a kind of temporal help, but it takes a different form than what the common person ordinarily understands as temporal help. The forgiveness of sin signifies that God has forgotten one's sin in time (JP 2:1123). Through forgiveness one is also made a new person, but this does not necessarily mean that one enjoys happier circumstances in life as a result of that transformation (JP 2:1205). Suffering and misfortune remain, but one's attitude toward them is significantly changed.

Faith in relation to this again means to hold fast to possibility, to believe that by virtue of the absurd God will help one temporally (JP 2:1123, 1124, 1126). Although the Christian striver understands this temporal help primarily in terms of forgiveness, faith extends even further to include also the possibility of help in relation to the ordinary sufferings of life. It is precisely this belief in the possibility of temporal help that distinguishes faith from, and makes it the inverse of, resignation. Resignation is based on the belief in the *impossibility* of being helped temporally. In contrast to the common person who seeks temporal help or alleviation from God for his or her temporal suffering, the person who becomes resigned to suffering when it persists in life no longer expects any temporal help from God. Thus resignation signifies a kind of despair in that person. Christians also accept their temporal suffering and, because of their greater concern over their sinfulness, are even indifferent toward it; but they also believe in the possibility of temporal help for these sufferings, *even if it does not occur.* This constitutes the highest level of existential faith, a hope and confidence that is possible to acquire only after all human capacity and expectation are exhausted (*JP* 2:1125). While human effort and expectation look to a *direct removal of,* or else a *resignation to,* temporal suffering, faith holds foremost to the possibility of a removal of spiritual suffering—the anguished consciousness of, or sorrow over, one's sin; then, as a *consequence* of this, it also believes in the alleviation of temporal suffering, since with God all things are possible. Kierkegaard's view on Christianity's relation to temporal misfortune, therefore, is not that it cannot or will not alleviate such distress but that this is not Christianity's primary concern with human existence, nor should it be a human being's primary concern in coming to Christianity. Christianity has to do first and foremost with alleviating the Christian striver's anguished consciousness of sin and only indirectly or secondarily with the alleviation of earthly sorrow.

2

THE POSSIBILITY OF OFFENSE / FAITH

In its positive definition Christian faith consists in a subjective passion of the highest pitch sustained in relation to the eternal in time and constitutes that ideal condition of the self wherein, by willing to be oneself, one is grounded transparently in God without despair. But in existence faith assumes a dialectical character inasmuch as it comes to expression in, and is defined by a relation to, the negative. This negative or indirectly positive factor in one context is constituted by the consciousness of sin, but Christian faith also stands in a complementary dialectical relation to the possibility of offense: "Just as the concept 'faith' is an altogether distinctively Christian term, so in turn is 'offense' an altogether distinctively Christian term relating to faith. The possibility of offense is the crossroad, or it is like standing at the crossroad. From the possibility of offense one turns either to offense or to faith, but one never comes to faith except from the possibility of offense" (PC 81). Like the consciousness of sin in the form of the anguished conscience, the possibility of offense is an essential condition of faith. It functions as a negative or dialectical element in the definition of faith and for the coming into existence and continuation of faith. It is experienced not only by those who turn away from faith but also by everyone who has faith. The Christian believer is not offended by Christianity but still must have encountered the possibility of offense in coming to believe. The possibility of offense arises in the very coming into existence of faith and poses a constant threat in the life of the faithful. As Anti-Climacus describes it in *Practice in Christianity,* "faith is carried in a fragile earthen vessel, in the possibility of offense" (PC 76). Only by facing and overcoming the possibility of offense throughout life does a person exist in faith. Actual offense signifies the lack or loss of faith, but the possibility of offense is a prerequisite for and a complementary dialectical correlative to faith.

This indirectly positive role of the possibility of offense in Christian existence is sometimes described by Anti-Climacus using such military meta-phors as "the guardian or defensive weapon of faith" and "the repulsion" or repellant force by which faith comes into existence (PC 105, 121). The consciousness of sin constitutes the way of entrance into Christian exis-tence, but the possibility of offense guards and protects the approach to this way of life. The goal of Christianity is naturally to attract believers, but it sets about this task *inversely* by first repelling, then attracting them; or rather, Kierkegaard says that it repels in order to attract, using repulsion as a "dynamometer of the inwardness" (*JP* 1:455; see also *JP* 6:6261). In its *first form*, therefore, Christianity appears so terrible that it threatens to drive people away. This repulsion, however, is designed first and foremost to guard against misunderstanding Christianity's true nature and taking its attractiveness lightly or in vain. In addition, it thrusts everyone backward in order to prevent a direct communication of, or transition to, becoming a Christian. In its deepest sense the possibility of offense is an expression for the necessity of emphasizing the great attention required in the decision to become a Christian (PC 140). Christianity requires a passionate response, a choice on the part of the individual, not merely a direct reception of its truth by means of reasons, proofs, enticements, threats, or warnings. Christianity repels precisely in order to exact such a choice or passionate response from everyone. Repulsion assures that when one decides to become a Christian the decision will be based on the infinite passion the hope of eternal blessed-ness excites in oneself, not upon its reasonable or immediately attractive fea-tures. In fact, it is precisely because Christianity appears *unreasonable* and *unattractive* that it raises the possibility of offense.

When Christianity is rightly presented in its first form, therefore, no per-son can avoid the possibility of offense, for it appears as "the greatest plague" (*den storste Plage*)[1] to which a person can be subjected, and the "treatment" or cure that it offers seems far worse than the "sickness" one already suffers from (cf. PC 62, 115). Every person must pass through the possibility of offense and then choose whether to be offended or to believe. In fact, Anti-Climacus goes so far as to claim that everyone who encounters Christianity, even the disciples of Christ, succumbs to offense at some point (PC 105). If one avoids offense at one aspect of Christ or Christianity, one will become offended at another. But just as one avoids actual offense by believing, one is saved from offense by regaining that belief and trust in Christ.

Kierkegaard insists on the necessity of the possibility of offense in Chris-tian existence particularly in opposition to the speculative philosophy and theology of his age. In his opinion, speculation turns Christianity into a doctrine, making it an objective or noetic matter and basing acceptance of that doctrine on its rationality or commensurability with human understanding. As Kierkegaard/Anti-Climacus sees it, however, the possibility of offense is precisely what defends Christianity against speculation (*SUD* 83). Ironically, the speculative philosophers think they are defending Christianity by removing the possibility of offense and making Christianity commensurable with human conceptions and expectations. Substituting doubt in place of offense, they convert the problem of entry into faith into a matter of overcoming one's intellectual reservations about Christianity rather than offense at its incommensurability. Then they propose to do away with this supposed obstacle to faith by showing the reasonableness of Christianity and providing proofs of its truth. In Kierkegaard's view, however, this procedure compromises and essentially abrogates Christianity. The more one tries to defend Christianity by making it reasonable, mundane, and worldly, the more one distorts and finally abolishes it (*WL* 200–201). The speculative philosophers take the possibility of offense out of Christianity, thinking they are performing an act of kindness. But in doing away with the possibility of offense they also do away with that which they set out to defend and preserve, which is Christianity itself. For that which tempts one to reject Christianity is, in Kierkegaard's estimation, precisely what preserves its qualitative peculiarity, and the factors in Christianity that raise the possibility of offense are in turn preserved by it.

In becoming commensurate with the world, or conversely, in the world's having become Christianized, Christendom too, in Kierkegaard's estimation, did away with the possibility of offense, thus making it imperative that this essential qualification of Christianity be reintroduced and reaffirmed. Kierkegaard points out that when Christianity first came into the world it did not have to call attention to the fact that it was an offense, for the world naturally took offense and discovered it without difficulty (*WL* 199). But now that the world (loosely speaking) has become Christian (loosely speaking), the offensive nature of Christianity needs to be shown and emphasized. Otherwise, Kierkegaard suggests, we may as well "close the churches" or else turn them into "places of amusement" (201). People have altogether missed the point of Christianity because they have missed the possibility of offense in it (199). They entirely miss the difficulty and danger in Christianity, its heterogeneity to worldliness and human understanding, and its initial repulsiveness, which make the decision to become a Christian a matter of the utmost significance, risk, and passion. If Christianity is to be freed from the "enchantment of illusion" and "deformed transmogrification" that Christendom's accommodation to worldliness has foisted upon it, then the possibility of offense must again be preached (200). Only the possibility of offense can help those who have fallen asleep to break the enchantment so that Christianity can be itself once again. Kierkegaard thinks that when true Christianity rises up again, "formidable with the possibility of offense," it will need no defense (200). Indeed, it ought not to be defended; rather, people should be required to defend or justify themselves when the choice is put to them either to be offended or to believe.

Exactly what in Christianity occasions the possibility of offense? And why is it unavoidable in becoming a Christian? Previous scholarly treatments of these questions have tended to focus primarily on Kierkegaard's earlier pseudonymous writings and to consider the relation of faith to the possibility of offense more broadly under the topic of the relation of faith to reason. Their approaches thus have tended to view the question entirely in an intellectual context, with Kierkegaard's view of faith being variously characterized as irrational, antirational, or suprarational.[2] My procedure in this chapter will be to shift the focus of attention on these questions to the later literature of Kierkegaard, particularly *Practice in Christianity*, although some preliminary consideration of *Philosophical Fragments* and *Concluding Unscientific Postscript* is necessary to establish the context for this discussion. In general, the later literature suggests that persons are repulsed by the *contradictoriness, absoluteness,* and *heterogeneity to the world* of Christianity and Christian existence. If one gets by these factors or comes to Christianity with them before one's eyes and chooses it in spite of them, then one's commitment is likely to be decisive, passionate, and proper.

The Absurdity of the Offended Consciousness and the Absolute Paradox in *Philosophical Fragments*

Kierkegaard first introduces the category of offense (*Forargelse*) in *Philosophical Fragments*, where Johannes Climacus, the pseudonymous author, discusses it in connection with an individual's encounter with the absolute paradox. Climacus identifies the Danish word *anstød* ("offense") with the Greek word *skandalon*, or "stumbling-block" (*PF* 5on). *At tage anstød* or *at tage forargelse* means "to take affront," but it is not offense that actively affronts (*støder an*) something, rather, offense passively takes affront (*tager anstød).* In other words, offense, or the possibility of offense, does not originate with the human understanding but is occasioned by the absolute paradox, which confronts the understanding as a paradox that the understanding cannot of itself conceive, understand, or resolve. The paradox proclaims itself as the absolute paradox in that it not only reveals itself to be absolutely unlike humans (thus outside human conception) because of human sin but also proposes to do away with that unlikeness through absolute likeness or an identification with humans through the entry of the eternal into time in servant form (47). But when the understanding protests that this is folly and absurd, its utterance, Climacus claims, is really only an "echo" of what the absolute paradox contends about the understanding, namely, that *it* is absurd, and this echo is reflected back upon the absolute paradox from the offended consciousness (52). This creates an "acoustical illusion," or the impression that the expression of offense is coming from the understanding as its discovery about the nature of the absolute paradox, whereas the understanding is merely parroting or mimicking what the absolute paradox declares about itself and the understanding by its coming into existence. It is this parroting or caricaturing of the absolute paradox in the form of an acoustical illusion, or more accurately, two acoustical illusions, that I want to focus on in *Philosophical Fragments* in order to show how a problem of interpretation with regard to the possibility of offense remains unresolved in this book and its sequel, *Concluding Unscientific Postscript,* but finds resolution in the later literature and journals.

The first acoustical illusion to which Climacus calls attention is prepared for and illumined by the use of an analogy of offense to unhappy love that is rooted in a misunderstanding of self-love. Like self-love, which deceptively appears to be active but is really a form of inner suffering, offense at its deepest level is a suffering (49). Climacus wishes to establish the passive or suffering character of offense in order to make the further claim that neither discovery of the absolute paradox nor taking offense at it originates in the understanding but rather comes into existence with the absolute paradox. Thus when he speaks of the understanding actively, passionately, paradoxically seeking to "discover something that thought itself cannot think" (37), the unknown against which the understanding collides in this instance is not something it has discovered on its own even though it is in active pursuit of that which it does not know. When the understanding then exclaims that it has discovered a paradox which it cannot think or comprehend and becomes offended at it, this is an acoustical illusion resounding in the form of an echo of what the absolute paradox announces to the understanding about itself, namely, that it is a paradox.

Like any echo or acoustical illusion, however, the understanding distorts that which it imitates. For this reason Climacus likens offense to a caricaturing or parroting of the paradox, a copying of it "in the wrong way," so that offense is reckoned as an "erroneous accounting" and a "misunderstanding" of the moment or paradox (51, 52). But what does this mean? Does it mean that the absolute paradox is not really a paradox? Does it mean that the understanding is wrong in thinking that it has discovered the paradox but right in declaring it to be a paradox? Or is offense simply the wrong response to the paradox?

Perhaps some light may be shed on these questions by considering another acoustical illusion that comes into play with reference to the absolute paradox. Offense declares that the paradox is absurd, foolishness. But according to Climacus, this claim of the offended consciousness about the absolute paradox is only an echo or counterclaim of what the absolute paradox claims about the understanding (52). This time, however, the echo is not a copying of something the absolute paradox announces about itself but rather of what the absolute paradox announces about the understanding. Instead of the paradox being the absurd, it is the understanding that is the absurd or has been declared absurd by the paradox. This would seem to be the conclusion to which we are drawn on the basis of the text so far. But the issue immediately becomes more complicated by the fact that Climacus goes on to say: "The understanding declares that the paradox is the absurd, but this is only a caricaturing, for the paradox is indeed the paradox, *quia absurdum*" (52). Now it sounds as if what offense says about the paradox is an echo or caricaturing of what the paradox is and proclaims about itself, not of the paradox's claim about the understanding as we were previously led to think. Climacus once again reiterates that this is not something the understanding has discovered but rather is a discovery made by the paradox, which "now takes testimony from the offense" (52).

But if offense constitutes an "erroneous accounting" of the paradox and copies it "in the wrong way," there must be some distortion in this testimony; otherwise offense is not wrong in its claim that the paradox is absurd, only wrong in thinking that it made the discovery on its own. Perhaps that is all the distortion amounts to, namely, the illusion on the part of the understanding that it has discovered the paradox. Climacus certainly leads us to think as much, since he continues to emphasize that the discovery belongs to the paradox and that the understanding merely parrots it. How the paradox "discovers" (*opdaget*) itself or something about itself to the understanding is unclear, but perhaps Climacus means only that the understanding becomes cognizant of the absolute paradox from the absolute paradox, which announces itself as the absolute paradox to the understanding. That this is the case is suggested by subsequent passages in which the understanding is ushered to the "wonder stool" by the absolute paradox and confirmed in everything it says about the absolute paradox: "Now, what are you wondering about? It is just as you say, and the amazing thing is that you think that it is an objection, but the truth in the mouth of a hypocrite is dearer to me than to hear it from an angel and an apostle" (52). This passage suggests that what the understanding says about the absolute paradox is true, even if it is parroted and intended as an objection. What then is the distortion that makes offense a wrong accounting of the absolute paradox? Does it consist merely in the mistaken idea of the understanding that its charge of absurdity against the absolute paradox constitutes an objection to, rather than a confirmation of, its divine origin? Is it only a matter of who discovers the absolute paradox? Surely there is more at stake than that.

Let us approach the problem, therefore, from another angle. Climacus states: "The offense remains outside the paradox, and the basis for that is: *quia absurdum*" (52). The first clause of this statement is reiterated twice in the course of the same paragraph, so it must be a claim Climacus wants to impress upon us. To illustrate what he means by this claim, Climacus introduces another term for the absolute paradox, describing it this time as "the most improbable" in order to draw a contrast between the absolute paradox and the understanding, which can deal only with the probable (52). The improbable is that which stands outside the realm of probability. Probability cannot deal with the improbable or rather can deal with it only by transforming it into something probable, ordinary, or trivial, hence abrogating it (52–53; cf. *CUP* 1:211). As that which is the most improbable, therefore, the absolute paradox stands outside the understanding as something it cannot understand. But Climacus's claim is stated in reverse fashion: it is offense or the offended understanding that stands outside the absolute paradox rather than vice versa. While the opposite is equally true, since it stands to reason that the absolute paradox remains outside the understanding if the understanding remains outside the absolute paradox, Climacus is primarily interested in determining how the understanding is related to the absolute paradox rather than vice versa. If the understanding stands outside the absolute paradox, the implication is that anything the understanding has to say about it is suspect or distorted in some fashion. Our problem is to determine the precise nature of this distortion.

The Absurd and the Absolute Paradox in *Concluding Unscientific Postscript* and in Kierkegaard's Response to Theophilus Nicolaus

Since *Philosophical Fragments* is extremely sparse in what it has to say about the absolute paradox and the absurd, it may help us to look briefly at Climacus's additional remarks about these categories in *Concluding Unscientific Postscript*. In this work he suggests that the eternal, essential truth becomes paradoxical either by being brought into relation to an existing individual, as in Socratic subjectivity, or by being placed in juxtaposition with existence by coming into existence itself, as encountered in Christian subjectivity (*CUP* 1:205, 209). In the first instance, Climacus claims, the eternal, essential truth is not a paradox in itself, but in the second instance it is. Furthermore, the second form of paradox is identified with the absurd, which is concretely defined here in terms of the historical fact "that the eternal truth has come into existence in time, that God has come into existence, has been born, has grown up, etc., has come into existence exactly as an individual human being, indistinguishable from any other human being" (210). The eternal truth in this instance is absurd, Climacus claims, because "it contains the contradiction that something that can become historical only in direct opposition to all human understanding has become historical" (211). Then he goes on clearly to equate this contradiction with the absurd: "This contradiction is the absurd, which can only be believed" (211).

These later comments by Climacus indicate, first of all, that the absolute paradox is constituted by the juxtaposition of the eternal truth with existence or the historical, and this is consistent with how he describes the paradox in *Philosophical Fragments,* where he says that "the paradox specifically unites the contradictories, is the eternalizing of the historical and the historicizing of the eternal" (*PF* 61). Second, they indicate that the absolute paradox itself is absurd because it involves the coming into existence of eternal truth or the god, whose being or essence is not subject to the contingencies of space and time. This would seem, then, to settle the issue about the absurdity of the absolute paradox. But if the absolute paradox is the absurd, why does it declare the understanding absurd for having declared that the absolute paradox is absurd? And why is this echo on the part of the understanding an "erroneous accounting" of the absolute paradox, a misunderstanding of it? Our original questions still stand, and neither *Philosophical Fragments* nor *Concluding Unscientific Postscript* answers them, at least not to my satisfaction.

Let us turn, therefore, to another source of commentary on the absolute paradox and the absurd, Kierkegaard's unpublished response to Theophilus Nicolaus (Magnus Eiríksson), written in 1849–50 and preserved in the journals (*SKP* X⁶ B 68–82; *JP* 1:9–12 [78–81]; 6:6598–601 [68–69, 77, 82]).[3] Although this response is directed to Nicolaus's review of *Fear and Trembling*, it ranges beyond the treatment of paradox and the absurd in that work to cover the use of these categories by other Kierkegaardian pseudonyms as well, including Johannes Climacus and Anti-Climacus. In fact, several of the journal entries constituting this response are attributed to Johannes Climacus. In the first of these, he points out that what he and Johannes de Silentio, neither of whom claims to have faith, call the absurd and the absolute paradox, Theophilus Nicolaus, who identifies himself in the title of his book as the brother of a knight of faith whose confidential communications to him are being used to assist in his reply,[4] does not regard as absurd but rather as "the higher rationality" in a nonspeculative sense (*JP* 6:6598). But Climacus points out that without the absurd serving as "the negative sign and predicate which dialectically makes sure that the scope of 'the purely human' is qualitatively terminated," there is no way of indicating that this higher reason lies on the other side of the human, "in the heavenly regions of the divine, of revelation," rather than on this side. The rationality of the content of faith might then be presumed to stand in continuity with human understanding and be subject to discovery through human reason rather than through revelation. In order to prevent this from happening, Climacus claims, the absurd is needed as a sign and category to exercise a "restraining influence" upon the believer. He then goes on to make the following crucial statement: "When I believe, then assuredly neither faith nor the content of faith is absurd. O, no, no—but I understand very well that for the person who does not believe, faith and the content of faith are absurd, and I also understand that as soon as I myself am not in the faith, am weak, when doubt perhaps begins to stir, then faith and the content of faith gradually begin to become absurd for me" (*JP* 6:6598). This statement contains two important implications. First, it suggests that the absurd is a category of interpretation employed by human understanding, not a qualification of the absolute paradox itself as the content of faith. Second, the absurd more specifically is a category employed only by nonbelievers, not by believers. For believers, faith and the content of faith are not absurd even though the believer, like Abraham, appears to believe "by virtue of the absurd" to those who stand outside faith. But Kierkegaard, speaking in another entry as Anti-Climacus in the response to Theophilus Nicolaus, goes on to point out that this is only how it looks *to a third person* who does not have the passion of faith (*JP* 1:10). Neither Johannes de Silentio nor Johannes Climacus is a believer; thus they illumine faith only negatively, from the standpoint of an outsider, and should not be understood as describing the positive content of faith.

The absurd as a negative sign or determination of faith is nevertheless regarded by Anti-Climacus/Kierkegaard as an essential element in coming to faith, for several reasons. First, it assures that one has not overlooked any possibility of explaining the absolute paradox or content of faith within the realm of what is possible from a merely human standpoint (*JP* 1:9). Second, it assures that faith is not a (higher) form of knowledge, for only the passion of faith, not a better or higher understanding of the absolute paradox, is able to overcome the absurd (*JP* 1:10; 6:6598). Third, and perhaps most important, it gives faith a *double-sided* or *twofold* character that is "more penetrating and dialectical and informed" than the view of faith as a higher form of rationality offered by Theophilus Nicolaus as a corrective to Johannes de Silentio's presentation of faith as being acquired by virtue of the absurd (*JP* 1:10). In another journal entry of 1850 Kierkegaard laments the tendency of his time to present faith directly and in continuity with human understanding without the tension of the dialectical, suggesting that it results in an "unholy confusion" in speaking about faith (*JP* 1:8): "The [immediate] believer is not dialectically consolidated as 'the single individual,' cannot endure this double vision—that the content of faith, seen from the other side, is the negative absurd."

In this duplex perspective, the absurd and faith are inseparable; one only comes to faith by way of the absurd and the possibility of offense, which always remains as a negative possibility in faith even though the believer no longer regards the content of faith as absurd (*JP* 1:10). This is the same position we find Anti-Climacus taking in the opening summary of his exposition of the possibility of offense in relation to Christ in *Practice in Christianity* quoted at the beginning of this chapter (*PC* 81).

Resolution of the Problem of the Absurdity of the Absolute Paradox

Factoring in these statements, let us now return to the problem of the absurd in *Philosophical Fragments* with which we began. The problem, to restate it briefly, concerns the charge and countercharge of absurdity echoing between the absolute paradox and human understanding. The offended consciousness charges that the absolute paradox is absurd, and the absolute paradox countercharges that it is the understanding which is absurd. But since the charge of the offended consciousness is only an echo of what the absolute paradox announces about itself, we are left wondering why the understanding is declared to be absurd in making this charge against the paradox, and further, why it is reckoned as an "erroneous accounting" of the paradox. *Concluding Unscientific Postscript* confirmed the absurdity of the absolute paradox but did not provide a satisfactory resolution of these questions. Kierkegaard's response to Theophilus Nicolaus carries us much further in this direction but further complicates the issue by requiring us to make a distinction between the believer and the nonbeliever when thinking about the absurd. Since Johannes Climacus is a nonbeliever, he speaks as one outside faith who nevertheless succeeds in articulating the negative or obverse side of faith and the content of faith as it appears from the standpoint of human understanding. From this perspective, to declare the absolute paradox to be absurd is undoubtedly a misunderstanding because human understanding stands outside the absolute paradox and thinks the absurdity of the absolute paradox constitutes an objection to it. Yet, according to Climacus, the absolute paradox proclaims itself to the understanding as the absurd and is the absolute paradox precisely because it is absurd. Is this perhaps a further misunderstanding on his part, because he is a nonbeliever? I think not, for Anti-Climacus is just as adamant as Climacus in proclaiming the contradictoriness and paradoxicality of Christianity. In fact, in the closing sentence of the response to Theophilus Nicolaus, Kierkegaard remarks: "Incidentally, I would be glad to have another pseudonym, one who does not like Johannes de Silentio say he does not have faith, but plainly, positively says he has faith—Anti-Climacus—repeat what, as a matter of fact, is stated in the pseudonymous writings" (*JP* 6:6601).

In Kierkegaard's view, then, there is congruence and continuity between the pseudonyms on the absurdity of the paradox. Perhaps a clue to how, in his mind at least, the apparent incongruities relating to the absurd in their accounts are resolved may be found in a journal entry of 1842–43, predating the writing of *Philosophical Fragments* (*JP* 3:3073). This entry contains Kierkegaard's reading notes on Leibniz's *Theodicy,* specifically, the distinction Leibniz makes between what is above reason and what is against reason. For Leibniz, faith is above reason, which in Kierkegaard's judgment is equivalent to his own claim that Christianity consists of paradox. Since reason, as Leibniz understands it, involves "a linking together of truths (*enchainement*), a conclusion from causes," Kierkegaard concludes that faith "cannot be *proved, demonstrated, comprehended*" because there is a missing link. This means faith is a paradox and does not stand in continuity with reason, or at least not immediately so. Here we reach the point I want to emphasize. Kierkegaard goes on in these notes to state that Christianity *does* stand in continuity with reason, but it has "continuity only in reverse" (*bagvendt Continuitet*), that is, "at the beginning it does not manifest itself as continuity." The paradoxicality and unreasonableness or absurdity of Christianity thus constitutes "the first form" of its appearance in world history and human consciousness.

Applying this dialectical structure to *Philosophical Fragments,* we may conclude, therefore, that Christianity appears in its *first form* as the absurd or absolute paradox to the understanding, but that is not its true or ultimate form, which is grasped only in faith. When the understanding declares the absolute paradox to be absurd, therefore, it is only an echo of what Christianity in its first form as absolute paradox proclaims about itself to the understanding. That echo is a caricature or distortion of the truth in being an acoustical illusion that originates from the absolute paradox rather than from the understanding and in constituting an improper response to the absolute paradox in the form of an offended consciousness rather than the happy passion of faith. But it is also a caricature because ultimately the absolute paradox, however improbable, absurd, contradictory, or paradoxical it appears to human consciousness, expresses only the *obverse* side of the truth, which is not only not improbable or impossible but is entirely possible because it is actual, having come into existence in the form of an individual human being in a decisive moment of time. From the standpoint of faith, all things are possible for God, even, we may presume, entering into the forms and substance of the temporal realm.

Our exploration of the perplexing little problem of the acoustical illusion in *Philosophical Fragments* has shown, therefore, that it is both appropriate and necessary to read both this book and *Concluding Unscientific Postscript* together with Kierkegaard's later writings and not in isolation from them. Otherwise one might be tempted to take Climacus's views as fully representing the Christian position, which he admittedly does not subscribe to or existentially reduplicate in his own life. Climacus gives us only one side of the truth as understood from a Christian perspective.

The Possibility of Offense as an Indirectly Positive Factor in Christian Existence

In the second period of Kierkegaard's authorship, the offended consciousness and its degrees of intensification are taken up in *The Sickness unto Death*, where as we saw in Chapter 1 the dialectical opposition between sin and faith becomes intensified to a higher form of opposition: offense/faith. In delineating the negative forms of offense, *The Sickness unto Death* suggests several ways in which Christianity presents the possibility of offense: (1) its assertion of an infinite qualitative difference between humans and God as a result of sin presents the possibility of offense because it contradicts human beings' essential understanding of themselves and of their relation to God or the eternal (*SUD* 117, 122, 126–27); (2) the Christian conception of the self, both in its ideal form (which appears too exalted) and in its actual form (which portrays the human being as a sinner), raises the possibility of offense because it contradicts the criterion and goal humans have projected for themselves and requires them to face themselves as they truly are, to repent for it, and to seek forgiveness in Jesus Christ (83–85); (3) Christ's offer of forgiveness of sin presents the possibility of offense first of all by its suggestion that one stands in need of forgiveness and then by the offer of forgiveness to an individual when, humanly speaking, forgiveness seems impossible (113, 116). Even more offensive in this last respect is (a) the fact that a human being presumes to forgive the sins of other human beings, and (b) the claim that God has come to earth, suffered, and died in order to help humans achieve selfhood and to live directly in the sight of God in fellowship with the divine. In each instance cited above the possibility of offense is either directly or indirectly related to the paradox of Christ, who in the later literature is generally referred to as the God-man, or more accurately, the God–human being (*Gud-Menneske*), rather than as the absolute paradox or the eternal in time.[5] Offense becomes possible through the knowledge of Christ or by existing before him. Christ represents a confirmed expression of the infinite criterion and goal that inversely reveals the infinite difference between human beings and God that convicts them as sinners. The denial of Christ as the paradox thus entails the denial of everything Christian.

Whereas *The Sickness unto Death* primarily elucidates the negative dialectic between faith and the possibility of offense, the indirectly positive dialectical relation between them is principally delineated in *Practice in*

Christianity. In the latter book Anti-Climacus works out his most thorough determination of how Christianity presents the possibility of offense and how it functions in an indirectly positive way as an inevitable and necessary obstacle on the way to faith as well as for existence in faith.⁶ While Christianity presents the possibility of offense in a number of ways, in this work Anti-Climacus suggests that it is primarily due to, or consists in, the *inversions* that characterize Christ and Christian existence.

In the opening discourse of *Practice in Christianity* Anti-Climacus reflects on Christ's invitation to come unto him. The invitation, he says, is extended to all—the poor, the wretched, the physically sick, the sick at heart, the unappreciated, the lost, and all those who have been treated unfairly, wronged, insulted, mistreated, despised, deceived, and victimized—and to each one individually, without regard to temporal differences between persons (*PC* 16–17). It urges those who have strayed and lost their way, those who have found human forgiveness but no rest, those who have found no forgiveness because they did not seek it, and those who have sought forgiveness in vain to *"turn around"* (*vende om*) and come to Christ without fear of the "difficulty of retreat" or the "laborious pace of conversion," which "however toilsomely . . . leads to salvation" (19). Christ's invitation stands at the crossroads or the parting of the ways—the way of sin, which leads one farther away from faith, and the way of conversion (*Omvendelse*), which leads one to, or back to, faith through Christ—and urges those who hear it to take the latter path.

Anti-Climacus points out two inversions that obtain in this situation. Normally those in need of help seek out someone who can help them, but in this instance the process is reversed: it is Christ who seeks out those in need of help. He assumes that they have been silenced by their suffering, that they are "so tired and exhausted and fainting that as if in a stupor they have again forgotten that there is comfort" (21). Thus he lovingly calls to them, alters his condition to likeness with theirs, and offers his help unconditionally to all those who will turn back and seek help from him. The second inversion follows as a consequence of the first. Christ issues the invitation to all who labor and are heavy laden, but instead of people flocking to him as one would expect, they run in the opposite direction. Christ offers help, forgiveness, rest, and life to those who suffer, but they turn back from him in horror and fly away. Anti-Climacus asks how this "frightful inverted relation" could have occurred, how one can explain that

> no one or almost no one accepted the invitation, but that all, almost all . . . are in agreement about opposing the inviter, putting him to

death, yes, even putting a penalty upon letting oneself be helped by him! It is certainly to be expected that upon such an invitation all, all who are suffering, would flock to him, and all who were not suffering, moved by the thought of such mercy and compassion, would flock to him, so that the whole generation would be in agreement about admiring and extolling the inviter. How can the opposite be explained? (PC 57)

The explanation lies, first of all, in the fact that Christ himself places an obstacle, the possibility of offense, in the way of those who would come unto him. He does not allow anyone to come directly to him, nor does he come directly to anyone. The possibility of offense interposes and is posed by Christ himself. Thus Christ is simultaneously the sign of offense and the object of faith. In fact, he must be the sign of offense in order to become the object of faith (23–24, 98).

Basically, Christ occasions two forms of offense. The first is essential, having to do with his person; the second is accidental, having to do with his relation to the established order. Both concern Christ's temporal existence, contemporaneity, or actuality, not abstract speculation about the union of God and humanity or the human race. Anti-Climacus criticizes Christendom precisely on this point, charging variously that it transforms Christ into the "speculative unity of God and humanity *sub specie aeterni* [under the aspect of eternity]," that it projects a fantastic image of Christ that does away with his concrete humanity and lowliness, or else that it ignores the importance of his person altogether and emphasizes only his teachings (81–82, 103, 123, translation amended slightly). For Kierkegaard and Anti-Climacus, offense and the possibility of offense pertain only to the individual, not to the human race in general. Offense becomes real or actual only when there is an individual who is offended or who encounters the possibility of offense. Likewise, the possibility of offense as it pertains to Christ has to do only with his existence as an individual human being (*et enkelt Menneske*). It is in the situation of contemporaneity with Christ, the moment when an individual human being meets Christ as an individual human being, that one encounters the possibility of offense (82). For it is precisely the fact that an individual human being claims to be God or acts and speaks in such a manner as to manifest the divine, and conversely, that God is identified with this lowly individual human being, that constitutes the essential possibility of offense in relation to Christ. The essential offense occasioned by Christ thus has to do with his *loftiness* and *lowliness* (82). Given the infinite qualitative difference between human beings and God, which for Kierkegaard and Anti-Climacus is axiomatic, both aspects of the essential possibility of offense derive from the fact that an individual human being, Jesus of Nazareth, acted and spoke in such a way that suggests that he is qualitatively the *inverse* of what he appears to be or of what people think his essential nature is. The essential possibility of offense is thus raised by the *composite* and *qualitatively contradictory* makeup of Christ's being. This combination of an individual human being and divinity, lowliness and loftiness, humanly understood, is unthinkable. Anti-Climacus goes on, therefore, to explore the possibility of offense in relation to Christ as a paradox or "sign of contradiction" in the form of a *qualitative contradiction* rather than as a logical or formal contradiction concerning the speculative unity of God and humanity:[7] "In Scripture the God–human being is called a sign of contradiction—but what contradiction, if any, could there be at all in the speculative unity of God and humanity? No, there is no contradiction in that, but the contradiction—and it is as great as possible, is the qualitative contradiction—is between being God and being an individual human being" (*PC* 125, translation amended slightly; cf. also 123 and 131).

As Anti-Climacus sees it, "humanly speaking, there is no possibility of a crazier composite than this either in heaven or on earth or in the abyss or in the most fantastic aberrations of thought"—a viewpoint which echoes that of Johannes Climacus concerning the absolute paradox (*PC* 82; *PF* 37, 46). For Anti-Climacus the essential possibility of offense is occasioned by the fact that an individual human being acts so as indirectly to suggest the quality of divinity in his being (in other words, one is offended by the "loftiness" of Christ) and by the fact that this man underwent humiliation and suffering, which are incongruent with the human conception of God (one is offended by his "lowliness") (*PC* 82). In neither instance does the contradiction of the Incarnation have to do with whether it constitutes a logical or formal contradiction but rather with the lofty actions and lowly condition of an individual human being that suggest an incongruous, qualitatively contradictory composition of his being. A logical or formal contradiction is governed by the principle of contradiction, which excludes the possibility of the opposite of a claim being true at the same time, whereas a paradox is distinguished precisely by the fact that both opposing terms are regarded as being simultaneously true. Like Vigilius Haufniensis, the pseudonymous author of *The Concept of Anxiety,* Anti-Climacus seems to assume a strict distinction between actuality and logic (*CA* 9–10 and note 14). Logic pertains only to the realm of thought and cannot think the particular or individual. Thus it can deal only with the concept of humanity in general; that is, it universalizes human being, whereas the union between the divine and human Anti-Climacus is talking about is between God and an individual human being, not humanity in general, which in his view poses no contradiction at all. The qualitative contradiction this union posits is the greatest possible contradiction because qualitative opposites in existence cannot be mediated as they are in thought. As Johannes Climacus points out in *Philosophical Fragments,* thought cannot conceive an absolute difference between God and human beings and tends, on the contrary, to assert a fundamental likeness rather than a contradiction between them (*PF* 45).

Misunderstanding of the qualitative rather than logical character of the contradiction pertaining to the paradox of the Incarnation generally has its source in a misperception of the earlier pseudonymous literature. In *Philosophical Fragments* Climacus describes the absolute paradox as being based upon a "self-contradiction," but this does not refer to a logical or formal contradiction. Rather, for Climacus it is the eternal's *going against its own nature* by coming into existence or inflecting the god's eternal essence "into the dialectical qualifications of coming into existence" that constitutes the self-contradiction (*PF* 87; cf. *CUP* 1:578). To the human understanding this event may appear to be a logical contradiction, but as C. Stephen Evans has pointed out, Climacus explicitly distinguishes his hypothetical assumption of the absolute paradox from the kind of self-contradiction, nonsense, or meaninglessness contained in the claim, for example, that "the god is the god for the contemporary, but the contemporary in turn is the god for a third" or follower at second hand (*PF* 101).[8] This claim, according to Climacus, "is unthinkable in a sense different from" how his hypothetical assumption and the individual's relation to it is "unthinkable" inasmuch as the former "produces a self-contradiction," whereas the latter is "unreasonable" (*urimelig*) and "the strangest thing of all" for thought to understand but "contains no self-contradiction," thus enabling thought to become preoccupied with it (101). Unless Climacus may be charged with having contradicted himself here (!), it must be assumed that he understands the self-contradiction pertaining to the absolute paradox to be different from that which obtains in the example given, which clearly constitutes a logical contradiction and which for that reason Climacus rejects as nonsense. In fact, Climacus consistently maintains, contra Hegel, that the principle of contradiction is not canceled in existence (*PF* 108–9; *CUP* 1:203, 304–5, 347, 351).

Like Anti-Climacus, therefore, Climacus is primarily concerned with the *duplexity* of the absolute paradox or how it unites qualitative opposites in existence, which in his view occurs in two senses. First, absolute unlikeness is annulled in absolute likeness to the human. God is the Unknown in the sense of being absolutely unlike human beings. In *Philosophical Fragments* Climacus attributes this unlikeness to human sinfulness, but in *Concluding Unscientific Postscript* he explains it more in terms of a basic ontological difference: "But the absolute difference between God and a human being is simply this, that a human being is an individual existing being . . . whose essential task therefore cannot be to think *sub specie aeterni,* because as long as he exists, he himself, although eternal, is essentially an existing person and the essential for him must therefore be inwardness in existence; God, however, is the infinite one, who is eternal" (*CUP* 1:217). Whether the qualitative difference is explained in terms of humanity's qualitative defection from an original likeness to God or through the inherently different nature of God and the conditions of existence, the historicity and qualitative contradiction this event engenders present the possibility of offense to the human understanding. Human understanding operates via the principles of analogy and correlation; it cannot conceive absolute unlikeness; it cannot negate or transcend itself absolutely. In trying to comprehend the absolute unlikeness of the divine that has come into existence in the absolute paradox, the understanding can only conceive the unlike in terms of the like. Thus it relativizes and abrogates the absolute paradox. The understanding is thus faced with another epistemological gulf that is based upon a qualitative rather than temporal barrier. Climacus says in *Philosophical Fragments:* "This human being is also the god. How do I know that? Well, I cannot know it, for in that case I would have to know the god and the difference, and I do not know the difference, inasmuch as the understanding has made it like unto that from which it differs. . . . The understanding has the god as close as possible and yet just as far away" (*PF* 45–46). True identification, or the establishment of an absolute likeness of the god with human beings, is achieved not through the reductive power of the understanding but through the historical appearance of the god in servant form, which combines the qualitative opposites of absolute unlikeness and likeness to human beings in an existential unity.

Second, the absolute paradox unites the eternal and the temporal in such a way as to be distinct from all other historical facts by virtue of its peculiar qualitative composition and its ability to take on transhistorical power and significance. Because of its contradictory qualitative composition, the absolute paradox is no simple historical fact, nor even an "eternal fact," but an absolute fact (*PF* 99–100). The simple or ordinary historical fact has only relative significance and involves no contradiction, only a qualitative change from nonbeing (*ikke væren*) to being (*væren*), or from possibility (*mulighed*) to actuality (*virkelighed*), in its coming into existence. An "eternal fact" is a contradiction in terms, since facts are historical and the eternal, by definition, is not. The absolute fact, by contrast, is historical. It does not differ from simple historical facts with respect to simple historicity, but rather on the basis of the qualitative contradiction between historicity and the eternal.

In the pseudonymous writings of Johannes Climacus and in *Practice in Christianity* by Anti-Climacus, therefore, the possibility of offense in relation to Christ is seen as being occasioned primarily by two factors: the historicity or coming into existence of the God–human being and the qualitative contradiction this engenders. Climacus emphasizes the element of historicity, Anti-Climacus the qualitative contradiction and the conditions attached to it. But this difference does not appear to be exclusive in Kierkegaard's mind. Just as in *Philosophical Fragments* the historicity of the absolute paradox is seen as uniting qualitative opposites, in *Practice in Christianity* Anti-Climacus is able to say that it is the *fact* of Christ's existence—the fact that God existed on earth as an individual human being—which is "the infinitely extraordinary, is the in-itself extraordinary" (*PC* 32).

In *Philosophical Fragments* and *Concluding Unscientific Postscript*, however, the possibility of offense sometimes seems to be raised more by the fact that the appearance of the eternal in time contradicts human beings' essential understanding of themselves, whereas in *Practice in Christianity* it is essentially related to the person of Christ. There is nothing in Christ's human condition or career, however, that would immediately convince people that God was present in this lowly man. That Jesus is God is certainly not *directly* obvious, and that is precisely what occasions the possibility of offense and the necessity of faith and contemporaneity with Christ. In Anti-Climacus's estimation, no accumulation of historical facts about this man, no proofs, and no assessment of him on the basis of his accomplishments can ever establish that he is God. This is why Anti-Climacus makes the notorious statement that nothing can be known about Christ through history or through the tools of historical investigation (*PC* 25). One cannot know that Christ is God; one must believe it. Certainly one may gather facts about the historical Jesus, but these in no way warrant the conclusion that, as Anti-Climacus expresses it, "ergo he was God" (29). If anything, Anti-Climacus suggests, the judgment of Christ on the basis of his earthly career would warrant the opposite conclusion. The natural human reaction to Christ was to regard him as mad, fantastic, foolish, ludicrous, an impostor. He started out attracting some favorable attention and admiration, but his career went steadily downhill or "instead of going forward in increasing esteem, goes ever backward in increasing disrepute" (53–54). He helped others with miracles (suggesting that, after all, he was a strangely extraordinary person), but he was unable to help himself when he encountered opposition from those in power. His condition in life was so unenviable that those who first idolized him soon gave him up, and those few who remained loyal could only be regarded as little more than madmen themselves. Historical research can establish that Christ was a human being, perhaps even an extraordinary human being, but nothing more nor other than a human being.

Kierkegaard was unshakably convinced that quantitative intensifications and the quantitative methods of measuring them do not yield a transition of quality. He applied this principle in the differentiation of Christian subjectivity from ethical-religious subjectivity, and it also underlies his view that Christianity is not directly the intensification of merely human conceptions, values, and passions. In the case of Christ, the proposal of such a logical conclusion or leap is, from Anti-Climacus's point of view, not only logically invalid but blasphemous. It proceeds from the notion (also invalid) that the consequences or achievements of Christ's life are more significant than his life or the fact that he existed (PC 31–33). This relegates Christ to being a mere human being and, ironically, defeats just what the inference set out to posit. Assessment on the basis of what one achieves in life may be appropriate for other human beings, but not for Christ. Neither the consequences of his life nor his historical achievements can establish that he is God, only the fact that God was present in him can do that, and that fact cannot be determined historically. This is what leads Anti-Climacus to make his other notorious claim, that Christ exists only for faith (25). Anti-Climacus does not intend to imply that Christ is a fiction or lacks historicity—far from it!— but only that his divinity must be believed rather than known or proved.[9]

The consequences of Christ's life may be used to point to his divinity only if one forgets the central fact of his existence (his lowliness), views him only as the Christ of glory, or regards his return in glory as the final consequence of his life. Anti-Climacus insists, however, that it is only through Christ's lowliness or humiliation that one apprehends his divinity. The return of Christ in glory is not a fact of history but a tenet of faith's expectation about the future. Therefore it cannot be used to judge the significance or the character of the life of Christ. The lowliness of Christ is an essential aspect of his existence. It is something Christ willed for himself and not something accidental to his being which may be forgotten in time. Christ's whole life falls essentially under the concept of lowliness. Consequently, in order to know and to believe in him, one must begin with his lowliness, not overlook it. When Christ's life of humiliation, suffering, lowliness, and powerlessness are taken into account, the infinite self-contradiction in the claim that God is this lowly human being, that the deity should suffer and be powerless as if the divine were a mere man, becomes apparent. The proper way of relating oneself to Christ, therefore, is not simply or directly to convert his humiliation into glory, thereby regarding him directly as the Christ of glory, but to learn to know him first in his lowliness, and then through that come to behold his loftiness. This is done by viewing Christ's lowliness and humiliation indirectly and inversely as a "sign of contradiction." It is also the means by which the possibility of offense is brought to the fore and more closely determined.

Anti-Climacus explains that being a "sign" means that something is different from what it immediately is or appears to be; being a "sign of contradiction" means in addition that the sign contains in itself, in its very constitution, a contradiction, that something is the *opposite* of what it immediately is (PC 124–25). Immediately, Christ is a lowly human being; the contradiction is that he is God, that his lowliness is a sign of loftiness. However, a sign is a sign only for the person who knows that it is a sign and what it signifies; to everyone else it is only what it immediately is. A sign of contradiction draws attention to itself and shows anyone who is attentive that it contains a contradiction. Attention is indirectly drawn to the contradiction in Christ's case by certain words and actions that are suggestive of the qualification of the divine: healing and blessing people, forgiving sins, showing infinite compassion with absolute self-abandonment. These provide no direct indication or proof of the contradiction in Christ's appearance. They can do no more than serve to make a person attentive, Anti-Climacus claims (126). In fact, because Christ is a sign of contradiction, he cannot communicate who he is directly. As Anti-Climacus understands it, "direct communication does indeed directly state what one essentially is," whereas "unrecognizability means not to be in the character of what one essentially is" (132). Thus, even when Christ spoke directly about himself, as when, for example, he said that he was the only begotten Son of the Father (and Anti-Climacus assumes that it is Christ, not the later church speaking), the fact that he is a sign of contradiction makes his *direct* utterances *indirect,* since he is not immediately perceivable as the begotten of the Father and must be believed to be such (135).

Apprehension of Christ as a sign of contradiction is important because it is what occasions the possibility of offense. Neither lowliness nor loftiness in itself is offensive. Only the person who senses that Christ is not what he immediately is, that is, simply and only a lowly human being, experiences the possibility of offense and faith. But the possibility of offense also arises from the fact that the contradiction in Christ's being is not directly recognizable. In the condition of lowliness Christ does not appear in his exalted role directly as God, but takes on a profound *incognito*. The possibility of offense lies precisely in the inversion that instead of immediately or directly appearing as God to such a degree that people could at once perceive it directly, he is God to such a degree that he is unrecognizable as such in the world. If he were directly recognizable as God, there would be no possibility of offense, no uncertainty or ambiguity about what his words and actions signify.

As Anti-Climacus sees it, however, the purpose of Christ's *incognito* is not to make it difficult for humans to know that he is God. Rather, Christ's loftiness appears in inverse form in the world in order to negate the worldly conception of loftiness and to prevent his spiritual loftiness from being taken in vain. By making himself a duplexity, a riddle, Christ commands the utmost attention to himself. By assuming a strict *incognito* and appearing in an unrecognizable and contradictory form in the world, he brings persons to a halt and presents them with a choice. Because he is a sign of contradiction, his lowliness being a sign of loftiness, the proper choice is not one or the other of his conditions—lowliness *or* loftiness—but *both*. It is precisely Christ's *contradictory compositeness* that creates the possibility of offense. There is no occasion for offense in affirming only one aspect of his being. It is not directly the fact that Christ is a lowly human being that arouses the possibility of offense, but the fact that this lowliness is inversely a sign of his loftiness.

The *incognito* is also assumed in order to enable Christ to know human beings, that is, to know what is in their hearts and to reveal it to them. This is ultimately why Christ is a sign of contradiction, and although Anti-Climacus does not actually say so, possibly the deepest reason why Christ occasions the possibility of offense. For in looking at the contradiction in Christ, "one sees as in a mirror, one comes to see oneself, or he who is the sign of contradiction looks straight into one's heart while one is staring into the contradiction" (*PC* 126–27). In choosing in relation to Christ, one is revealed to oneself, for what dwells within oneself is made evident by how one chooses.

This leads to another way in which Christ poses the possibility of offense. One might even say that this other possibility of offense arises out of this self-revealing encounter with the contradiction in Christ. When Christ issues the invitation for all to come unto him and people run from him instead, it is because the invitation comes from a lowly human being, not from the Christ of glory. But the invitation that comes from this lowly man properly belongs to the Exalted One, who is clearly in a position to help human beings, whereas a lowly man can do nothing. It is quite incongruous that someone in his condition should presume to offer help to others, for he clearly stands in need of it himself. But the kind of help Christ offers and his absolute expression of love and compassion through complete self-abandonment for others also repel people because he introduces the divine conception of love, compassion, and human sickness. Ordinarily one would have expected people to flock to someone who offers to help them, but instead they avoided him and even conspired to have him put to death, which presumably would not have happened if Christ had conformed to a merely human conception of compassion and human misery (PC 57, 65–66). It was because he displayed divine compassion or an unlimited, reckless concern for others and none for himself, quite literally making himself one with the most wretched, that he was rejected. From a merely human standpoint, such compassion is "madness," "too much," and "too lofty" (58–59). People do not know what to make of someone who acts so recklessly, and they are inclined to laugh when they see it. They are willing to practice compassion and self-denial themselves, but only "to a certain degree" (59–60). Consequently they are not accustomed to seeing such loftiness in actuality, in their daily lives; for them, loftiness is only a subject for poetry, far removed from actuality and lasting for only a brief time. "That the loftiest of all has become the everyday" thus constitutes "an enormous contradiction" that presents the possibility of offense for them (60).

A similar incongruity obtains between Christ's conception of human misery and a merely human conception of it. Christ invites the poor, the sick, and the suffering to come unto him, but instead of healing their ordinary sufferings he promises forgiveness of sin, which in his view is what essentially constitutes human corruption and sickness (PC 60–61). From a merely human perspective, Anti-Climacus exclaims, this would be "cruel," "shocking," "outrageous," embittering, and even laughable if it were not so serious (60–61). Moreover, he accuses the inviter of employing "almost a kind of cunning" or deception in coming "in the guise of compassion" for ordinary human suffering when what he really wanted to talk about was sin: "It is cunning of the inviter to say: I heal all sicknesses, and then when one comes says: I acknowledge only that there is one sickness—sin—of that and from that I heal all of those 'who labor and are burdened'" (61). So ludicrous and incongruous to all human expectation is this that Anti-Climacus likens it to "breaking one's leg and going to a physician who specializes in diseases of the eyes" (61–62). Thus a corollary of the essential possibility of offense is the contradiction that the appearance of God in an individual human being constitutes to human beings' earthly needs, priorities, conceptions, self-understanding, expectations, actions, and goals. If Christ had behaved in a merely human way and in accordance with his lowly station, he would not have occasioned the possibility of offense.

This aspect of the essential possibility of offense in Christ is related in a way to what Anti-Climacus identifies as the second or accidental forum of offense occasioned by Christ. This form has to do with Christ's collision with the established order of his day. It has its source in the fact that Christ refused to "deify" the established order and subordinate himself to it. Anti-Climacus cites as an instance of this the time when Jesus and his disciples refused to wash their hands before eating bread, a custom of Jewish piety (PC 85). Jesus saw that such a practice was really an expression of secularization in which there was complete commensurability and congruity between the outward or external practices of Judaism and its adherents' professed inwardness. Ordinarily, Kierkegaard praised the achievement of a correspondence between the inner and the outer, and he projected it as the goal of the Christian life. But in the case of Judaism in Christ's time, at least as Kierkegaard understood it, inwardness had become dissolved into outwardness, making worship of God into a sham, mockery, and contempt. In contrast to this Christ made the individual God-relation of absolute significance and pointed out that piety or inwardness is not directly commensurable with the outer. The establishment regarded this disparagement of itself as the action of someone who was trying to make himself more than a human being, although in this instance it was inversely the establishment that had usurped the position of God. When the establishment has thus deified itself, any form of opposition or nonconformity by an individual occasions the possibility of offense. Anti-Climacus says this form of offense in relation to Christ "is a historically vanishing possibility that vanished with his death, that existed only for his contemporaries in relation to him, this individual human being" (PC 94). But it can become a present possibility for Christian strivers as they contradict the established order's tendency toward self-deification and its emphasis on external conformity: "Every time a witness to the truth transforms truth into inwardness (and this is the essential activity of the witness to the truth), every time a genius internalizes the true in an original way—then the established order will in fact be offended at him" (87). This form of the possibility of offense may be assured of vicarious continuation because it is precisely "this deification of the established order" that constitutes "the perpetual revolt, the continual mutiny against God" (89).

Christian strivers face not only the possibility of reacting to Christ with offense, but also the possibility of being offended at the Christian life themselves and of serving as the occasion of offense for others. To be like Christ is the most exalted life a person can strive for, but it is also a life of insult, hardship, and derision from others who regard the Christian striver as no more than a criminal, madman, or misanthrope. The possibility of offense in relation to this aspect of the Christian life is derived from, and corresponds to, the possibility of offense that has to do with the lowliness and humiliation of Christ, only now it is the Christian who becomes the occasion of offense to others because his or her conceptions, values, actions, and goals conflict with theirs. But the abasement and humiliation of the Christian life present the possibility of offense in a *double* sense: not only do Christian strivers become repulsive to others by exemplifying the Christian life and values in the world, they are likely to be repulsed or put off by this form of life themselves. One discovers that being a Christian involves a self-contradiction that intensifies the possibility of offense. One comes to Christ for aid to bear the normal sufferings of life, then learns that one must voluntarily give up all and take upon oneself the responsibility of exposing oneself to suffering that one could easily avoid.

The remedy that Christ prescribes as *salvation from offense,* therefore, is inversely the very thing that constitutes the *possibility of offense* (PC 110–11). Help appears as a torment, relief as a burden. To outsiders it is madness to expose oneself to such a precarious existence. Yet the offense lies not so much in the painfulness such an existence brings as in the fact that one is exposed to tribulation and persecution only because one has had recourse to this particular "physician" (114–15). Help from any other source would seek to make things better for one in the world, but help from Christ only makes matters worse. One could perhaps understand it if life were to go badly in the world for the offended person, but the dialectic of offense in Christianity is such that it is the believer for whom things go badly and who is regarded with scorn. All the proper relationships and conditions are completely reversed or inverted. A person with forbearance could perhaps put up with such treatment for a while, but the believer is required to sacrifice his or her entire life. One's human understanding is thus brought to a standstill by the inverseness of Christian existence, the why and the wherefore of the requirements in relation to the benefits, for indeed, there seem to be *no* "wherefore" and *no* benefits. But just this stage of puzzlement is necessary before a person can be helped by Christ in the manner in which he offers help. Only when one is willing to accept Christianity on any terms, no matter whether it is a help or a torment, does one properly attach oneself to Christ and receive his benefits.

Faith in this context means, therefore, *to let go of probability*. In Chapter 1 it was shown that Kierkegaard defined faith as *holding on to possibility* in the face of, and in spite of, seeming impossibility or absurdity. The dialectical correlative we have just examined underscores the absurdity of the fact that becoming a Christian may bring hardship and defeat in the world just as much as victory and success. One must be prepared for either destruction or victory and desire attachment to Christ regardless of which comes. In fact, the probability that holds in relation to faith is that one will be defeated by the world. The possibility of offense in Christian existence requires an intensity of passion and commitment of everyone who would come to Christ. If after seeing the possibilities of offense a person still desires to come unto Christ and to be helped by him in the manner in which his help is offered, then Christ will help that person and he or she will find the consolation, joy, and benefits of the Christian life. The possibility of offense assures, however, that these positive aspects of Christianity are not understood as the world understands them, that it is only after the human understanding has been confounded by the inverseness of Christ and Christian existence that the positive appears indirectly in the negative. The worldly conception of Christianity as a direct intensification of the worldly contains no distinction, no contrast, no possibility of offense. Thus a person in Christendom, Anti-Climacus says, "becomes a Christian in the most pleasant way of the world without being aware of the slightest possiblity of offense" (PC 111). But if any persons are willing to venture the Christian life based on Christ's historical reality, they will immediately discover the possibility of offense themselves, and Christendom will discover it from them in turn.

Through conditions pertaining to both Christ and Christian existence, therefore, the possibility of offense becomes a complementary dialectical factor in faith and is essential for a proper understanding of faith and existence in it. Actually being offended is a hindrance to faith, but the possibility of offense is something every Christian striver must pass through and overcome. In this way the possibility of offense guards against taking faith lightly or in vain. Offense is the opposite of faith, but the possibility of offense is the negative sign of faith or expresses the negative criterion for faith: that humanly understood what Christianity proposes is impossible, absurd, contradictory, and completely heterogeneous to most people's way of thinking and acting. Over against this, faith is the belief in possibility that arises in response to the expression of impossibility, absurdity, contradiction, absoluteness, and heterogeneity contained in, or projected by, those factors that constitute the possibility of offense.

Whereas the offended person holds to the impossibility, contradictoriness, and absurdity of Christianity and is repulsed by Christ and the highness, severity, and inverse values of Christian existence, the believer affirms possibility and makes an unconditional commitment to Christ. Offense and faith are opposite responses to whatever presents the possibility of offense, but faith is not properly Christian faith unless it arises out of the tension of this dialectical moment. The tendency, however, is to present faith directly as the positive correlative to reason or common sense and values, to portray it as the probable or as belief that is above reason but compatible with it. Christian strivers, however, must keep themselves in a life of tension, maintaining a "double vision" of the content of faith as being, on the one hand, the negative absurd to their own understanding and that of those outside faith, and on the other hand, the positive and true source and assurance of eternal blessedness. The Christian striver understands that to human reason the content of faith is absurd, contradictory, and yet he or she still believes and clings to it. The possibility of offense provides this negative side of faith, while the will to believe forms the positive expression of faith. To the believer the content of faith is not absurd, but this positive vision of faith lies on the other side of the dialectical. Faith must be maintained every moment in the recognition and overcoming of the possibility of offense. Consequently, faith is not faith without the possibility of offense.

3

DYING TO THE WORLD AND SELF-DENIAL /
NEW LIFE, LOVE, AND HOPE IN THE SPIRIT

In *Works of Love* Kierkegaard asserts that to love human beings is the only thing worth living for, that without such love we do not really live, and that to love others is the only true sign of being a Christian (*WL* 375). There and elsewhere in the later religious writings he looks upon Christian existence as a new form of life, full of faith, hope, and love. God is Love itself. True hope and genuine love of others are grounded in this divine love and are formed through a relation to God or love of God. Moreover, part of the spiritual qualification of a self, or becoming a self, is learning to love oneself in a Christian manner. Kierkegaard thus views Christian existence positively as being essentially a life of love for God, for one's neighbors, and even for oneself, but as in everything Christian, the positive is known and expressed through the negative and must be viewed as the inverse of the merely human or natural conception of this quality. Therefore, Christian love must be distinguished from the merely human conception of love and understood in terms of its dialectical expression in self-denial or self-renunciation (*Selvfornægtelse* or *Selvfornegtelse*).[1]

The dialectical relation between Christian love and self-denial is such that the first is not possible without the second. As Gene Outka has pointed out, for Kierkegaard "self-renunciation or self-sacrifice is the only fully appropriate 'temporal' embodiment or the inevitable 'historical' manifestation of agape."[2] Christian love is self-denying love. Proper self-love is achieved inversely through the renunciation of selfishness; love of others is expressed by the transferal of one's own desires and love of oneself to the neighbor through self-sacrifice and a willingness to endure any amount of ill for the neighbor's sake; and love of God is shown by inwardly realizing one's nothingness before the divine and becoming an instrument in the deity's service. Love and self-denial are so interrelated and interdependent in Kierkegaard's thought that the disregard of either expression results in a simplistic and one-sided understanding or misunderstanding that does an injustice to Kierkegaard and, from his point of view at least, to the correct representation of Christianity and Christian existence. Characterizations of his thought as entirely negative, radically individualist, acosmic, misanthropic, abstract, and void of any social ethic do not provide a balanced account of Kierkegaard's position or sufficiently appreciate the inverse dialectic that informs his thought.[3] By the same token, however, descriptions of his thought that portray Christian existence in a directly positive manner distort his views as well.[4]

I have maintained from the beginning of this study that Kierkegaard's understanding of Christianity and Christian existence contains both negative and positive qualifications that are intimately related through the operation of inverse dialectic or the dialectic of inversion in his thought. Nowhere is this more true than in his understanding of love and self-denial. In his reflections on the relationship between these qualifications in Christian existence, Kierkegaard set out to correct the tendency of people in his day to view Christian love in a superficial and directly positive manner and to assume its commensurability with the universally human forms and understanding of love. His intent was not to negate the positive understanding of Christian existence as a life of love but to show how this must necessarily include the act of self-denial in order to be rightly understood and genuinely achieved.

The same perspective informs Kierkegaard's understanding of Christian existence as a new form of life. In the third discourse of For Self-Examination, "It Is the Spirit Who Gives Life," Kierkegaard states that "there is not one, not one Christian qualification into which Christianity does not first of all introduce as the middle term: death, dying to [at afdøe]—in order to protect the essentially Christian from being taken in vain" (FSE 76–77). The Spirit gives life, but only "on the other side of death," so that it does not stand in immediate or direct continuity with the natural life of a person but constitutes instead a new life for the individual (76). In like manner, the Spirit brings faith, hope, and love, but only after death has come in between, after all purely natural or merely human confidence, understanding, hope, and self-centeredness have been extinguished (81–84).[5] Into this darkness, this night of hopelessness, this self-hatred (for "not until you in love of God have learned to hate yourself, not until then can there be talk of the love that is Christian love"), the Spirit comes with the gift of faith that is able to conquer the world, the gift of hope that is a hope against hope understood as a purely natural hope, and the gift of sacrificial love for an unloving world (82–85).

To become a Christian and to love God and one's fellow humans is to live the life truly worth living, but the promise of life that Christianity brings to a person is a life on the other side of death. Thus it is a new life, not the culmination or direct continuation of one's natural existence. Death must intervene. Christianity changes death to life, but first changes life to death (*SKP* X⁴ A 460). The Christian requirement, of course, is not literally to die (*at dø*) but metaphorically "to die to," or more precisely, "to die away from" (*at afdøe*).⁶ Physical death is unavoidable and final, whereas "to die to" is spiritual and voluntary and consists fundamentally in the transformation of one's attitude toward, and attachment to, oneself and the world. "To die to" is primarily a qualification of inwardness and denotes not so much an end as a qualitative change from one's old way of life to a new life, from the natural life to spiritual life, from life oriented in and toward the finite to a life concerned absolutely for the eternal. The new life of Christian existence is therefore obtained indirectly and inversely by means of its opposite. It comes only through and after death. The dialectical factor of death prevents a person from confusing the Christian form of life with the immediate understanding and desire for life, of conceiving it as a kind of "intensified lust for life" and consequently taking it in vain (*JP* 3:3097). For people are eager enough to appropriate anything that promises life. There is, Kierkegaard says, no feeling that a person clings to more firmly than "the feeling of being alive" (*FSE* 76). But the inverse requirement of Christianity that one must "die to" in order to receive life places a constraint upon this desire and turns the immediate appeal of the gospel into repulsion. People are eager to have life, but there is nothing they shrink from more than death. Thus, in its first form, Christianity appears to the natural person as cruelty rather than as a blessing and as a contradiction to human understanding. The natural human being understands a "life-giving spirit" as one that gives life, as being directly what it is. But Christianity manifests itself first of all conversely as "the Spirit who kills, who teaches dying to" (76, 98). Its formula is "first death, then life." The Spirit does indeed bring the blessedness of new life, but only indirectly by first teaching one to die to one's old life. Christianly understood, death is not a cruel affliction but the sign of a transition to new life, a sign that one is related to eternal life. Kierkegaard thus asks rhetorically: "Is it cruel to be, if you please, cruel when it is unconditionally the only thing that can save from ruin and help pull through? So it is with dying to" (81).

The dialectical relationships between self-denial and love, on the one hand, and between dying to the world and new life and hope, on the other, together constitute the third set of correlative qualifications in Christian existence. In Kierkegaard's thought, self-denial and dying to the world are essentially identical and therefore should be considered together. They are synonymous expressions for the negative movement by which religious individuals relate themselves in an indirectly positive manner to the positive nature of Christianity as a new form of life characterized by Christian love and hope. These qualifications thus further illustrate the inverse dialectic that informs and distinguishes Christian existence. Even more important, they serve to clarify this dialectic with respect to the natural, immediate, human, pagan, and worldly. In its expression of love, new life and hope through dying to the world and self-denial, Christianity stands in the sharpest possible opposition to these dimensions of life. But as Kierkegaard sees it, Christianity does not simply set itself against them; rather, it seeks to qualify or transform one's understanding and expression of them by informing them with the Christian mode of understanding and action.

These inverse dialectical relationships are primarily worked out in the writings of the second period of Kierkegaard's authorship, although a preparatory basis for this discussion is laid in the earlier upbuilding and pseudonymous literature.[7] Since *Concluding Unscientific Postscript* constitutes the transition to this period, we shall begin our examination in this chapter with a brief look at how that text presents the concept of resignation or dying away from immediacy before turning to the themes of dying to the world and self-denial and their correlative relation to love and new life and hope in the later literature. This nexus of related concepts also poses several critical questions that will be addressed in the course of examining the *Postscript* and later literature together: Does Kierkegaard see things differently from Johannes Climacus in his later religious writings, regarding dying to immediacy and self-denial as strictly and solely Christian determinants rather than as ones understood and required in common with ethical-religious inwardness? Does he reflect a different attitude toward the ethical-religious, now including it in, or interpreting it in terms of, those characteristics and conceptions to which Christianity is qualitatively heterogeneous and opposed? Or if he maintains a line of continuity between immanent religiousness and Christianity and admits that Christianity shares certain characteristics or qualifications in common with the ethical-religious, how is he able to establish the distinctiveness of Christianity in these respects? These questions resonate in other recent scholarship concerned with the more general question of whether Kierkegaard should be regarded fundamentally as a humanist thinker, a Christian thinker, or perhaps a combination of these, namely, a Christian humanist.[8] As C. Stephen and Jan Evans have perceptively pointed out, "the key to understanding Kierkegaard's authorship as a whole lies in understanding his view of the relationship of the 'merely human' to the 'specifically Christian.'"[9] Nowhere is this more apparent and true than with the concepts of "dying to" and self-denial, which are essential to both ethical-religious and Christian existence and thus provide common qualifications by which to illumine more specifically the similarities and differences between these two forms of religious existence in Kierkegaard's later religious writings. I shall show that Kierkegaard understands Christian self-denial as taking *two forms* in the later literature. The first corresponds formally to the ethical-religious but is nevertheless peculiarly Christian in that it presupposes the inner motivation of the second, which constitutes the decisive expression of Christian self-denial and introduces an external dimension to living Christianly. Consequently, I shall argue that Kierkegaard's thought undergoes a process of development in the later literature, but not a fundamental shift or change, inasmuch as the second form of self-denial provides the indirectly positive outward response that is commensurable with the inwardness of the Christian striver's new life, love, and hope in the Spirit.

Dying to Immediacy in *Concluding Unscientific Postscript*

In the *Postscript* the pathetic and dialectical factors that issue in death and new life for the existing individual are brought to the fore in the concept of resignation.[10] Climacus asserts that the ethical qualification of an individual consists in a transition from life oriented in and toward the finite to a life concerned absolutely for the eternal. Existential or ethical pathos comes to expression in the active transformation of an individual's entire mode of existence into conformity with the object of his or her passionate interest. For the ethical individual this object is eternal happiness. The initial expression of existential or ethical pathos consists in the acquisition of an absolute respect toward the absolute *telos,* which cannot be put on a level with other things or mediated by a "both/and" attitude toward it and the finite (*CUP* 1:400, 406). When eternal happiness is projected as the highest good in life, then all finite satisfactions must be relegated to a relative status of what may have to be renounced in order to gain that happiness. If the absolute does not transform one's life absolutely, so that there is nothing one is unwilling to give up for its sake, then one is not truly related to the absolute. A relation to a relative *telos* can transform a life partially, but Climacus points out that it is a contradiction to will the finite absolutely, since everything finite must have an end and at some point can no longer be willed (394). Only the infinite or the eternal can be willed absolutely. To will eternal happiness is to will the infinite because it is an end that can be willed every moment for itself and is never finished; that is, it is never possessed in time but constitutes the object of striving for the whole of one's existence.

The ideal task for the existing individual, then, is to maintain an absolute relation to the absolute and a relative relation to the relative (407). In their immediate existence, however, human beings are rooted and have their existence wholly in the finite. They may desire eternal happiness, but they also want temporal good fortune. Consequently, instead of renouncing the finite for the absolute they transform eternal happiness into an added "gift of good fortune" for their finite existence and relegate it to the level of "an unusually fat livelihood" (392). In their immediacy, therefore, human beings are committed to relative or finite ends, and so long as they remain in immediacy only succeed in relativizing (thus abrogating) the absolute. When one ventures to commit oneself to the ideal task, one cannot begin at once or simultaneously relate oneself absolutely to the absolute and relatively to the relative, for in one's immediate state one is in precisely the opposite situation, relativizing the absolute and absolutizing the relative. Consequently, one must first establish oneself in the proper absolute relation through a renunciation of the finite before one can turn to the ideal task of relating oneself positively to both the finite and the absolute, that is, to each with the appropriate level of passion and commitment.

According to Climacus, one severs one's roots in the finite by a resignation of it (395, 404, 431). This preliminary act of renouncing the finite is what Climacus understands as *afdøe* or "dying to." It is essentially a dying to immediacy, to a life dominated by one's natural propensities toward pleasure, the seeking of good fortune, the satisfaction of selfish desires, and the sense of power or a belief that one can do anything one sets out to do in life. Dying to immediacy forms the initial expression of existential pathos, which is characteristic of both Religiousness A and B, or immanent religiousness and Christianity, in contrast to aesthetic pathos. However, there are differences between the two forms of existential or religious pathos which condition the expression of this movement in each sphere. In Religiousness A the absolute *telos* remains abstract and undefined, and one relates oneself to it only pathetically through the decision to venture all in spite of its objective uncertainty. Religiousness B or Christianity makes the task more difficult by adding the dialectical to the pathetic, requiring one to believe and venture all not only in the face of uncertainty but against one's understanding as well (568). In Religiousness A there is a growing sense of impotence in relation to the possibility of performing the ideal task. Religious suffering, the essential expression of existential or religious pathos, is thus characterized as the suffering of impotence or an incapability to unite in existence the absolute *telos* and relativity, or as Climacus puts it more concretely, the God-idea with an outing in the Deer Park (461, 472–74). One never gets beyond the initial task of resignation, for as soon as one has succeeded in doing it once, one is faced with the same task all over again. Consequently, religious suffering culminates in the consciousness of total guilt or utter failure to realize the eternal in existence and thus in self-annihilation, which is Climacus's somewhat exaggerated expression for the realization that one is nothing or can do nothing before God (461).

Dying to immediacy comes to expression precisely in this inward suffering or feeling of impotence and nothingness. Immediate individuals manifest a youthful sense of power in the belief that they can do anything. Religious persons, by contrast, harbor a sense of failure and impotence in the realization that they can do nothing, particularly as regards the transformation of themselves into conformity with the absolute. However, as Climacus points out, the greatest difficulty lies not so much in the constant failure of religious individuals to combine the absolute and the relative in existence as in annulling the illusion that they *can* combine them (486). So long as one assumes an immanent relation to the eternal this illusion is not absolutely dispelled. In Religiousness B this sense of impotence is intensified and absolutized through the consciousness of sin. This has the effect of completely destroying the illusion of one's continuity with the eternal as well as one's ability to transform oneself inwardly so as to sustain a positive relation to it. By making the absolute venture and commencing the process of dying to immediacy in Religiousness A, one is no longer the same as before. Yet Climacus claims that Religiousness A does not make one a new person (532, 534, 584). This transformation occurs only in Religiousness B or Christianity. In Religiousness A the individual is decisively changed, but the individual's self-identity remains intact inasmuch as "it is he himself who becomes conscious of guilt by joining the guilt together with the relation to an eternal happiness" (534). Moreover, the eternal "embraces the existing person everywhere" so that "the misrelation remains within immanence"

(532). Christianity, by contrast, asserts an absolute breach between the existing individual and the eternal or eternal happiness (532, 576, 584). In Religiousness A the breach with the eternal is viewed as being *relative,* while in Christianity it is conceived as *radical.* In both forms of religiousness a positive relation to the eternal is sustained inversely and indirectly through the consciousness of one's distance and separation from the eternal and through dying to immediacy, but the expression of this sense of separation and death is conditioned by differing estimates of the extent and implications of the individual's breach with the eternal.

These similarities and differences between Religiousness A and B are important to bear in mind as we progress to an examination of Kierkegaard's understanding of "dying to" and self-denial in the later religious writings. For in the later writings and journals Kierkegaard contrasts Christianity and its qualifications to natural, immediate, pagan, merely human, and worldly viewpoints, and he bases its qualitative distinctiveness on the fact that the Christian qualifications are in a sense peculiar to Christianity and the inverse of the common conception and experience of these factors. Determinants such as the consciousness of sin and the possibility of offense are clearly distinctive to Christianity and present no problem in differentiating it from ethical-religious pathos and religiosity. But in its requirements of "dying to" and self-denial Christianity is not so entirely or clearly distinct from ethical-religious or immanent religiosity.

There is some question as well whether Climacus's understanding of dying to immediacy in the *Postscript* is consistent with Kierkegaard's later interpretation of it. The classic debate on this issue is between two Swedish scholars, Torsten Bohlin and Valter Lindström.[11] Although Bohlin finds a "marked lack of agreement" in the authorship as a whole, he thinks Kierkegaard is consistent in his understanding of dying to immediacy.[12] Immediacy in the *Postscript* must be understood, he claims, in terms of Kierkegaard's later, more explicit and inclusive identification of it with the "natural human" sphere, against which Christianity is opposed.[13] Dying to immediacy thus means dying to the natural human sphere, and on this basis it becomes a peculiarly Christian act.

Lindström, by contrast, interprets dying to immediacy in the *Postscript* in a more restricted sense as a dying to selfishness, not from the natural human sphere as such. As evidence for this view he cites the *Postscript* itself: "All the passions of finitude must be dead, all selfishness rooted out, the selfishness that wants to have everything and the selfishness that proudly turns away from everything. But that is just the trouble, and here is the suffering in dying to oneself" (*CUP* 1:472).[14] Lindström criticizes Bohlin for citing Kierkegaard's late journals to establish the meaning of dying to immediacy in the *Postscript,* and conversely points to the journals and other writings of that period as proving that Kierkegaard was not consistent on this issue. Lindström claims that Kierkegaard's thought undergoes a change or "gliding away" from his earlier view that results in a different understanding of "dying to" and self-denial in the later works.[15] Bohlin in turn criticizes Lindström for interpreting immediacy in a univocal fashion. He does not deny that dying to immediacy involves a dying to selfishness, but he insists that it also means to give up everything worldly. Thus he detects an ascetic tendency in Kierkegaard's thought.[16] Lindström agrees that Kierkegaard's thought more and more takes on the character of a rigorous asceticism, but he disagrees as to when this appears in the literature. While Lindström does not take this change to signify a fundamental shift or revision of Kierkegaard's overall perspective in the authorship, in which "seemingly opposed tendencies are in some way held together" by a unitary, general view, Bohlin sees it as evidence of a major shift in Kierkegaard's ethical thought.[17] He thinks Kierkegaard moves from a positive social ethic in *Either/Or,* part 2, emphasizing a realization of the universal human or "common lot" to an increasingly negative and individualistic one in the later pseudonymous works and religious writings that culminates in a "rigidly ascetic and misanthropic" ethic in the *The Moment.*[18] Bohlin thus finds Kierkegaard inconsistent in the authorship as a whole but consistent in his view of dying to immediacy in the *Postscript* and later literature, while Lindström finds him inconsistent in his view of dying to immediacy in these writings but consistent in the general view that informs his thought and writings overall.[19]

On the nature of dying to immediacy Bohlin is surely correct in claiming that immediacy is a broader concept than selfishness in the *Postscript,* but he is not justified, as Lindström has rightly pointed out, in establishing this on the basis of the later writings. The *Postscript* itself speaks of dying to immediacy as a "difference from worldliness" (*CUP* 1:410). However, it is debatable whether one should label this as "ascetic," given the medieval conception of asceticism usually associated with the term. Dying to worldliness means dying to one's selfish attachment to the worldly. It is an overcoming of the "vital power" and dominance of the finite or relative goals in one's life (411). One gives up or renounces the finite or worldly in the sense that one is no longer absolutely attached to it or essentially has one's life in it. This does not mean, however, that one literally denies oneself the things of the world or avoids intercourse with the world, becoming, as it were, "otherworldly."[20] The ideal task of the existing individual is to maintain an absolute relation to the absolute while continuing to live in the finite. The difference is that one no longer has one's life essentially in the finite. Climacus expressly contrasts this understanding of "dying to" to the medieval ascetic way of renouncing the world. One does not become indifferent to the finite or express renunciation of it in outward forms. The ethical-religious individual's separation from worldliness is *incognito,* since he or she continues to look and act like other human beings. Dying to worldliness is essentially an inward movement that cannot be directly, unambiguously, or unconditionally expressed in outward forms and identified with or by external actions.

While dying to immediacy in the *Postscript* should be seen, then, as dying to both selfishness and worldliness, the question of whether it also means dying to the "natural human" remains open. Much depends on what one interprets that term to mean or include. Both Bohlin and Lindström interpret it broadly, but they form opposite views of Kierkegaard's estimation of Christianity's relation to it. Bohlin does not associate the term merely with the aesthetic stage but views both immediacy and the natural human as being more universal and inclusive. Presumably for him the natural human incorporates the expression of both aesthetic and existential pathos within the sphere of immanence. In effect, then, Bohlin makes no decisive distinction between immediacy and immanence in the *Postscript* and views Christianity as representing spiritual life in opposition to them. For Lindström the natural human corresponds to the human in general or the ordinary human values of life.[21] It is not identical to selfishness, immediacy, or the aesthetic outlook on life, although human values may be appropriated by the immediate or aesthetic outlook and expressed in terms of that orientation. But they may also be sanctified through Christianity. This possibility suggests to Lindström that Kierkegaard asserts a positive rather than a negative relation between Christianity and the human values of life. When the natural human has been purged of selfishness, it reflects the kind of human values Christianity affirms and seeks to establish in the world. The natural human in itself, however, seems to be a neutral category in Lindström's view; it is the immediately given sensual life of human beings that is capable of becoming either an expression of sensuality or spirituality, aestheticism or Christianity.

Lindström's distinction has a certain theoretical validity or else Kierkegaard's characterization of faith as a second or new immediacy would not make sense and other human values such as love, hope, and joy would find no expression in Christianity. But in actuality human beings do not find themselves to be in a neutral state. Their immediate, natural, unqualified state in existence is already a life characterized by selfishness and worldliness, and this more nearly corresponds to Kierkegaard's description of the natural human. Bohlin's identification of immediacy, selfishness, and worldliness with the natural human, therefore, more closely reflects Kierkegaard's general view. Bohlin's error, however, lies in viewing immediacy too broadly in the *Postscript* and in not taking sufficient notice of the fact that there are two breaches identified in that book, first with immediacy and then with immanence. Christianity is decisively opposed to both, but on quite different grounds, and it is joined by immanent religiosity in its opposition to immediacy. It is not accurate, then, simply to contrast Christianity to the immediate as if it included the ethical-religious. Climacus shows a quite positive appreciation of ethical-religious subjectivity in the *Postscript,* so much so that he views it as the kind of inward development every individual must undergo before there can be any possibility of becoming a Christian.

In order to gain a clearer perspective on this issue, one needs to distinguish among three senses in which Kierkegaard understands and uses the category of "the human" in his writings: the natural human (immediacy), the universal human (the ethical-religious), and the transformed human or new being (the Christian). The first designates human beings as they are prior to any spiritual qualification or transformation. The second represents what every person can become, the purely human, or human beings viewed essentially and potentially within the limits of a finite vision of what it means to be human. The universal human is the stage in which subjectively concerned individuals undertake to enact their own inward transformations in order to bring their being into conformity with the eternal and express it in their lives. However, we have seen that this stage culminates in a sense of failure, impotence, and guilt-consciousness in the struggle to effect such a transformation, although it assumes that essentially human beings possess the eternal and will ultimately achieve eternal happiness. In the end, therefore, the ethical-religious individual and the immediate person "go equally far" (*CUP* 1:582). The latter does not try to become anything other than what he or she immediately is; the former tries to transform him- or herself but ultimately fails.

The third conception of the human represents what human beings can become through Christ. Whereas in the universal human or ethical-religious perspective human beings seek to become themselves through an inward self-transformation, Christian strivers become themselves through a paradoxical transformation of the self. Christianity begins by intensifying the sense of impotence in persons through sin-consciousness by revealing the radical alteration in human beings that accounts for their inability to transform themselves. Ethical-religious individuals become conscious of what it means to exist *qua* humans by themselves. Christians gain a consciousness of their essential identity as human beings through a relation to the eternal in time, or the eternal outside themselves, which gives them the requisite condition for transformation and new birth. As sinners they recognize that they are not merely different from themselves in their essential humanity but this essential humanity itself has been so radically altered that it no longer possesses the eternal potentiality it was assumed to have. The Christian estimate of human actuality and potentiality thus conflicts with both the natural human and universal human conceptions. It differs from the natural human in viewing human actuality negatively and in envisioning the need for a qualification or transformation of human beings that would enable them to die to their attachment to selfishness and worldliness. It goes beyond the universal human in viewing the human condition as being radically altered rather than merely relatively different from human beings' essential conception of themselves and in projecting a reality for the human self that is infinite, having God for its criterion rather than what human beings by themselves are able to project as the goal of their self-transformations (*SUD* 79). The natural human being is satisfied in being what he or she already is, seeking merely to enjoy life and to perpetuate that state. The ethical-religious human being ultimately fails in effecting a positive transformation of his or her existence, depending at last upon recollection of the eternal through immanence. The Christian human being is decisively transformed, becoming a new creature whose existence is redefined and qualified through a relation to the eternal in time or Jesus Christ.

In Christianity, therefore, "dying to" not only issues in new life but is further defined and qualified as a dying to purely human or immanent motives, presuppositions, and viewpoints as well as from immediacy. Christianity requires the killing of every selfish desire in oneself, every drive to conquer and succeed in the world, every expectation of divine assistance in accomplishing worldly ends, as well as all reliance upon oneself or presumption of an eternal potentiality within oneself to bring about the death of immediacy and the transformation of one's existence. The existential pathos for eternal happiness is not extinguished, but the illusion that one can ultimately win it by one's own effort must be dispelled and the motivation with which one expresses self-denial must be purified. This is the viewpoint that is emphasized in the writings and journals after the *Postscript* and which enables Kierkegaard to contrast Christianity not only to immediacy or the natural human but also to the broader range of immanence or the universal human, even its comparable expressions of religiousness or existential pathos. Kierkegaard continues to express the opposition of Christianity to immediacy or the natural human, but coupled with it is a concern to sketch out in more detail Christianity's distinctiveness from the ethical-religious as well.

Dying to the World, Self-Denial, and Love in Kierkegaard's Later Religious Writings

In the writings of the second period of Kierkegaard's authorship dying to the world and self-denial are equivalent concepts that may be seen as taking two forms. The first corresponds formally to the ethical-religious, the second is peculiarly Christian. In conformity with the *Postscript,* the first form of self-denial consists in dying to selfishness and worldliness. In *For Self-Examination,* for example, Kierkegaard makes it perfectly clear that these conditions go hand in hand, that it is only through selfishness that the world has power over a person, and that if one has died to selfishness, one has died to the world: "You must die to every merely earthly hope, to every merely human confidence; you must die to your selfishness, or to the world, because it is only through your selfishness that the world has power over you; if you are dead to your selfishness, you are also dead to the world" (*FSE* 77). The immediate or natural human being seeks to enjoy life, to acquire its goods, and to receive God's help in securing them (*JP* 3:3774). But this is precisely what constitutes worldliness. Kierkegaard does not limit worldliness to a narrow pietistic understanding of it as indulgence in "vices" such as card playing and dancing. He defines worldliness essentially as the desire to acquire honor and esteem in the world, to seek to be "on top" or to succeed in the world, to want to possess those things that the world assumes every person should want to possess (*CD* 227). Christianity's attitude is diametrically the opposite of this. It holds that it is more blessed to do without than to get, to suffer than to enjoy life, to lose than to win in the world (*JP* 3:3774). Its concepts of life, honor, and value are just the converse of those held by the world.

Thus it is very difficult for a Christian to combine religiosity and worldliness. Kierkegaard concedes that Luther could do it because he had an inner truth and certainty that enabled him to engage in worldliness yet be entirely free in doing it—he could marry yet be as not married in relation to God, take part in everything in the world yet be as a stranger in it (*JP* 3:2518). Luther did not embrace worldliness but expressed religiosity in the midst of it. The usual result, however, is that religiosity simply collapses into worldliness, and this is what Kierkegaard thought had happened to Christendom in his day. Human beings want to use Christianity to help them live in the world and to enjoy life, to have its consolation for misfortunes and misery and its assurance of a brighter future. Thus they remain essentially attached to the world.

In "An Occasional Discourse," the first part of *Upbuilding Discouses in Various Spirits,* Kierkegaard characterizes worldly persons precisely in this vein. Double-minded persons do the good for the sake of some positive worldly reward or else because they fear that if they do not do it, they will be punished by the loss of some worldly good, such as money, success, or reputation. Such persons do not truly will the good because they will it out of self-centered motivations rather than out of a purity of heart that wills the good simply because it is the good. Ethical individuals, by contrast, will the good disinterestedly, without thought of reward, or rather, they "cheerfully" understand that their reward will be opposition from the world rather than its approval and material benefits (*UDVS* 36–60).

While "An Occasional Discourse" does not strictly identify the ethical individual who wills the good with the Christian, the correlation is everywhere implied. Here the broad sense of the ethical is pitted against immediacy, but it receives a distinctly Christian characterization. Part 3 of *Upbuilding Discourses in Various Spirits,* "The Gospel of Sufferings," subtitled "Christian Discourses," develops this perspective further in a specifically Christian context and defines the Christian and Christian discipleship by it. Being a Christian means to follow Christ, and following Christ means to go the same way he went: "indigent, forsaken, mocked, not loving the world and not loved by it" (*UDVS* 223). It means to take up the cross, to deny oneself by renouncing the world or worldliness and any relationship that would tempt or obstruct one's love and devotion to Christ. It means to be willing to sacrifice and suffer everything, not for one's own gain or selfish purposes, but for the sake of following Christ.

In "The Gospel of Sufferings," therefore, Kierkegaard equates dying to selfishness and worldliness with Christian self-denial. Christian self-denial thus is understood in conformity with the ethical-religious conception of "dying to," but it is also distinctive because in Christian existence self-denial is performed for the sake of following Christ and is patterned after Christ, whose whole life was one of self-denial (*UDVS* 224–25). In congruity with Johannes Climacus in the *Postscript,* Kierkegaard stresses here that self-denial or renunciation of selfishness and worldliness is essentially an inward act, or is "the inwardness to deny oneself," although the establishment of Christ's life as the pattern for Christian self-denial would seem to require some form of outward expression of this inward act (323). But Kierkegaard does not develop that implication at this point. Instead he stresses that self-denial is something that every person can do, regardless of one's circumstances in life. Beggars can just as unconditionally deny themselves as kings or queens. The giving up of worldly goods, as in the gospel example of the rich young man (Mark 10:21), is viewed as no more than a preliminary step (222). Taking up the cross and following Christ is a daily and life-long task and is primarily determined by one's inner disposition toward oneself and the world.

It is in Kierkegaard's next publication, *Works of Love,* that the correlation between love and self-denial in Christian existence is established, the decisive differentiation of Christian love and self-denial from both aesthetic immediacy and the ethical-religious is worked out, and the intent of Christianity's dialectic with these spheres is significantly clarified.[22] Inverse dialectic shows itself once again in this work in the expression of the positive in terms of the negative and in the opposition of the Christian conception and expression of these qualifications to the natural, pagan, worldly, and universal human understanding of them. The heterogeneity of the temporal and the eternal, the natural and the spiritual, the purely human and the Christian qualities and viewpoints is strongly drawn and emphasized throughout *Works of Love.* Although some distinction between the ethical-religious and the immediate or natural sphere is still evident, over against Christianity this distinction now begins to break down as it is made clear that only in Christianity does the true ethic, true sacrifice, complete transformation of the eternal, and spiritualization of love come to expression. Kierkegaard regards the ethical-religious as being "like a tentative running start" toward transformation and spiritualization inasmuch as it projects the eternal as humanity's goal in existence, but it "stops halfway" and becomes only a "half-heartedness" because the eternal is envisioned from a finite perspective and assumed to be essentially already in humanity's possession or capable of being actualized in and by human beings themselves (*WL* 121, 131, 196).

Whereas in his early writings Kierkegaard had contrasted the ethical, religious, and Christian to the aesthetic or immediate without making any decisive distinction between them, the distinctions achieved in the *Postscript* made it necessary to contrast Christianity to the ethical-religious or universally human as well. Both the natural human and the universal human stand in need of transformation, for while the process of inward transformation is begun in the ethical-religious sphere, it is not carried through, death does not occur, and one is not made a new person. Judge William, the ethical spokesman in *Either/Or*, for example, also envisions love as the eternal, believes in the religious significance of marriage, calls for the transfiguration or spiritualization of romantic or erotic love, and contrasts earthly love to spiritual love. There the ethical, religious, and Christian are all compressed into one ethical or universal human perspective. Judge William urges the aesthete to carry through with his despair in order to arrive at the point where he may choose himself in his eternal validity rather than remain in his immediacy. But the Judge's belief that one *can* choose oneself through despair is the flaw in his vision. It reflects just the immanent viewpoint that Christianity denies: that human beings can effect their own self-transformations and adequately conceive and define what it is they are to become in life. In *Works of Love* Kierkegaard says that "Christianity begins immediately with what *every* human being *should become*" and agrees that "to be a human being is the fundamental category" of persons, but it proposes to define the universal human or purely human Christianly rather than immanently (*WL* 141, 180). The transformation or spiritualization of human beings truly takes place in Christianity because it has the power, authority, and responsibility to make transformation actual. It achieves the transformation of human beings through self-denying love that is consciously based on and grounded in the eternal outside human beings as well as within them. Ethical-religious self-denial does not fully break with selfishness and worldliness because it is limited by a finite, purely immanent determination of what constitutes these conditions and the renunciation of them. Thus, while the first form of Christian self-denial is defined as identical to ethical-religious self-denial and dying to the world, it may also be distinguished from them in that it actually achieves the death of immediacy, whereas they do not.

Part of the problem Kierkegaard wishes to address in *Works of Love* is the error of confusing Christian love and self-denial with or subsuming them under purely natural, pagan, and universal human conceptions of them. The common practice is to regard erotic love as the highest form of love and Christian love as the highest expression of *eros*. Kierkegaard agrees that Christian love is the highest form of love, but it is not the highest in direct continuity with merely human forms or expressions of love. Rather, Christian love is qualitatively different from, even the opposite of, merely human love and is distinguished by placing it against, not on, the comparative scale with natural, pagan, and universal human expressions of love. Far from representing the highest expression of merely human love, it constitutes an offense to the natural, pagan, and merely human understanding. Natural and merely human expressions of love consist in immediate, spontaneous feelings or inclinations toward others that take the form of friendship (*Venskab*) or erotic love *(Elskov)*, although these may contain an "alloy of duty" and be regarded as a worthy aspiration that people ought to attain as a matter of convenience and advantage (*WL* 143–44). Christian love (*Kjerlighed*) is grounded in the hidden depths of inwardness and God's love but seeks outward expression as action. It is what it does, that is to say, it is inwardness that reduplicates itself inversely in outwardness and thus is known by its fruits, the works of love. Whereas Religiousness A consists in hidden inwardness and can find no satisfactory outward expression of its pathos, Christian love, although ultimately hidden in inwardness, is not "such a hidden feeling that it is too exalted to bear fruit, or such a hidden feeling that the fruits demonstrate neither for nor against" (15). Christian love has an inherent desire or need to manifest itself, to express itself in acts, and to make itself recognizable by its fruits, for it is truly itself only in going beyond itself. Thus it is not sufficient, and even promotes the very confusion Kierkegaard hopes to dispel, to portray Christian love simply as hidden inwardness in conformity with the characterization of true religiosity as hidden inwardness in the *Postscript*.[23] Kierkegaard does say that works do not provide any direct or unconditional demonstration of the presence of love, but works at least indirectly indicate the presence or lack of love (14). One must believe, one cannot know, that they are expressions of love. Belief in love is possible, Kierkegaard thinks, only when one is oneself loving. By abiding in love one is able to recognize love in others, and one's own love becomes recognizable in the same manner. The important task, however, is not to seek recognition but simply to produce the fruits that manifest love, which make it *knowable* even if it cannot be unequivocally known. It is not so much recognition as *recognizability* that Christian love seeks in the works of love. The outward expression of love is more important than the outward recognition of love.

Christian love is also distinguished from natural, merely human, and pagan love by its eternal nature, whereas these other forms of love are essentially transient, perishable, and subject to change even if change does not occur. For this reason temporal love is always uncertain and requires continual reaffirmation of its existence between lovers. Christian love, by contrast, is love that has won not merely continuance (*Beståen*) but enduring continuance or *continuity* (*Bestandighed*) (*WL* 31). Continuity is gained by love's having undergone the transformation of the eternal to become consciously grounded upon the eternal. Christian love is love that is no longer something spontaneous but has been made a duty through Christ's command to love. Furthermore, the continuance of love is no longer dependent on the test of time, for when love is a duty, it is forever decided that one shall love and that love shall abide (33–34).

The qualitative heterogeneity of Christian love to other forms of love is most evident in its converse view of what constitutes genuine love and self-love. Paganism also rejects direct love of self and affirms erotic love and friendship as genuine expressions of unselfish love inasmuch as they are passionate preferences for other persons. But Kierkegaard regards both erotic love and friendship as forms of self-love. He points out that even when pagan love devotes itself to another and admires that person, the relation has the effect of turning back to the lover's advantage, for just as the beloved is the lover's object of admiration, so the lover forms the beloved's object of admiration in return (54). To relate oneself to others in order to make demands upon them, to use them, or to get something from them, Kierkegaard contends, is really self-love.[24]

Yet it is the selfishness in erotic love, not the immediacy or spontaneity as such, that Christianity directly opposes and excludes (52–53). Christianity presupposes that persons naturally love themselves. It sets out to do away with selfish self-love by using a person's natural self-love against itself, or more precisely, to rid it of selfishness. That is, Christianity requires one to love one's neighbor as oneself. Self-love is mastered by *redoubling* (*Fordoblelse*)—by the duplication of oneself in the neighbor (21).[25] Pagan love also involves redoubling, Kierkegaard concedes, but it is quite different from what takes place in Christian redoubling. In pagan love redoubling of oneself in the other means that the loved one becomes one's "other-I" (53). Thus it is not really the other person who is loved but oneself as projected into and benefiting from the relation. Erotic love culminates in two becoming one to create a new selfish self. In contrast to this, Christian redoubling involves duplicating oneself in the other in such a way that love for oneself is transformed into love for the other. Every demand in the relationship is placed upon oneself rather than the other, and what one would have desired for oneself, one desires for the other. In Christianity one regards the other not as an "other-I" but as an "other-you" who is distinct from oneself and who is loved not on the basis of his or her personal attractiveness (preferential love) but because the beloved is a spiritual being like oneself (*WL* 57).

In Christian redoubling, therefore, one denies oneself, or more accurately, one renounces the selfish self-love or egocentricity in oneself by loving others as oneself. Only Christian redoubling is real redoubling, Kierkegaard claims, for self-love cannot abide two, and even in its projection to the other essentially maintains a single concern for itself (21, 57). The "as yourself" in the Christian command, however, implies two, that there is another whom one loves as one loves oneself. At the same time it implies that self-denial in Christian love does not mean total renunciation of oneself but only the renunciation of selfishness in oneself. As Kierkegaard understands it, Christianity is not opposed to love of self *per se* but demands that one love oneself in the right way. If one cannot do this, then neither does one love one's neighbor, for "to love yourself in the right way and to love the neighbor correspond perfectly to one another; fundamentally they are one and the same thing " (22). Proper self-love, then, is to love oneself in the same way one loves one's neighbor when one loves that person as oneself, namely, without selfishness.

Christianity also preserves erotic love and friendship, only these must be incorporated within the higher universal command to love all persons, even the beloved or friend, as neighbors. This is consistent with the view expressed in Kierkegaard's earlier pseudonymous writings, that the aesthetic and the ethical must be dethroned by the religious, then reincorporated into the individual's life at a subordinate level. Kierkegaard does not advocate an unqualified opposition of the religious to the ethical and the aesthetic, nor of the Christian to the natural and universal human. Christianity does not simply set itself against or exclude these dimensions but rather seeks to qualify or transform one's understanding and expression of them so as to lead one out of the snare of selfish self-love. T. W. Adorno has characterized Kierkegaard as advocating the "breaking down" of nature, but actually his view is better expressed in the opposite manner as the "building up" or upbuilding of nature.[26] Kierkegaard devotes a whole chapter in *Works of Love* to a discussion of how love "builds up." Christianity seeks only to dethrone inclination and to make Christian or spiritual love the highest ruling factor in one's personal relations with others (50).

Christianity, therefore, does not prohibit one from entering into special relationships with one or more individuals (*WL* 140–42). Friendships, erotic love, and marriage are still permitted, but one must express neighbor or spiritual love within and in addition to these relations. To love only selectively and to call this "loving one's neighbor" is to make platonic and erotic special relations the highest and to confuse them with Christian love. First and foremost one should love all persons as neighbors. The Christian rule, according to Kierkegaard, is that "what is the eternal foundation must also be the foundation of every expression of the particular" (141). Being a friend, beloved, or spouse is a "more precise specification" of one's position in a special relation (141). Every special relation must be informed by the broader conception of the other party as a neighbor. Thus, while one certainly loves one's friend, beloved, or spouse differently from how one loves others, that difference is not essential, since fundamentally one loves that person as one loves others, as a human being or neighbor. If one does not love one's spouse, beloved, or friends as neighbors, then one does not love one's neighbor. For to love one's neighbor is to love all persons without exception and to love them as human beings, which all persons are equally and in common. Being a human being is the fundamental qualification of a person; his or her particularity or distinguishing characteristics are secondary and cannot serve as a basis for making any person an exception to the commandment of neighbor love (141–42).

The task first of all, then, is to love all persons on the basis of their common humanity and without distinction. This means that one must learn, as it were, "to shut [one's] eyes" to the differences between persons, to become "blind" to them and to look "away from the dissimilarities" (*WL* 68). Christianity does not literally do away with distinctions but seeks instead to make one victorious over the temptation of distinctions by teaching one to lift oneself above them (70–72). Neither does it attempt to reduce everything to one distinction as does a "well-intentioned worldly effort" (71). In Kierkegaard's view, worldly similarity (*Lighed*), or the establishment of one social condition or class for all, is not the same as Christian equality (*Ligelighed*) (72). Christianity "allows all the dissimilarities to stand but teaches the equality of eternity" and locates the decisive change in the way one views them (72). Distinctions between persons begin to "hang loosely," enabling that which is common to all persons, namely, their essential humanity, their "eternal resemblance" or likeness, to shine through (88). Then, while making no distinction between those whom one loves, one must turn around and at the same time make infinite distinctions between them. That is, one must love each according to his or her own individuality or individual characteristics (270). This consists primarily in helping those one knows and sees to become authentic selves or individuals before God by enabling them through one's relations to them to become independent and stand on their own as individual selves. This is, Kierkegaard says, "the greatest, the only beneficence one human being can do for another" (277–78).

Central to the possibility of Christian love and self-denial is the requirement that one allow one's relation to God to penetrate and become a middle term in one's relations to others. Christianity recognizes only one kind of love—spiritual love—and insists that it "lie at the base of and be present in every other expression of love" (WL 143, 146). Kierkegaard maintains that every special relationship must be based upon and in a relation to God: "Every person is God's bond servant; therefore he dare not belong to anyone in love unless in the same love he belongs to God and dare not possess anyone in love unless the other and he himself belong to God in this love—a person dare not belong to another as if that other person were everything to him; a person dare not allow another to belong to him as if he were everything to that other" (108). Before God one learns what it means properly to love oneself, to love one's beloved, and to be loved in return. Initially in Works of Love Kierkegaard defines proper self-love as love for self that excludes selfishness. Later he further qualifies this definition by adding that the "true idea" of what it is to love oneself is to love God (107). God is the only proper object of love. This does not mean that one should become solely occupied with love of God or that the love of neighbor is effaced by a concern for one's individual relation to God.[27] The true conception of what it means to love another person is to help that person to love God, and vice versa, to be loved means to be helped by another human being to love God. Since in Kierkegaard's view "love is God," this means that the object of every love relationship is God or love itself rather than either party in the relation (121). Christianity seeks to transform every love relation into sacrificial love, to teach both the lover and the beloved to help each other to love rather than to seek to be loved through their relation to one another. Christian transformation consists finally in being made wholly an active power in the service of God or love, of becoming dedicated to the well-being of others rather than to one's own self-elevation and promotion in the world.

This is how Christianity proposes spiritually to qualify and transform erotic love and friendship. It does not seek the discontinuation or modification of special relationships but rather wants to qualify and inform all human relationships with a third dimension by making God or the neighbor a middle term in them (WL 119). Thus Kierkegaard says: "Christianity has not changed anything in what people have previously learned about loving the beloved, the friend, etc., has not added a little or subtracted something, but it has changed everything, has changed love as a whole" (147). The fundamental change that Christianity brings to love relations is not external but internal. Externally everything remains the same, but it has been inwardly purified, sanctified, and made new (145). Even the speech of the person whose love has been spiritually qualified undergoes transformation so as to become metaphorical speech (*overført Tale*) or speech that is "carried over" by the spirit (209). One does not appropriate a new language but rather uses the old in a "transferred" fashion. That is, one can say the same words as before but will mean something quite different by them. This is the *paradox* of Christian transformation, that love is the same yet infinitely different, old yet marvelously new. Christianity seeks to inform all forms of love with spiritual love, but it allows the outward distinctions between forms of love to persist, simply requiring "infinity's change" or the transformation of the eternal to take place in the inner being or conscience of lovers (138). The worldly understanding of transformation envisions change in the external realm in a *direct* manner through a reformation or revolution of social-political-economic structures, but in Kierkegaard's view Christianity seeks only to bring about an inward change in the individual's mode of existence in the world. It does not require one to cut oneself off from one's former relationships and flee the world but rather to express Christian love in one's relationships in the world. As Kierkegaard sees it, Christianity's goal is to bind the temporal and the eternal, to make the temporal a reflection of the eternal rather than simply to exclude it (6).

This ethic of transformation has the effect of significantly qualifying the inverse dialectic of Christian existence with regard to the immediate, natural, pagan, worldly, and merely human perspectives. For while Christianity stands uncompromisingly opposed to these conceptions and expressions in their unqualified forms, the intent of the dialectic points beyond mere differentiation and opposition to an eventual union of the natural and the spiritual, the temporal and the eternal, the human and the Christian, through the transforming power of self-denying love. Moreover, while Kierkegaard does not call for a direct transformation of society on a Christian basis (although that may be justified on other grounds), this does not mean that he lacks a social ethic or that there are no social implications of his views on Christian love.[28] On the contrary, I would argue that this text in particular contains quite a radical social ethic in that it challenges and inverts the natural and merely human viewpoints in such a way as to bring about a fundamental change in social relations, if not social structures also, were it to be followed. As Kierkegaard sees it, Christianity *is* out to change the world but goes about it in a very different manner than most social programs would recommend inasmuch as it envisions social transformation effected first and foremost by a change in the attitudes and actions of individuals in their personal relations, which in turn inevitably will have social consequences. Indeed, as Kierkegaard sees it, serious external consequences will surely result from the attempt to mediate one's temporal relationships with Christian love. This is just the point where *outright collision* between the divine and merely human conceptions and expressions of love develops and where Christian love must be expressed and made recognizable through a *second form* of self-denial that has the effect of heightening the radicality of Kierkegaard's social ethic.

If to love another person means first and foremost to help that person to love God, or what amounts to the same thing, to become a more self-denying lover in relation to other human beings, the extreme implication of this requirement is that if only one party in the relation understands love in this way, then that person may need, as it were, to "hate" the beloved out of love, even break off the relationship in order to prevent the other from loving one in return as if one were God or "everything" to the other. In the context of love, this is what Kierkegaard understands by Christ's teaching that one shall, if necessary, hate one's father and mother and loved ones. Christianly understood, such an extreme action is not really hate—"far be this abomination from Christianity!" he exclaims—but it would be regarded as such by others (*WL* 108). From the world's point of view, to call such an act the expression of love and to sacrifice one's own happiness and that of the beloved is sheer madness. Thus the *double inversion* develops that precisely what Christianity regards as the ultimate expression of love is regarded by the world as self-love and unkindness, while conversely what the world regards as genuine love Christianity considers to be the expression of self-love (113). There is, then, an infinite difference between the divine and human conceptions of love. When one ventures to run counter to the worldly conception in order to hold fast unconditionally to the divine conception, a painful and terrible collision inevitably occurs. It is precisely in this situation that one becomes aware of the Christian requirement of another form of self-denial and becomes exposed to what Kierkegaard calls "the double danger" of Christian existence and the "double mark" of Christian self-denial (194–95, 204).

Christian strivers face not only the internal difficulty of coming to believe in Christ and undergoing an inward transformation of their attitudes and actions vis-à-vis the world, they also potentially face opposition from the world as a consequence of venturing to express Christian love in their relations to others. The second danger of Christian existence is thus brought about by the practice of self-denial in the external realm in one's relations to others in the world, where the inward movement of dying to the world has outward, indirectly recognizable consequences for the Christian striver. What the world understands and approves as sacrificial love, Kierkegaard says, is a personal sacrifice of a portion of one's selfishness for the sake of an alliance (*WL* 119). But as Kierkegaard sees it, this is nothing more than the subordination of personal selfishness to a larger group-selfishness. It does not constitute true sacrifice because it has as its reward, if not also its goal, the approval of others. True sacrifice has no reward, or rather, it has as its reward precisely the opposite of what could be expected through the performance of a sacrifice. For the Christian discovers that as a reward for one's love one is hated by one's beloved and abominated by the world. But voluntary submission to being hated and scorned in return for love is precisely the decisive distinction of Christian love and the "double mark" of self-denial (195). The Christian not only expects opposition from the world but "knows in advance that this will happen . . . and freely chooses it" (195).

In the merely human expression of self-denial one gives up one's own selfish desires, longings, and plans, but with the expectation that for doing so one will become admired and honored by the world (*WL* 196). In *Judge for Yourself!* Kierkegaard cites as an example of this the medieval practice of self-denial in which persons were accorded worldly esteem for their acts of sacrifice (*JFY* 205). The Christian conception of self-denial, however, is to give up one's selfish desires, longings, and plans in order to work disinterestedly for the good and to submit by free choice to being abominated, insulted, ridiculed, perhaps even executed, for this act (*WL* 194). From the world's point of view, to be willing to be forsaken and treated in this way is stupid and insane. It hardly warrants admiration and approval. Christian self-denial thus involves *two forms of self-denial:* first, the giving up of selfishness and worldliness, and then self-denial in the form of submission to the world's denial of oneself in return. This negative reception by the world constitutes an indirect indication that one stands in a genuine relation to God and one's fellow human beings, while conformity with the world's conception of love, self-denial, and sacrifice leads one at the critical point to sacrifice the God-relation in order to remain in worldly esteem.

Thus Kierkegaard cautions: "But if your ultimate and highest goal is to have life made easy and sociable, then never become involved with Christianity, shun it, because it wants the very opposite; it wants to make your life difficult and to do this by making you alone before God" (*WL* 124). He even advises ministers of the gospel that they should be prepared to preach against Christianity, if need be, so as to warn people of the dangers to expect in becoming a Christian instead of enticing them to Christianity by a fraudulent depiction of the Christian life (198). Anyone who chooses Christianity should know its difficulty and what kind of life he or she is choosing. Christianity should not be *directly* recommended to people; on the contrary, sermons should open with the possibility of offense contained in Christian existence. The common practice in the preaching of Christian love, however, is to leave out the added danger that if one ventures to express such love in one's relations to others it will go hard for one in the world (191). In Kierkegaard's estimation such a presentation of Christian existence is deceptive and false. Opposition between the world and Christianity is essential, not accidental (194).[29] If one ventures to express Christian love unconditionally in one's relations to others, then opposition from the world will surely result, since the Christian and worldly concepts of love are converse and qualitatively heterogeneous to one another. Thus Kierkegaard says that Christians who get through life without any opposition should be suspicious of themselves. One must at least expect and be willing to accept opposition, not enter upon the Christian life with the thought of avoiding opposition and leading a happy life as a consequence of one's decision. The earnest Christian does not seek to avoid danger but willingly chooses it. One does not seek worldly happiness in Christianity but conversely chooses to make oneself unhappy—doubly unhappy—by constraining one's own self-love and then, as a reward for not acting like the crowd, by reaping the world's ridicule, hatred, and scorn (204).

The second form of self-denial in Christianity thus presents the "final difficulty" in becoming a Christian and is what distinguishes both forms of Christian self-denial from merely human self-denial (*WL* 194). In the first form of self-denial one gives up selfishness and worldliness in order to work disinterestedly for the good, but disinterested devotion is not really possible unless one's renunciation of selfishness and worldliness extends to the *inner motivation* or *expectation* that informs one's outward expressions of sacrifice. In purely human forms of self-denial one gives up one's selfish desires for the sake of the community, for example, but with the expectation of some positive reward in return. But the expectation of a positive reward for sacrifice is not consistent with altruism. The true expression of self-denial in the first form thus depends upon one's willingness to express self-denial in the second form. Without the frame of mind that informs the second form, self-denial is not Christian.

Although Kierkegaard begins with a definition of Christian self-denial in conformity with the merely human or ethical-religious definition of self-denial, it becomes clear in *Works of Love* that the two are ultimately quite different, that ethical-religious self-denial is performed with the expectation of understanding, encouragement, and honor from the world, although this is not always forthcoming and purely human self-sacrifice may also result in ridicule from the world (120, 193–94). Ethical-religious individuals, however, do not anticipate a collision with the world over their actions because they believe that their basic understanding of love is essentially held in common with others (113). Christian strivers, by contrast, express self-denying love with open eyes, knowing in advance that their acts will provoke opposition because their understanding of love is qualitatively different from the purely human understanding of love. They do not expect to be understood and honored for their actions, but conversely expect and receive misunderstanding and scorn. They not only anticipate collision where the merely human or ethical-religious individuals do not, their collision is precisely with the purely human conception of love and sacrifice (118).

Kierkegaard's conviction that Christians inevitably face opposition from the world as a result of expressing Christian love has been pointed out by numerous scholars, most notably by Valter Lindström in his studies of *Works of Love*.[30] Lindström's studies are particularly noteworthy because he sees in this work the genesis of a fundamental change in Kierkegaard's understanding of Christian self-denial, whereas it is more properly viewed, in my estimation, as constituting a second form of Christian self-denial that, together with the first form, defines and distinguishes Christian self-denial for Kierkegaard throughout the writings of this period. Lindström does not think the two aspects of self-denial identified in *Works of Love* are incompatible or really even dual, but he thinks they become so as Kierkegaard progresses to his later writings. Lindström concludes that Kierkegaard gradually came to identify Christian self-denial with suffering and relegated the earlier definition of self-denial in terms of unselfishness and disinterested service to God to the level of human self-denial. Although Lindström thinks this essentially different view of self-denial comes to the fore in *Christian Discourses*, he points to a journal entry from 1847 (the year *Works of Love* was published) where it is already evident: "But to what purpose is all this? First of all in human self-denial to renounce everything of body and of mind which a human being otherwise holds dear and then in Christian self-denial to reap scorn, disdain, persecution, and death as a reward—is this not madness?" (*JP* 1:463). Here Kierkegaard appears to define human self-denial in terms of his earlier definition, while Christian self-denial is distinguished by the reception of hate and scorn as a reward for sacrifice. Lindström thinks this means that self-denial first becomes Christian when one receives opposition in return for dying to the world and that this contradicts the view in *Works of Love,* where Christian self-denial consists in giving up selfishness and becoming nothing in God's hands in order to become His servant, and where human self-denial is based on the hope for a positive reward for sacrifice. In comparison with *Works of Love,* then, Kierkegaard appears in this journal entry to have changed his view of both Christian self-denial and human self-denial. Lindström interprets Christian self-denial in *Works of Love* primarily in terms of its first form and views the opposition it elicits from the world merely as an unavoidable consequence of self-denial rather than a final and essential part of its definition.

If this were an accurate interpretation, the journal passage would indeed conflict with the understanding of self-denial expressed in *Works of Love.* But Christian self-denial in *Works of Love* is defined by both forms, not just by the first form. Without the second form, self-denial is not Christian: "As soon as the double-mark is missing the self-denial is not Christian self-denial" (*WL* 195). Thus the journal passage does not contradict, but on the contrary reiterates, the definition of Christian self-denial expressed in *Works of Love.* It may be presumed that Kierkegaard regards the Christian in the journal passage as having expressed self-denial in the first form as well. If the Christian had not first renounced everything inwardly, he or she would not be reaping scorn, disdain, persecution, and death as a reward. While the preliminary act of Christian self-denial is formally identical to human self-denial, in the context of the whole journal entry cited by Lindström it is, as in *Works of Love,* peculiarly Christian. For the entry emphasizes that Christian self-denial appears to others as madness; nothing is to be gained from it; there seems to be no purpose in it. Self-denial seems quite unnecessary, since all humans are going to be saved, somehow or other, whether they do anything or not. Thus the passage does not contradict the negative estimate of merely human self-denial in *Works of Love* but actually reinforces it by contrasting the Christian, who answers that he or she cannot do otherwise, regardless of the consequences, to the general run of humans who are not about to make sacrifices without some good reason or positive reward for their actions.

Lindström's misunderstanding, I think, is rooted in his failure to take sufficient account of the importance Kierkegaard attaches to the second form of Christian self-denial for defining and distinguishing Christian self-denial in *Works of Love.* Lindström tends to link *Works of Love* with the *Postscript* rather than with the later religious literature, stressing the hidden inwardness of Christian love and the dying to selfishness that is the dialectical expression of it. Both of these characteristics were prominent in the *Postscript.* But in introducing the element of double danger and the double mark of self-denial in Christianity, *Works of Love* really belongs with the later writings and provides the full and decisive definition by which Christian self-denial is to be understood in the other writings and journals of the second authorship. In the later writings Kierkegaard sometimes refers to Christian self-denial in terms of the first form, as in the passage from *For Self-Examination* quoted earlier, and sometimes in terms of the second form.[31] These are not seen as in any way contradictory, as one may find Kierkegaard speaking of Christian self-denial in both contexts in the same book, even within the same part of a book. When he speaks of Christian self-denial in terms of its second form, this does not represent, as Lindström thinks, a different view of Christian self-denial from the one advanced in *Works of Love,* but only a reiteration or sharper statement of it. *Practice in Christianity* even explicitly refers back to *Works of Love* as the point where the second and decisive form of Christian self-denial was introduced: "Magister Kierkegaard has shown (at the end of Part One of *Works of Love*) what is to be understood by Christian self-denial, that there is Christian self-denial only when there is double-danger, that the second danger, the danger of suffering because one denies oneself, is the decisive qualification" (PC 222). This statement flies in the face of Lindström's interpretation. He locates the turning point in Kierkegaard's thought in the *Christian Discourses,* where Kierkegaard expounds upon the gospel theme that it is more blessed to suffer derision for a good cause. Thus he thinks that Kierkegaard has shifted from the view advanced in *Works of Love,* that it is no longer good works done unselfishly as such but the reward of suffering which accrues from those works that is decisive for the definition of Christian self-denial. But actually suffering is also decisive for the determination of Christian self-denial in *Works of Love;* it does not replace but is coupled with unselfish devotion to God as the proper understanding of Christian self-denial and dying to the world in that work.

Marie Thulstrup also thinks that Kierkegaard changes his view of self-denial and dying to the world, but she attributes the shift to a change in

Kierkegaard's view of nature rather than locating it, as Lindström does, in his emphasis on suffering.[32] Whereas Lindström points to *Christian Discourses* as representing Kierkegaard's revised, external understanding of Christian self-denial as suffering, Thulstrup points to it as advocating "dying to" in an inward spiritual sense, as the dying to one's own will, or what I have called the first form of Christian self-denial. Actually *Christian Discourses* refers to Christian self-denial or "dying to" in both forms, not just one or the other as these scholars suggest. Thulstrup thinks that in *Christian Discourses* Kierkegaard regards nature in a positive light and does not consider the world or creation in itself to be evil, but in his very last publication, *The Moment,* Kierkegaard came to view evil as lying not only in the human heart but also as forming the very law of nature, making it unthinkable for a Christian to marry and have children. Dying to the world is thus no longer a dying to self-will but a dying to the world as such. Thulstrup therefore locates the change in Kierkegaard's understanding of "dying to" as occurring sometime between his middle period and the last year, rather than, as Lindström dates it, near the beginning of the middle period. To emphasize the distinctiveness of this shift vis-à-vis the *Postscript* and *Christian Discourses,* she coins the designation "Religiousness C" for the stricter Christian expression of dying to the world and self-denial.

Apparently unaware of Thulstrup's designation, Merold Westphal more recently has adopted the same label to characterize what he regards as a "teleological suspension of Religiousness B" in Kierkegaard's later writings, such as *Practice in Christianity, For Self-Examination,* and *Judge for Yourself!* in which (presumably) a "basic difference expresses itself in radically disparate meanings for such basic Kierkegaardian categories as *offense, objectivity,* and *outwardness.*"[33] Westphal equates "teleological suspension" with the Hegelian concept of *Aufhebung,* in which an immediately given or posited moment in a dialectical movement or progression is negated, transcended, restored, and preserved as a limited, relative, subordinate truth in a higher moment that constitutes the absolute or whole truth. According to Westphal's interpretation, Religiousness B is preserved in Religiousness C but is relegated to subordinate status in it with respect to the three categories of offense, objectivity, and outwardness.

With regard to the category of *offense,* Westphal strangely but somewhat hypothetically suggests that Religiousness B is subject to repudiation or negation because it only offends human reason, requiring the sacrifice of our "epistemic autonomy" while retaining the possibility of striking a "negotiated compromise" with the divine that leaves our "ethical autonomy," and thus the established social order, intact, whereas in Religiousness C "what matters" is not the facticity of Christ as the Paradox but the content of his life as the Pattern, which poses a threat to the established order (116–17). Such a characterization of Religiousness B, however, totally misses the sense of impotence or ethical incapability that is not merely intensified but abso-lutized in the consciousness of sin, since it is only through the power of God that one is able to do anything relating to one's salvation in Christianity. Moreover, Westphal elevates to a position of priority what Anti-Climacus in *Practice in Christianity* regards as an unessential and vanishing form of offense in relation to Christ, the essential possibility of offense being pre-sented by the loftiness and lowliness of his being rather than by his conflict with the established order. With regard to the essential possibility of offense, however, Westphal further claims that "Religiousness B knows the offense of loftiness, that an individual human being should claim to be God," but "only Religiousness C knows the offense of lowliness, 'that the one who gives Himself out to be God shows Himself to be the poor and suffering and at last the impotent man'" (117). Again, such a characterization of Reli-giousness B totally ignores the emphasis Climacus places on the god's ap-pearance in time "in the form of a *servant*," which in his estimation is "not something put on like the king's plebian cloak . . . but is his true form" (*PF* 31–32).

With respect to the category of *objectivity*, Westphal claims that Reli-giousness B attempts to "make Christianity into a doctrine" (119), thus identifying (that is to say, confusing) it with Christendom (or at least Lu-theranism) and associating it with objectivity rather than subjectivity. On the contrary, I would argue that the aim of the *Postscript* is precisely the opposite, to aver that Christianity is to be understood as subjectivity, in-wardness, not as some form of objectivity, although it does incorporate ob-jectivity in reflecting on what Christianity is for the purpose of becoming a Christian.

Finally, with respect to the category of *outwardness*, Westphal claims that inwardness (which he associates with Religiousness A and B even though both are subject to the temptation of objectivity, albeit in different ways) is "teleologically suspended in outwardness" in Religiousness C (123). According to Westphal's Hegelian view of teleological suspension, this means that inwardness is present in, but relegated and subordinated to, outwardness in this stage, which in my view is highly questionable with re-gard to Kierkegaard's understanding of Christianity. It is true that in *Prac-tice in Christianity* Anti-Climacus is critical of collapsing Christianity into "hidden inwardness," which in established Christendom too easily can be used to avoid any discernible expression of the Christian life (PC 252–53), but the hidden inwardness of Religiousness B is not to be equated with the spurious inwardness of Christendom. Moreover, Kierkegaard never rejects the definition of Christianity as inwardness, nor does he relegate or subordinate it to outwardness. Rather, in the later religious writings, that inwardness is shown to be given its proper outward expression in works of love and voluntary suffering.

The most important point in this whole debate, however, is not where the shift or change in Kierkegaard's thinking occurs or what one calls it (although I think the designation Thulstrup and Westphal adopt is inappropriate, for reasons I shall make apparent) but the fact and significance of its occurrence. Lindström, Thulstrup, and Westphal all agree that Kierkegaard moves from an internal to an external determination of Christianity and/or Christian self-denial, although they disagree over when that change takes place in the literature. Lindström dates it after *Works of Love,* and Thulstrup places it still later, while Westphal thinks the emergence of Religiousness C begins before *Works of Love* in part 3 ("The Gospel of Sufferings") of *Upbuilding Discourses in Various Spirits.* Both Lindström and Thulstrup regard this change as signifying a shift from a positive determination of the norm for being a Christian to a negative one, and Lindström claims further that Kierkegaard ends up, albeit against his intention, with an essentially two-level, medieval view of Christianity in which there is one level composed of those who practice dying to the world or self-denial in a mild form and a higher level for those who practice it in a stricter sense in an attempt to fulfill the absolute demand.

Certainly the external dimension of Christian self-denial represents a new element in the literature of the second period, although it appears already in germinal form in "The Gospel of Sufferings" with the establishment of Christ as the pattern for self-denial (as Westphal notes) and is brought to prominence in *Works of Love* rather than after it as Lindström, Thulstrup, and Westphal think. To be sure, this dimension is emphasized more and more, and in an increasingly stark and shrill manner, in the later religious writings. By the time of Kierkegaard's last years (1854–55) the delicate dialectical balance established in *Works of Love* had been relaxed; and as both Lindström and Thulstrup point out, Christianity is seen as being simply and directly opposed to marriage, procreation, and other forms of participation in the world that earlier served to bind the temporal and the eternal.[34]

It is debatable, however, whether the incorporation of an external dimension in the definition of Christian self-denial represents a shift or change in Kierkegaard's point of view in the second period of his authorship. Strictly speaking, Kierkegaard does not move from one view to another on this matter. He does not discard the inward definition of self-denial in the later writings but simply adds the external to the internal, the outward response that is commensurable with inwardness, and views it as decisive for the determination and recognition of the Christian's inward self-denial or dying to selfishness and worldliness. In like manner, he does not shift from a positive determination of the Christian life-form (unselfish devotion to God) to a negative one (sacrifice and suffering for the Christian doctrine) but in accordance with the "Christian formula" that obtains in the determination of every Christian qualification, views the positive as being expressed and made recognizable in and through the negative (*JP* 4:4680). Sacrifice and suffering are not merely negative determinants in Christian existence but are indirectly positive qualifications. Moreover, in comparison with the world's understanding of what is positive and negative, even the first form of self-denial must be characterized as a "negative" qualification.

Lindström's characterization of Kierkegaard's view of self-denial as medieval distorts his position. In order to fit Kierkegaard into the medieval framework, Lindström correlates Christian self-denial with the apostle life-form and the stricter requirement of self-denial in suffering. Then he correlates human self-denial with the relative, milder Christian life-form and the positive act of following Christ through sacrificial love. However, this kind of dichotomy between the two forms of self-denial and the life-forms associated with them does not hold up. In Kierkegaard's view the person who practices sacrificial love inevitably suffers for it, and the suffering which the apostles or Christians in a stricter sense submit to is the result of their positive act of following Christ in expressing Christian or sacrificial love. Kierkegaard's view is more complex than the medieval model with which Lindström seeks to align it, and differs from that model in some important respects, as Kierkegaard himself takes pains to point out. In Kierkegaard's estimation Christianity advances the absolute requirement for all Christian strivers, and although some are more successful in fulfilling it or strive to conform to it in a stricter sense than others, all fall short and need to take refuge in grace. Grace is not merely for those who practice Christianity in a milder form, as Lindström suggests, nor are they exempt from the obligation to conform to the absolute requirement.

Moreover, as Kierkegaard understands the practice of self-denial in the Middle Ages, it was untrue and worldly, not really Christian self-denial, because it was done with a view toward receiving reward or profit—the approval of God and humanity, merit, and honor, all of which are worldly motivations. Kierkegaard's view, by contrast, is once again informed by inverse dialectic. The higher one ranks in fulfilling the absolute requirement, the more one suffers and is rejected by the world. In the direct order of rank which in Kierkegaard's estimation characterizes medieval religiosity, one strives and suffers for honor, rank, and esteem, whereas in the inverse order that characterizes true Christianity, one suffers only for the truth (*JP* 4:4666). The first is outwardly positive but really negative; the second is outwardly negative but really positive. Finally, Kierkegaard does not propose that one should leave the world or separate oneself from it in some external form such as medieval monasticism, but rather that one should remain in the world and express there what it means to be a Christian.

Kierkegaard's definition of Christian dying to the world and self-denial in terms of double danger thus has the effect of significantly qualifying his understanding of Christian existence as a new form of life. While he holds a positive view of the Christian life as being on the other side of death, in existence this life is characterized by death and double danger. The worldly, immediate person's goal in life is to live a "beautiful, rich, and meaningful life in friendship and joy," without strain or sacrifice except where it promises a positive reward for oneself, one's beloved or friends, or society at large (*WL* 127). The Christian conception of life posits an ethical task, making it a duty to love and to make every sacrifice in order to help others to love God. Whereas the worldly person's "ultimate and highest goal is to have life made easy and sociable," Christianity makes life difficult, dangerous, and unhappy (124). In *Works of Love* Kierkegaard likens the second danger of Christian self-denial to being on one's deathbed and suggests that the Christian must live in the world as a deceased person (133). In *For Self-Examination* he continues this line of characterization with the claim that "the apostles were indeed dead, dead to every merely earthly hope, to every human confidence in their own powers or in human assistance" (*FSE* 77; see also *JFY* 132). In one sense, then, the Christian life must be viewed inversely as a kind of living death, inasmuch as one has to go on living in the world after one has died to it and continue to suffer the consequences of this death. In coming to love God and the neighbor, however, one truly lives for the first time and possesses the highest good to be gained in human life. At the same time one is on one's deathbed in the world, then, one is required to "walk forward upright" and to procure hope for the future in and through one's life of tribulation (*WL* 133). For as Kierkegaard understands it, hardship does not take away hope but rather recruits it (*CD* 106).

There is, then, a strongly positive dimension in Kierkegaard's understanding of the Christian life, but it is informed by the negative and must be defined in relation to death and self-denial. The Christian has been brought to the extremity of hopelessness through despair and sin, to that point where, humanly speaking, no possibility exists, where all confidence in oneself and the world is lost, where every source of comfort, even God's help in any direct sense, is unavailable, where all human hope is gone. It is precisely in this "night of hopelessness" that death occurs, but for the Christian it is an indirectly positive movement, the "last phase" of his or her sickness unto death, not the last thing (*FSE* 82). For the Christian, death is a transition to a new life and a new hope won and asserted over against one's previous life of selfishness and worldliness and over against both human hope and despair. While the expression of Christian love and self-denial inevitably meets with opposition from the world and is entirely misunderstood as being an expression of hate, self-love, and misanthropy, the Christian striver is able to hold to the possibility of the good, reconciliation between human beings, the victory of love in the world, and the triumph of self-denial.

4

SUFFERING / JOY AND CONSOLATION

Suffering constitutes the crowning mark of Christian existence in Kierkegaard's thought. It is integrally related to the determination of every aspect
of becoming a Christian, whether that be acquiring an anguished consciousness of sin, facing the possibility of offense, dying to the world, or expressing Christian love through self-denial and sacrifice. But suffering is also a
qualification of Christian existence in its own right that stands dialectically
related to joy and consolation. This dialectical relationship illustrates once
again the Christian formula that the positive is inversely recognized by the
negative. Yet the very feature that most distinguishes Kierkegaard's view of
Christian suffering, namely, its inverse dialectical relation to joy and consolation, has often been neglected or overlooked in interpretations of his
thought.[1] Most interpreters do not go so far as to reduce Kierkegaard's view
of Christian existence to suffering, but they frequently fail to relate suffering
to joy and consolation or else mention this relationship only incidentally in
their discussions of suffering in his thought.[2] The effect of this, as in the case
of the other Christian qualifications, is that Kierkegaard's understanding of
Christian existence is given a one-dimensional representation in terms of the
negative, whereas it should be given a dialectical construction in terms of
the positive that is expressed in and through the negative, or what amounts
to the same thing, in terms of the negative seen as an indirect sign of the
positive. Kierkegaard's understanding of Christian existence is informed by
inverse dialectic in every facet, and thus its qualifications should always be
viewed in terms of that dialectic.

In the process of delineating this negative or indirectly positive qualification in the writings of the second period of his authorship, Kierkegaard was
especially concerned with differentiating between various types of suffering,
and in particular with bringing conceptual clarification to specifically Christian suffering, which he believed had been confused with other forms of suf-

fering and completely abolished in Christendom. Accordingly, the present chapter will undertake to show how Kierkegaard progressively worked out his understanding of specifically Christian suffering and its inverse dialectical relation to joy and consolation in these writings. In line with the procedure followed in previous chapters, it will begin with a brief consideration of the general notion of religious suffering in *Concluding Unscientific Postscript* before turning to the writings of the second period. In these later works I shall focus first on the delineation of ethical suffering, Christian suffering, and the latter's inverted dialectical relation to joy in *Upbuilding Discourses in Various Spirits* and *Christian Discourses*. Then I shall flesh out the definitive definition of specifically Christian suffering set forth in *Practice in Christianity, For Self-Examination,* and *Judge for Yourself!* and conclude with a discussion of the themes of consolation and the redoubling of divine love in the strife of suffering.[3] I shall seek to show that while Kierkegaard's thought on suffering undergoes a process of development from 1847 through 1851, it is more *consistent* in the course of that development, more *complex* in its recognition and differentiation of several kinds of suffering, more peculiarly *dialectical* in its use of inverse dialectic to show the essential relation of suffering to joy and consolation in the Christian life, and hence more (indirectly) *positive* in its understanding of Christian suffering than many critics and general readers have realized.

Religious Suffering in *Concluding Unscientific Postscript*

A common misunderstanding and misleading practice in the interpretation of suffering in Kierkegaard's thought is the tendency to view Christian suffering primarily in terms of religious suffering as delineated in *Concluding Unscientific Postscript*. While Christian suffering is formally synonymous with religious suffering in its initial form, its most decisive form and definition are not worked out until Kierkegaard's later religious writings, and even as a form of religious suffering it may be distinguished from the general kind of religious suffering described in *Concluding Unscientific Postscript*. In the *Postscript* suffering is seen as the essential expression of existential pathos and as the distinguishing mark of religious action. That is, suffering is viewed as the expression for the attempt of religious individuals to transform their inner existence in order to sustain an absolute relation to the absolute. Suffering becomes the essential expression for this attempt because religious individuals are continually prevented from actualizing such a relationship by the fact that they remain in existence and are constantly faced with the task of bringing their immediacy into subjection. For as soon as they have succeeded in renouncing their selfish attachments to relative ends, immediacy reasserts itself and the process must be repeated, so that they seemingly get no further along by their efforts. In Climacus's view, religious suffering is not something accidental, nor is it something that comes from without. Rather, it is the point of departure for a view of life that recognizes that the persistence of suffering is essential for the maintenance of a pathetic or passional relation to the absolute *telos*. Suffering is an inverse sign of striving toward that *telos*. Thus, an end to suffering would signify either that one had ceased to exist or that one had given up one's pathos for eternal happiness. Eternal happiness is the highest *telos* of human existence, but it can never be fully possessed in time. Religious individuals must always live in the expectation of eternal happiness while suffering inwardly from continuous failure to actualize it in existence (*CUP* 1:402).

Climacus contrasts this understanding of suffering to that of aesthetic or immediate individuals, who are not able to comprehend the essential role of suffering in existence. Rather, they consider it a misfortune and regard it as "something alien" in their lives which they hope will soon end (434). Aesthetic individuals view suffering only as an external event that affects their lives, and they think that when the external manifestations of suffering are dispelled, suffering itself will end. Their view of life is based essentially on good fortune; misfortune is regarded as external, temporary, and accidental, "a narrow pass on the way of immediacy" that bears no essential significance for existence and must be overcome (434). If suffering does not cease, despair ensues and immediacy is brought to an end. However, it is precisely at that point when the life-view of immediate individuals fails to comprehend suffering that "the transition to another understanding of misfortune is made possible" (434). This new understanding consists in the realization that "life lies precisely in suffering" when it has been internalized and made the sign of one's pathos for eternal happiness rather than an accidental and external barrier on the path to temporal good fortune (436). Religious suffering is inward suffering concerning one's relation to the absolute *telos* rather than an internal reaction to external misfortune. Consequently, it is present in religious individuals even when external misfortune is absent (435). Religious suffering is never overcome but persists as long as the religious individual lives and sustains a relation to the absolute *telos*.

Climacus nevertheless asks whether it might be possible for religious individuals to transcend suffering through joy over the fact that they are related to eternal happiness, in which there is no suffering. He denies this possibility, since it would mean they have become eternal rather than existing individuals, and although they may experience joy over being related to the eternal, Climacus maintains that it would not be a direct form of joy but rather an indirect one grounded in "the consciousness that the suffering signifies the relation" (452). Consequently, the perfection of joy in existence would always be frustrated, since it is "possessed in an imperfect form," that is, indirectly through suffering (452). It is not possible, therefore, for religious individuals to overcome suffering with joy and thus to sustain a directly positive relation to eternal happiness, for as long as they are separated from this happiness in existence their suffering cannot be transcended without terminating the relation and thereby eliminating the rationale for joy.

How, then, does one explain the New Testament statements that the apostles were joyful when they were flogged and gave thanks to God for being accounted worthy of suffering for Christ's sake? Climacus also raises and addresses this question, suggesting that such suffering, like aesthetic suffering, must be distinguished from religious suffering (452–53). Not everything an apostle suffers is, strictly speaking, religious suffering. Even pagans have been known to express joy while undergoing bodily suffering. What an apostle suffers outwardly at the hands of others is not religious suffering, nor, conversely, does the absence of such maltreatment signify that one is not religious or free from suffering. When persons suffer outwardly for their faith, they may very well be able to experience a joy that enables them to transcend the bodily pains they must endure, but inward religious suffering cannot be transcended or annihilated through such joy (453–55).

Climacus's distinction between inward religious suffering and the outward suffering experienced by religious individuals is an important one to bear in mind as Kierkegaard proceeds to the delineation of specifically Christian suffering in his later writings, where it will become apparent that religious suffering and Christian suffering are not simply identical. What is said about religious suffering in the *Postscript* is not even intended to be a description of Christian suffering but is presented, if one is careful to note the context in which it is discussed, as a description of suffering in immanent religiousness. Insofar as Christianity reincorporates and intensifies the distinguishing expressions of existential or ethical-religious pathos, it includes inward religious suffering but is not limited to it or most decisively defined by it.

Ethical Suffering and the Dialectic of Christian Suffering and Joy in *Upbuilding Discourses in Various Spirits*

In *Upbuilding Discourses in Various Spirits,* the first ethical-religious publication after *Concluding Unscientific Postscript,* Kierkegaard considers suffering in a general ethical-religious perspective in part 1, "An Occasional Discourse," and in an explicitly Christian context in part 3, "The Gospel of Sufferings." In the first discourse, written "on the occasion of a confession," he explores the theme of purity of heart, which is to will one thing—the good—by renouncing all double-mindedness (*UDVS* 7–36). The double-minded person, Kierkegaard claims, stands at the crossroads where two heterogeneous prospects or visions appear: (1) willing the good for the sake of the good, or (2) willing it for the sake of reward, out of a fear of punishment, or in the presumption of victory through one's own effort (41, 56, 63). If one is to will the good in truth, one must be willing either to *do* everything for the good or to *suffer* everything for the good (78). But regardless of whether one is essentially a doer or a sufferer, the requirement is equally the same: to decide to be and to remain with the good (79–81, 99). Of these two ways of willing the good, however, Kierkegaard suggests that it is proper to dwell on the latter, since "one learns more profoundly and reliably what the highest is by reflecting on suffering than by reflecting on achievements" (100). Accordingly, in putting the focus of reflection on suffering in this discourse he concentrates on *three* aspects of suffering for the good: *its spiritual usefulness, its volitional character,* and *its emancipatory effects.* Along with other negative factors such as remorse, punishment, and the sense of shame, suffering can be an indirectly positive aid in willing the good (101–4). Persons who truly will the good even hope for punishment and suffering when they see that these can lead them back to the good when they falter. Thus, even if it seems to have no purpose in the eyes of the world, suffering can be useful in helping persons reach the highest and find spiritual health. But as in other matters, one must draw a distinction between the merely human or temporal viewpoint and the eternal perspective and adopt the latter in order to perceive the spiritual usefulness of suffering. The merely human or temporal attitude regards suffering as useful only when it can be shown to serve some (temporal) good cause and to be a benefit to others. The eternal view sees things *inversely:* the usefulness of suffering is determined by whether sufferers are willing to let it help them to the highest, and instead of their suffering being a benefit to others it is a burden to others as well as to themselves (103–4).

Kierkegaard still has inward suffering in mind here as the true or essential suffering experienced by ethical-religious strivers. Inward sufferers are distinguished from active persons whose suffering is externally determined (116–17). Whereas activists work outwardly to establish good in the world, inward sufferers are primarily concerned with their own internal condition, working to let the good conquer first of all in themselves rather than in the world at large. But while true suffering is essentially inward and passive, it may also contain an outward dimension; and concomitantly, although active persons are not, strictly speaking, sufferers (even though suffering is incurred in their actively seeking the good), their outward actions are informed by an inner commitment to the good. Active sufferers must have allowed the good to conquer in their own hearts in order to work for it outwardly. Correspondingly, inward sufferers may be said to work for the good outwardly by the power of personal example. Because they are committed to the good and are denied much in life for this reason, their lives serve as a judgment on others. Active persons are committed to do all for the good, and in acting for the good they will surely incur suffering, for in dedicating themselves to the good they lose the approval of the world and face opposition from it. Inward sufferers, by contrast, are committed to suffer all for the good, but the occasion of their suffering comes from within. It is the pain or "tender spot" of the wish, or suffering that comes from their wish for the eternal, that they must endure (99). Suffering is a sign of one's wish for the eternal, but in another sense to wish for the eternal means to wish to be cured from suffering. In order for this to happen, however, sufferers must assent to their suffering. They must accept and persevere in it because only as suffering continues does healing come. Healing by the eternal is not something that is gained all at once but is given continually as long as one remains firm in one's wish for the eternal and in one's commitment to the good. Suffering is a sign that this wish and commitment remain in effect.

Consequently, inward suffering is not something forced upon ethical strivers against their will but something *voluntarily chosen* (*UDVS* 117–18). By courageously willing suffering that could be avoided or terminated and by patiently accepting suffering that is imposed or unavoidable, inward sufferers are able to unite freedom and suffering in their lives. Through patience they are able to achieve *freedom within suffering*. This is precisely the healing power of the eternal, that through one's willingness to suffer all one is made able to accept even compulsory suffering, and then, through this submission, become emancipated within it. Through courage the free person becomes bound; through patience the prisoner becomes free. In each one finds the purity of heart that in truth wills the good and receives the salvation of eternity.

In pointing out the spiritual usefulness, volition, and emancipation to be found in inward suffering, Kierkegaard makes an advance upon Climacus's elucidation of religious suffering in *Concluding Unscientific Postscript.* There, as we have seen, suffering was regarded as the negative indicator of a positive God-relation. It was the expression for dying away from immediacy and for the individual's sense of impotence, failure, and distance from the absolute *telos,* which remained abstract and undefined. In "An Occasional Discourse" this *telos* receives closer definition as the good, and while suffering still indicates that one is separated from the eternal, the indirectly positive nature of suffering is emphasized in additional ways. Suffering is not only a sign that one is related to the eternal but constitutes an indirectly positive aid toward willing it. Although suffering is essential to ethical-religious existence, it is the result of a positive choice, and although it is persistent, there is a possibility of emancipation and healing within it. Climacus, we may recall, rejects the possibility of transcending suffering through joy because it would mean the annihilation of suffering in existence, which is impossible. "An Occasional Discourse" goes further by suggesting that although one cannot place oneself beyond suffering in existence, one can at least find freedom within it. Suffering remains, but now it begins to be viewed in a dialectical relation to the positive not merely as an abstract ideal but in existence as well through the determinant of freedom. This possibility of emancipation from suffering, however, is internal rather than external. Thus it is not analogous to, but should be distinguished from, the merely human or natural viewpoint that seeks freedom from suffering and equates that with the termination of external misfortune in life. The healing which the eternal brings through suffering is contrary to the kind of healing that the world desires. The world wants relief from temporal distress and expects it to occur all at once, while the eternal deals principally with spiritual suffering, which is in the process of being healed life-long.

In "An Occasional Discourse" Kierkegaard draws no distinction between the ethical, religious, and Christian perspectives. When he returns to the theme of suffering in "The Gospel of Sufferings," part 3 of *Upbuilding Discourses in Various Spirits,* however, he brings the discussion of suffering under an explicitly Christian perspective, although as he points out in his journals, the concept of suffering is still left indefinite (*JP* 5:6101). Jesus Christ is introduced as the paradigm for Christian sufferers, inasmuch as being a Christian means to follow Christ, assuming the lowly form of a servant, walking the same road he walked, taking up the cross, and bearing it daily in self-denial (*UDVS* 217–25).[4] In the eyes of the world Christian strivers will be considered fools and regarded as wretched because, like Christ, they choose not worldly advantages but trouble and hardship. Yet they are to bear the abuse of the world with *meekness*. This is the quality that Kierkegaard identifies at this point as "the Christian's most specific mark," since meekness such as Christ displayed is not to be found, he thinks, in paganism (245). But Christians may also be required to be *bold*. They may be required to confess Christ openly and to suffer for this act if the necessity arises, only now the occasion will be marked by the *inversion* that confession will be directed toward those who profess Christ rather than to those who oppose him (322, 324–25). That is, confession may be required as a judgment against other so-called Christians rather than for the proclamation of Christianity to its enemies. But the consequences of such an act may be just as serious as when the apostles proclaimed Christ to a hostile world. Kierkegaard does not say that confession and the suffering attendant to it are unconditionally required of every Christian. In fact, he observes that it is seldom that there are persons like the apostles who suffer for the sake of Christ, but it could happen to every Christian striver, and thus all Christian strivers should prepare themselves for it in case the need arises (340). Such suffering is in one sense peculiar to Christians inasmuch as it is suffering for the sake of Christ, but in another respect it is not suffering restricted to Christians. Pagans have also been known to suffer innocently at the hands of others for the sake of truth and righteousness (Socrates, for example). Insofar as Christian suffering has been presented as innocent suffering, then, it has not yet received its distinguishing mark from other forms of suffering but has been shown to share a general category with them.

Another distinction that Kierkegaard brings out in these discourses requires a similar sort of general application. While it can be said that Christians suffer innocently when others insult and persecute them for confessing the truth, they always suffer as guilty before God (UVDS 264–88). There is no such thing, therefore, as innocent suffering before God.[5] This applies not only to Christians but to all human beings—pagans, Jews, and Christians alike—whether they are conscious of such a relationship to God or not. In fact, Kierkegaard says that no person is conscious of such a relation at every moment, for no human being could endure it (285).

Two kinds of suffering (innocent and guilty) have now been attributed to Christians who follow Christ, although in relation to both kinds Christ does not serve so much as a pattern for imitation as a standard by which "an eternal chasmic abyss" and "eternal difference" are fixed between his suffering and that of other human beings (*UDVS* 281, 287). The innocent suffering that Christians undergo because of opposition against them is inflicted suffering, or suffering that is occasioned outwardly, while the suffering of guilt before God is a form of inward religious suffering that calls for repentance and sets them apart from Christ, who is the only person of whom it can be said that he suffered innocently before God. Yet Kierkegaard emphasizes the *positive* implications of this inward suffering of Christians. He points out that the fact that persons always suffer as guilty before God makes it certain that God is love, for the consciousness of guilt leads one to doubt oneself rather than God (280).[6] Thus one can find a kind of relief and comfort in understanding that one is guilty before God, and one can acquire hope through it—the hope that everything will improve as one becomes "more diligent, more prayerful, more obedient, more humble, more devoted to God, more heartfelt in . . . love, more fervent in spirit" (275).

This attempt to show the positive in the negative is really the central concern of Kierkegaard in "The Gospel of Sufferings." While suffering is in a general sense identified and shown to be essential in Christian existence, Kierkegaard is most intent to uncover and enumerate the *occasions for joy* in suffering and to show how Christians are able to conquer suffering while remaining in it. The title of every discourse but one begins with the phrase, "The Joy of It" (or a variation thereof), and each explores an occasion for joy derived from knowing what suffering signifies in a particular context. Unlike Climacus, who has very little to say about joy, Kierkegaard finds many possibilities for joy through showing what suffering signifies, but he agrees with Climacus that such joy does not allow us to transcend suffering so as to terminate it. Suffering remains and life becomes harder and harder for Christians, but even that is a source of joy in Christian existence.

Suffering becomes a source of joy in following Christ first of all because it signifies that one has chosen rightly, that one is advancing on the right way, and that the way of hardship is the way of perfection (*UDVS* 227, 291). There is joy in the thought that when hardship is the way, the task is immediately clear and the way is certain for all eternity (293). One need neither doubt nor delay in assuming the task of following Christ. Joy is also to be had in the thought that Christ has gone before to prepare a place for his disciples (227). Christ does not "lead people out of the world into regions of paradise where there is no need or wretchedness at all or by magic to make mortal life into worldly delight and joy" (233).[7] Nor does he make the way easier. On the contrary, it is essentially "equally difficult for every follower" and becomes harder and harder as each progresses along the way (228). When hardship is the way, suffering is not merely a difficulty or barrier along the way that is to be overcome. Suffering cannot be taken away without also taking away the way. Thus *Christ does not remove the burden of suffering in life.* In this respect everything remains as it was before. But *Christ does make this heavy burden light or easy to bear, first* by offering himself as a prototype of one who bore his suffering lightly; *second* by evoking faith in his followers that their burdens can be made light through the belief that suffering is beneficial; and *third* by replacing an even heavier suffering peculiar to the Christian—the consciousness of sin—with the light burden of the consciousness of forgiveness (231, 234–37, 246).

Thus far in elucidating the occasions for joy in following Christ, Kierkegaard has claimed that suffering is *essential, beneficial, perpetual,* and (externally at least) *unmitigated* for Christian strivers. The attempt to combine joy with suffering in no way compromises the necessity and persistence of suffering. On the contrary, the experience of joy encourages them in the strife of suffering by providing them with the vision or perspective that will enable them to endure hardship and at the same time to bear it lightly and profit from it. Suffering contains prospects of joy, but joy elicits suffering in turn. Thus these determinants are dialectically related in a complementary sort of way. But joy can also signify an *inward defeat* of suffering even as it serves as suffering's source of perpetuation. Kierkegaard suggests that when one uses one's reflective power to weigh the eternal against the temporal, one will discover that temporal suffering, like temporal bliss, "amounts to nothing" in comparison with eternal happiness, and it is precisely this happiness that suffering procures (*UDVS* 318–19). Second, he suggests that courage in suffering will enable the sufferer to conquer suffering, to bring victory out of the external defeat that suffering imposes (328). In "An Occasional Discourse" Kierkegaard had already indicated that one can conquer inward suffering, achieving freedom within suffering by accepting it. Now he adds that when Christians are subjected to persecution by the world for confessing righteousness and truth, they can even conquer outward suffering, not externally but internally by their attitude toward it, which is not merely to accept suffering but to *invert its meaning,* to take pride in it and regard it as an honor rather than as a disgrace (328–30). In this inverse way one takes power from the world, turns defeat into victory, and triumphs over suffering not in the next life but in the very day of suffering (331).

The Inverse Dialectic of Christian Suffering in *Christian Discourses*

"The Gospel of Sufferings" thus brings Kierkegaard to the application of inverse dialectic in the definition of Christian suffering. As Kierkegaard continues to sound out the "joyful notes" (*Stemninger*)[8] in the strife of suffering in part 2 of *Christian Discourses,* he employs this dialectic full force, drawing a sharp distinction between the Christian attitude toward suffering and the worldly or merely human conception of suffering and showing how the former is informed by it. He expounds the various *inversions* that characterize Christian suffering: that suffering does not take away hope but recruits it; that the poorer Christians become, the richer they make others and themselves as well; that the weaker they become, the stronger they become; that to lose is to gain; and that misfortune is really good fortune. These are all the antithesis of the human conception. Humanly understood, suffering is thought to take away hope, but Christianity converts affliction into hope by awakening the spirit in persons and directing them inward, away from their close attachments to the world, their environment, external circumstances, and relationships that ordinarily make up their waking life, in order to be schooled in how to grasp the eternal. Eternally viewed, life turned outward is really a dream life, while "to be awake is to be turned inward eternally in inwardness" (*CD* 108). This inversion is made even more complex in that, with regard to sense perception, the Christian is "like one who is sleeping, is absent-minded, has died—in him the spirit is awake and the lower nature sleeps; therefore he is awake" (108).

Christians find joy in the knowledge that the poorer they become, the richer they make others, and they also find that poverty is the road to riches for themselves. But this is not a way or form of understanding the world would know or recommend (114). What the world regards as riches is not what the Christian calls riches. The difference is determined by how one views one's temporal goods and losses. From the Christian point of view, Kierkegaard says, all worldly goods and the possession of them is selfish, envious, and of necessity makes others materially poorer (115). What one person has, another cannot have; if one has much, another must have little; and time spent selfishly laboring to acquire things for oneself contains no thought for others (115–16). To become poor in the possession of these worldly riches, then, frees them for use by others, and the Christian views loss of them as a blessing. Yet even this does not constitute, in the strictest sense, the Christian conception of riches and of how to make others rich. It is through the possession of *spiritual goods* such as faith, love, hope, insight, knowledge, capacities, and gifts that one is enabled to benefit others, for in possessing these goods one does not deprive others of anything but instead labors for them, communicating by one's possession of these goods that they are goods that every person can possess (116–20). In possessing these spiritual goods Christians also benefit themselves without being selfish, since in Kierkegaard's opinion anyone who would possess them selfishly does not truly possess them (118).

The initial strife of suffering for Christian strivers, therefore, is not the kind that occurs between human beings but is an inward strife with God over whether they are going to exist for God or for themselves, whether they will become weak through suffering so that God might become strong—not merely in the external sense of being triumphant over them through divine omnipotence but in the inward sense of becoming stronger within them (*CD* 127–28). God desires a reciprocal relationship with humans and thus gives them the freedom to choose in this matter. If, aided by hard suffering, they choose to give up the freedom to exist for themselves in order to live for God, they become utterly weak and God becomes strong in them. But then another inversion obtains in that the stronger God becomes in them, the stronger they become. Thus, *weakness is really strength.* When Christians are reviled or put to death by other humans and they submit to such treatment out of the weakness of perfect obedience to God, it cannot harm them eternally. Before other humans they will appear to be weak, but before God and in God they are made strong in weakness. Conversely, the stronger persons become in a worldly sense, the weaker God is in them and the weaker they really are in themselves, for "to be without God is to be without strength; to be strong without God is therefore to be strong—without strength. It is like being loving without loving God, that is, to be loving— without love, for God *is* love" (130).

The same sort of complexity is contained in the inversion that *to lose is to gain.* By losing the temporal one may gain the eternal (one may also lose the temporal and fail to gain the eternal, but in that case there is only loss and the inversion does not obtain). In order to convert loss into gain Kierkegaard says that one must lose the temporal in such a way that it is lost only temporally; that is, in losing the temporal one must not treat it as more than it is (merely a temporal, not an eternal loss) or despair over losing it (*CD* 139–41). To lose the temporal while treating it as the eternal is really to lose the eternal, or more precisely, it is to be lost because one has abandoned the eternal by seeking to abuse it, to reduce it to the temporal by the presumptuous wish to gain the eternal temporally, that is, "in order to have *earthly* advantage from it" (137). The eternal can only be gained eternally by losing temporality, not by seeking the eternal for earthly profit or for regaining lost temporal possessions over which one suffers grief. What is lost temporally through suffering may be gained eternally, but it is regained in an eternal sense rather than in a temporal one, so that what is gained eternally is not the same as what is lost temporally. If, for example, one loses the riches of temporality, one gains the riches of eternity, which are of infinitely more value (139–40). In reverse fashion, yet saying essentially the same thing, Kierkegaard also claims that in gaining the eternal, one loses nothing at all, for in gaining the eternal one gains "the true everything," while in losing the things that the world values and strives to gain—gold, goods, power, might, honor, prestige, health, vigor, mental power, friends, erotic love— one really loses nothing, since they constitute "the false everything" to which Christians have died and regard as nothing (145–46).

Just as the inverse dialectic of the temporal and the eternal requires re-definition of false and true values to be discarded or gained in the strife of suffering, one must also re-examine the definition of prosperity in order to see the basis for the inverse claim that *adversity is prosperity* (CD 150–59). If one defines prosperity as that which helps one to attain one's goal and adversity as that which prevents one from attaining it, then everything de-pends on the definition of the goal, of acquiring a true conception of the goal or of attaining the true goal. Kierkegaard distinguishes essentially two possible goals toward which persons can strive: the goal they *desire* to attain and the goal they *ought* to attain, or the goal of temporality and the goal of eternity (152). Since these goals are mutually exclusive, one must also *invert* or *turn around* one's understanding of adversity and prosperity. When eter-nity is the goal, one becomes unconcerned about the path, whether it is pain-ful or hard, as long as it takes one to the eternal goal. Whatever the path is, it is good fortune if it leads one to that goal. Thus Christians are indifferent to what is ordinarily called adversity or prosperity. Only that which brings one to the eternal is looked upon as being good fortune, and what is ordi-narily called misfortune is precisely what leads to the eternal goal. If pros-perity (humanly understood) and adversity led equally to the eternal goal, or if prosperity could lead one to the goal more easily, the temptation would be to see prosperity as the way to the goal. But prosperity (humanly under-stood) is the way to the temporal goal, and it is precisely the temporal that prevents one from attaining the eternal. Prosperity, then, delays rather than aids one in attaining the eternal and is, in truth, adversity. Conversely, ad-versity (humanly understood) hinders one from attaining temporal goals and thus is precisely that which can bring one to the eternal goal, if one views loss of the temporal as a good. That adversity is really prosperity is the comfort of the eternal and the occasion for joy in the strife of suffering.

One can see that in these discourses the inverse dialectic that informs Christian suffering is the product of an inner disposition or attitude of mind, that externally there is nothing that gives suffering the positive connotations and implications Kierkegaard ascribes to it. This inverse attitude is applied to the proper understanding of inward suffering and external or temporal suffering without making any distinctions or restrictions regarding whether it is unavoidable suffering, innocent suffering, guilty suffering, or a specifically Christian form of suffering to which the dialectic pertains. In fact, these distinctions had not yet been firmly established, and the way inverse dialectic applies to strictly Christian suffering contains dimensions that had not yet been explored in these discourses.

Kierkegaard moves closer to differentiating specifically Christian suffering from other forms of suffering in part 3 of *Christian Discourses* when he disrupts the joyful mood of the previous part with "Thoughts that Wound from Behind—for Upbuilding," which focuses principally on the realization that Christianity requires one to die to the world, to forsake all to follow Christ, and to do this voluntarily. Kierkegaard points out that not even in Old Testament times did God require humans to give up everything—it was not demanded of Job, and even of Abraham it was required, as a test, only that he give up Isaac (*CD* 178–79). Christianity makes self-denial both a requirement and an act of freedom, but it is the voluntary that constitutes "the essentially Christian" (179). "Moreover, the voluntary, voluntarily to leave everything, is in every case the essentially Christian only when . . . it is done in order to follow Christ" (186). The requirement itself contains the qualification that one give up everything voluntarily, thus revoking or negating any connotation of external imposition or deprivation that might be associated with the idea of a requirement. Furthermore, insofar as the decision is left to freedom, the requirement is not advanced unconditionally; that is, God may not require one to forsake all, or at least not require it in the same way as was required of the early Christians. Kierkegaard says that "I do not know that it is anywhere unconditionally required of a person in Christendom that in order to be a Christian and in order to be blessed he must in the literal sense leave everything, or indeed that he must even sacrifice his life, be put to death for the sake of Christianity" (187). Both the person who does this and the person who does not do it—if the latter is humbled by the requirement and is sincere and penitent before God—can be said to act

Christianly. Thus the requirement remains in force for every person, but the decision whether it will be fulfilled, and in what manner, is determined by the individual and the status of his or her relation to God, whether that person will be helped by grace to forsake all or to take refuge in grace by failing to do it.

The voluntary is not the only factor that qualifies one as a Christian, but it is the main factor which in Kierkegaard's view distinguishes Christianity from paganism and Judaism on the matter of suffering: "Reconciling oneself to unavoidable loss is also seen in paganism. Reconciling oneself to unavoidable loss in such a way that one not only does not lose faith in God but in faith worships and praises his love—that is Jewish piety. But to give up everything *voluntarily*—that is Christianity" (*CD* 178). It is the voluntary that creates offense and decisively reveals the heterogeneity of Christianity to the world and to Christendom:

> The world can well comprehend that little consolation is found for those who suffer unavoidable loss. But that one should voluntarily expose oneself to loss and danger, this is madness in the eyes of the world—and it is altogether properly the essentially Christian.
>
> Voluntarily to leave everything in order to follow Christ, which the world neither wants nor is able to hear without being offended, is also that which so-called Christendom prefers to have suppressed or, if it is said, would very much like to ignore, or in any case hears in such a way that something different comes out of it. (*CD* 179)

The "thoughts that wound from behind" thus introduce the decisive and distinctive factor in Christian suffering and the serious consequences attendant to it that distinguish it from other forms of suffering, although the voluntary character of Christian suffering in itself is not unique to Christianity inasmuch as the inward suffering of ethical-religious individuals in "An Occasional Discourse" is also voluntarily chosen. The decisive and "essentially Christian" factor for Kierkegaard, however, lies in the fact that the Christian voluntarily leaves everything "in order to follow Christ."

In spite of the fact that these thoughts constitute an attack from behind, they are intended for upbuilding, as the title of part 3 indicates. Thus, instead of mitigating the comfort and joy to be gained in Christian existence, these sobering reminders of the rigorous requirement and earnestness of Christianity enable one to discover the inverse source of joy and blessedness in the Christian life in another respect. Contrary to the worldly conception, these positive experiences are to be found precisely in doing a good deed and being derided for it rather than doing a good deed and being rewarded for it. Blessedness consists in suffering mockery for a good cause, since the only time a person can be said to have real merit is when she or he suffers for doing the right thing (CD 223). For this reason, according to Kierkegaard, Christianity is suspicious of any honor and esteem gained in life and associates it with worldliness (227). Thus self-denial is requisite in this respect "even more definitely than with regard to money," since money is "something purely external," whereas "honor is a concept" (227). This being the case, the renunciation of honor becomes essentially an inward act on the part of the Christian and is not to be unequivocally identified with an outward relinquishing of high office or position. A person may very well retain such a position yet inwardly renounce the worldly conception of honor and esteem normally associated with it.

Although it is blessed for one to be derided for doing the good, Kierkegaard stops short of suggesting that Christians are required to follow Christ in suffering to the point of allowing themselves to be put to death for the truth.[9] The suffering of martyrdom comes to constitute for him the ultimate but not the only expression of what it means to be a Christian. In *Practice in Christianity,* in the voice of Anti-Climacus, he states:

> I have never asserted that every Christian is a martyr, or that no one was a true Christian who did not become a martyr, even though I think that every true Christian should—and here I include myself—in order to be a true Christian, make a humble admission that he has been let off far more easily than true Christians in the strictest sense, and he should make this admission so that, if I may put it this way, the Christian order of rank may not be confused and the no. 1 place completely disappear as place no. 2 takes over its position. (PC 227)

Kierkegaard thought the only way this order of precedence could be preserved was to stress severity over gentleness, to advance the requirement of suffering over against the laxity that had prevailed and resulted in the dethroning and abolition of true Christianity in the world. Thus, even if one does not become a martyr, to follow Christ must mean at least actually to incur suffering "in a way akin to Christ's suffering," which is "to suffer evil at the hands of people because as a Christian or in being a Christian one wills and endeavors to do the good: thus one could avoid this suffering by giving up willing the good" (*PC* 173).

Specifically Christian Suffering in *Practice in Christianity*

Thus far we have seen that the distinguishing marks of specifically Christian suffering are its voluntary character, its likeness to Christ's suffering, and its inverse conception and contradictory consequences that run counter to our natural or merely human desires, understanding, and values. In *Practice in Christianity* Anti-Climacus reiterates all of these distinctions and emphasizes that specifically Christian suffering is a "whole scale deeper" than ordinary suffering, with which it has been confused in a "masterpiece of upsidedownness" and completely abolished in Christendom (*PC* 108–9). The fact that a person suffers the usual adversities in life does not constitute suffering in likeness to Christ but is simply part of the universal human experience in which pagans as well as Christians are tried. It is characteristic of Christian strivers that they have learned to bear such earthly suffering patiently, but this is not an ability that only Christians possess. One may very well have turned to Christianity initially in search of help to bear one's earthly suffering, but precisely by this, as a contrast to it, one encounters the inversion and self-contradiction that peculiarly characterize Christian suffering: One comes to Christianity for refuge, then finds that one must suffer for turning to it for help. One turns to Christ, who issues the invitation to "all who labor and are heavy laden" to come unto him for rest, and then learns that Christ does not propose to alleviate one's ordinary sufferings but only the sickness of sin. Or one gives up all to follow Christ, then discovers that one must suffer as a result. Specifically Christian suffering is distinguished, therefore, not merely by the *inverse interpretation* Christians bring to ordinary and innocent sufferings in life as Kierkegaard had indicated earlier, but also, and primarily, by its *inverse character* and the *contradictory consequences* that entails. It is suffering that occurs as the result of turning to Christianity, and it constitutes a contradiction to what one would ordinarily expect as the result of becoming a Christian, which is the alleviation of suffering rather than a seemingly endless and unnecessary perpetuation and increase of it. This kind of suffering one could well avoid in life; it comes only because one has had recourse to Christ and has elected to stand fast to his truth when opposition from the world arises.

On the one hand, Christian suffering is entirely voluntary and as such is a choice that appears as madness in the eyes of the world, for no person, humanly understood, chooses suffering when one can avoid it, escape it, or expect no earthly reward for it. Yet this is precisely what the Christian does. On the other hand, this suffering must also be seen as an inevitable conse- quence of attaching oneself to Christ, given the heterogeneity of the Chris- tian conceptions to those of the world and the world's negative reaction to the outward expression of Christian ideals. We have already seen how the inevitability of outward suffering is advanced in *Works of Love* and tied to the decisive determination of Christian self-denial as voluntary submission to ill treatment at the hands of a hostile world. But because Christians must suffer for their relation to Christ and in addition voluntarily do it, Christian suffering presents the possibility of offense not only to the world but to the sufferers themselves. If Christian strivers thought their earthly suffering was such a heavy burden that it required assistance, now they are faced with having to bear new suffering (and, moreover, bear it willingly) simply be- cause they went to this particular "physician" for help.

This suggests that the possibility of offense, as it relates to specifically Christian suffering at least, continues to arise even after one has accepted Christ's invitation. The crucial decision then is whether one will be offended or accept Christianity "on any terms," regardless of whether it is "a help or a torment" (PC 115). This decision is made even more difficult by the fact that Christianity appears to be *misanthropic*, "the greatest curse and tor- ment upon what it is to be human," not only to "the natural human being" (*det naturlige Menneske*), whom Anti-Climacus describes as being "wom- anly," "effeminate," and "weak" in wanting to "have an easy life in the world," but also to "the more profound person" and "even the strongest person" who in a moment of weakness find the requirement of suffering to be too much and senseless to the understanding (116–18).[10] This association of woman and the feminine with the natural life of immediacy, weakness, and an unwillingness to suffer and struggle reflects a negative attitude toward the female sex that is evident in other works in the Kierkegaardian corpus as well, and it suggests that Christianity (or Anti-Climacus/Kierke- gaard at least) is *misogynous* as well as misanthropic.[11] One may also add to this list, as Julia Watkin does in regard to Kierkegaard's late writings gen- erally, the charge of *misogamy*.[12] For Anti-Climacus explicitly states that

> it is also quite certain and true that Christianity has an uneasiness about marriage and also desires to have among its many married servants an unmarried person, someone who is single, because

Christianity is well aware that with woman and erotic love [*Elskov*] etc. also come all the weaker, softer elements in a person, and that insofar as the husband himself does not hit upon them, the wife ordinarily represents them with an unconstraint that is extremely dangerous for the husband, especially for the one who is to serve Christianity in the stricter sense. (*PC* 117)

While Anti-Climacus does not rule out marriage per se in this passage, he certainly makes it clear that the single life is preferable in Christianity, and while he associates "the weaker, softer elements" in a person's makeup with "the natural human being," which includes both sexes, the discussion that follows clearly puts the bulk of blame for seeking "coziness and comfort" in marriage on the shoulders of the wife, who is portrayed as trying to talk her husband out of exposing himself to the danger of Christian suffering and persecution (*PC* 117–18). Indeed, the wife brands such teaching as not only misanthropic but also unchristian, disparaging it as "the invention of some sallow, grumbling, misanthropic hermits who have no sense for the feminine" (118)!

Of course, from Anti-Climacus/Kierkegaard's point of view, neither Christianity nor Christ is really misanthropic or cruel. Quite the contrary, "Christ is in himself leniency and love, is love and leniency itself; the cruelty comes from the Christian's having to live in this world and having to express in the environment of this world what it is to be Christian, for Christ is not so lenient, that is, so weak, that he wants to take the Christian out of this world" (*PC* 196). Likewise, "Christianity may seem cruel to one. But it is not so: it is the world that is cruel—Christianity is leniency and love" (196). Once again the *inversions* that characterize the life of Christ and the Christian life of his followers come into play as Anti-Climacus tries to answer charges brought against Christianity by the natural or merely human mentality and by Christian followers facing the possibility of offense at the awful suffering entailed in the imitation of Christ. For as Anti-Climacus so astutely points out, "there is one thing to which no one ever felt naturally drawn, and that is to suffering and abasement" (167). However, there is an element of irony to be noted in his characterization of Christ and Christianity as being lenient, thus essentially like the natural and the feminine that he so disdains!

Specifically Christian suffering as Anti-Climacus has defined it thus far is primarily *outward suffering* that occurs as a result of turning to and following Christ. But in addition to the outward suffering involved in becoming and remaining a Christian, Anti-Climacus identifies two forms of *inward suffering* in *Practice in Christianity*. The first has to do with the inward suffering of Christ, which has a parallel, up to a certain point at least, in human life, and the second with a form of inward suffering peculiar to his followers in which Christ was not and could not be tried.

With regard to the first form of inward suffering, Anti-Climacus suggests that it constitutes "an entirely different kind of suffering" that "seems to be forgotten," which is "the suffering of inwardness, suffering of soul, or what might be called the secret of the sufferings that were inseparable from [Christ's] life in unrecognizability from the time he appeared until the very last" (*PC* 137). This hidden, inward suffering on Christ's part is painful for two reasons, first because it is an inwardness that has to be concealed, and second because he must appear to be other than he really is (137). In both respects it corresponds to the most grievous human suffering, which according to Anti-Climacus is *psychical* rather than physical in nature, being greater in one day "than [suffering] from all physical tortures combined" (137). Such psychical suffering results from a collision out of love for another person in which the pain of suffering becomes compounded and intensified in *three* respects: *first,* there is the pain that comes from having to keep the suffering to oneself; *second,* there is the pain of suffering endured on behalf of the other person as a result of having to express "love's solicitude" or one's willingness to do everything, even sacrifice one's life for the other, in a manner that appears to be "the most extreme kind of cruelty" to the other; and *third,* there is the pain of responsibility that one assumes in expressing love in such an inverse or contradictory manner (137). In the case of Christ, whose divinity is not directly recognizable and thus must be the object of faith, the inward suffering he endured in expressing divine love and compassion for others goes beyond anything merely human suffering can endure or understand. Just as Christ suffered betrayal and desertion by his friends as well as the infliction of physical pain and mistreatment from his enemies, other humans can suffer in these ways too, but "then no more," Anti-Climacus points out (138). For in addition to this "first time of suffering" which others may also experience, Christ had to undergo "the second time" of inward suffering in that his suffering constitutes an occasion for offense, which is something no human being can do or comprehend, not even Anti-Climacus, who in spite of being an extraordinary Christian claims to have only a purely formal awareness of "concealed inwardness" or "the suffering of real self-denial" (138–39).

Christ's inward suffering, then, is in one sense unique and as such poses a stumbling block for faith by presenting the possibility of offense to actual as well as potential followers. But there is also a form of inward suffering that is unique to the followers of Christ, who unlike him suffer inwardly over how far they are from the truth (*PC* 196). Since Christ *is* the truth, he does not and cannot suffer "in his innermost being" in this respect, although he is persecuted for being the truth (196). His followers, however, are not the truth, nor in Anti-Climacus's opinion would it ever occur to them to commit blasphemy by wanting to be the truth (196). Before God they are lowly, sinful beings who are only imperfectly related to the truth; consequently, the more they stand before God "in the fear and trembling of inwardness," the more they are beset with anxious self-concern and self-accusation over their lapses from the truth, and the harder they work "in new fear and trembling" to be "wholly unselfish, sacrificing, and loving" (196–97). With respect to their differing relations to the truth, then, Christ does not function as the prototype of Christian suffering for his followers. His role as prototype does come into play, however, with respect to their increased striving to fulfill the Christian ideal, but not quite in the way one might expect. *Ironically* and *inversely,* Anti-Climacus suggests that the more Christians strive to be unselfish, self-sacrificing, and loving like Christ, the more they will be accused by others of being selfish, evil, and even unchristian in their refusal to "let Christianity be something one supposedly should only have hidden in one's innermost being" (197). This has the effect of making them even more anxious and self-doubting inwardly, so that, if it were not for the prototype, who "expressly manifested that love is hated, truth is persecuted," they would not be able to believe in themselves and persevere (197).

Inward suffering serves to humble Christian strivers before God and to confirm them in the state of lowliness, and the disregard of the world enhances this sense of lowliness and abasement. But the suffering of both inward and outward abasement is again subject to an *inverse interpretation* in Christianity. Abasement is not "sheer abasement" but "a depiction of loftiness"; it is the appearance of loftiness in converse form in the world (*PC* 198). Abasement is naturally not recognized as such by the world, which understands everything to be directly what it is. For the Christian, abasement signifies not only that one is lowly before God and in the eyes of the world but also that it constitutes the proper negative form by which one stands related to the truth and, in a certain sense, already enjoys the exhaltation or loftiness that relation confers. Anti-Climacus thus emphasizes that one must become contemporary with Christ in his abasement, know him first of all in his lowliness, and desire to share that abasement and lowliness with him.

There is one other important aspect of suffering that Anti-Climacus addresses in *Practice in Christianity:* the inability of the imagination to portray human suffering in general and Christian suffering in particular. In *The Sickness unto Death* Anti-Climacus identifies the imagination as "the capacity *instar omnium*" or the fundamental capacity in human beings on which all other capacities such as feeling, knowing, and willing depend inasmuch as it is the medium for infinitizing or relating oneself to possibility, especially the possibility of the self (*SUD* 30).[13] In *Practice in Christianity* imagination is still regarded as "the first condition for what becomes of a person," but here Anti-Climacus stresses *the will* as constituting "the decisive condition" for "a person's upbringing in the school of life" (*PC* 186).[14] Since in Anti-Climacus's view "imagination is strongest in youth," he uses the examples of two youths to show both the *positive function* and the *limitation* of imagination in this regard (186). Through imagination, whether based on some actuality or concocted by itself, the first youth (*Yngling*) projects an image of perfection or an ideal self that he strives to become.[15] While such projection is a necessary step for human development, as Anti-Climacus sees it the imagination is nevertheless problematic with respect to its ability to depict actuality adequately, especially the actuality of suffering. For the depiction of suffering by the imagination is always an idealized suffering that is already finished or perfected, which has the effect of mitigating, toning down, and foreshortening the actuality of suffering, making it appear to be easier and less enduring than it really is (187). Thus the suffering that the imagination is able to depict "is still nonactuality; with regard to adversities and sufferings, it lacks the actuality of time and of temporality and of earthly life" (187).

Moreover, the perfected image of suffering depicted by the imagination is not really true perfection, since in Anti-Climacus's view true perfection exists in the present, not in the past (it *"is—not was"*), and consists in being "tried day after day in the actual suffering of this actuality," which is something that can only be lived, not depicted (187–88).[16] Anti-Climacus likens the illusion of suffering depicted by the imagination to "an actor dressed in rags," which "is something totally different from being the one in rags in the daily life of actuality" (188). Were one really able to grasp actuality through the imagination, that would render actuality meaningless, as there would be no need to live through what one had already experienced fully through the imagination. Anti-Climacus goes on to point out "the frightful contradiction" involved in the condition that true perfection "exists in something infinitely less perfect," which is actuality, while the imperfection of the perfect image of suffering depicted by the imagination consists precisely in the fact that "the imperfection [of actuality] is not depicted" (188). This contradictory condition is also tragic, inasmuch as "in actuality, the only place where true perfection can truly be, it is so rare, because there it is so hard and exhausting to be that, so hard, yes, so hard that to be that is for that very reason true perfection" (189).

However, in Anti-Climacus's opinion Governance or God, who is love, "never tries a person beyond his ability" (190). Thus the youth who embraces the (imperfect) image of perfection projected by the imagination may gradually become so transformed in likeness to it that eventually he is trapped or caught in a "tight corner" or Catch-22 situation by the incongruity between this image of perfection, which he loves and cannot give up, and the imperfect world in which he lives (189–90). Now the earnestness of life really begins, and the decisive importance of the will begins to come into play as the youth discovers that "the earnestness of life is to *will* to be, to *will* to express the perfection (ideality) in the dailyness of actuality" and that this must unavoidably involve suffering on his part (190). If the youth wills this task for himself and "cheerfully" accepts the suffering it entails, the imagination may be credited with having deceived him, but not adversely, inasmuch as it will have "deceived him into truth" (190–91). Finally, however, Anti-Climacus suggests there will come a moment when everything will become clear to the youth and he will understand that not only is suffering unavoidable in carrying out this task but also that it will increase as he goes forward in life (191). But when he has learned "to live under or to endure life under this pressure," he will then have discovered what it means to exist as a human being, and if he succeeds in becoming the image of perfection he loves, he will not have been truly deceived by the imagination or by God (191).

In much the same manner as the first youth, the second youth imagined by Anti-Climacus projects an image of perfection and undergoes a process of transformation, entrapment, and clarification, but in this instance the image of perfection that lures and captures him is Christ in his loftiness, which unlike other images of perfection appears inversely in history as lowliness and abasement (PC 192). The second youth tries imaginatively to visualize the suffering Christ endured as a result of his earthly condition, but given the capacity of the imagination to relate itself essentially to perfection or ideality and only imperfectly to actuality, it falsely downplays the world's opposition to Christ, making his suffering look easy and less inward than it really was (192–93). However, as the second youth goes out into the world with the image of Christ before him, it leads him, in likeness to Christ, "to the very opposite of loftiness and glory," that is, to abasement and lowliness (198). But just as it is with Christ, this "abasement is not sheer abasement"; rather, it is a depiction of loftiness as that must appear in the world, which is always "inversely as lowliness and abasement," so that "in a certain sense the abasement is loftiness" (198).

Like the first youth, therefore, the second youth has the task of realizing his image of perfection in the world, but unlike the first youth, he must realize it in *contrary* form. For both youths suffering is unavoidable, continuous, and increasing as they move forward in life, but the second youth also faces the possibility of an intensification of suffering that is lacking for the first youth, inasmuch as the second youth's prototype of perfection, Christ, was forsaken in the end not only by humanity but also by God (195). The possibility that suffering might entail abandonment by God never even arises for the first youth, who remains convinced that God is loving and gentle, never trying him with more than he is able to bear. The second youth finds abandonment by God unimaginable but nevertheless trusts that even if it were to happen, it would be only for a moment, since for him too God is love, even if that love must sometimes appear inversely as cruelty to the world (190–91, 195). Thus the second youth, like the first, refuses to abandon his image of perfection, and just as the first youth succeeds in the task of becoming human by persevering in suffering from the attempt to express ideality or perfection in the context of an imperfect actuality, so the second becomes and continues to be a Christian by persevering in suffering that entails not merely imperfection but the inverse condition of lowliness and abasement on his part (195).

By means of these two examples, Anti-Climacus is also able to delineate both the similarities and the differences between merely human suffering and the suffering that is specifically Christian in nature. In his view, to become and continue to be a Christian is "a suffering with which no other human suffering can be compared in pain and anguish," although, as we have seen, there is still much in common between the two (196). In fact, the two examples provide an interesting parallel to the distinction between Religiousness A and B in *Concluding Unscientific Postscript,* in which the first form of religiousness constitutes a universal human subjectivity that is presupposed by the second even though the latter is pathetically intensified and dialectically distinguished from the former by the consciousness of sin and the possibility of offense. In comparable manner, Anti-Climacus's first example illustrates the existential task and process that must be undergone by everyone who wants to exist as a human being, while the second depicts more narrowly what is required to become and continue to be a Christian. While the two youths undergo virtually the same process of upbuilding, the primary difference between them is determined by their differing images of perfection, both of which entail suffering in the process of being realized/imitated in existence. But only the second image of perfection manifests its perfection or loftiness inversely as lowliness and abasement in the world, with the result that Christians become "inversely recognizable" by the suffering they receive in opposition from the world (PC 212, 215).[17]

Anti-Climacus contrasts this *inverted recognizability* of the Christian in and through external suffering inflicted by the world to the "hidden inwardness" of established Christendom, which in his view nurses the illusion of being "a Church triumphant" in the assumption that "the time of struggling is over," whereas in actuality Christianity is always "the Church militant," in which suffering persists and is intensified as a result of being a Christian "within an environment that is the opposite of being Christian" (PC 211–20). At first blush, Anti-Climacus might seem to be rejecting the hidden inwardness and inward religious suffering attendant to it that constitute for Johannes Climacus the very essence of true religiosity in both its forms, Religiousness A and B, or immanent religiousness and Christianity, in *Concluding Unscientific Postscript*. But that can hardly be the case, since Climacus also contrasts the hidden inwardness of immanent and Christian subjectivity to the aesthetic pathos of Christendom, distinguishing both from the "*wohlfeil* [cheap] edition of a Christian" that prevails in Danish culture (CUP 1:557). Concomitantly, Anti-Climacus does not deny that Christianity is inwardness or that much of the suffering essential to becoming and continuing to be a Christian is inward and hidden or secret in nature; on the contrary, we have seen that he takes time to elucidate two such forms of inward suffering. But he does make an advance upon Climacus in recognizing that there is an outward or external dimension of Christian suffering that is not merely accidental but essential to the definition of becoming and being a Christian. This aspect of Christian suffering introduces the "double danger" of Christian self-denial identified earlier in *Works of Love*: the danger of suffering outwardly as well as inwardly because one denies oneself for Christ (WL 194; PC 222). Since Anti-Climacus explicitly refers to *Works of Love* as having provided the definition and decisive qualification of Chris-

·denial in the double danger of suffering, it is clear that his perspec-
ds in continuity with that work rather than departs from it.[18]

As we have seen in the course of this chapter, the recognition of an outward as well as an inward dimension of Christian suffering is not unique to
Anti-Climacus, inasmuch as in both "An Occasional Discourse" and "The
Gospel of Sufferings" of *Upbuilding Discourses in Various Spirits* Kierkegaard recognizes that inward suffering may have an outward dimension in
the form of external opposition from the world. Even Johannes Climacus in
Concluding Unscientific Postscript is aware of such external suffering, although he does not regard it as religious suffering, which for him is entirely
inward in nature. But as Kierkegaard moves to a closer determination of
specifically Christian suffering in *Christian Discourses* and *Practice in
Christianity*, associating it as he does with inverse dialectic, voluntary suffering, the possibility of offense at Christ's loftiness and lowliness, and the
enormous self-contradiction these pose for those who accept Christ's invitation at the crossroads of offense or faith, the outward dimension of Christian suffering is accentuated more and more. We have also seen that
Kierkegaard does not regard Christian suffering as being merely negative,
for he finds numerous occasions for joy in Christian suffering as he progressively identifies the inverse dialectic that informs that suffering and the decisive factors that distinguish it from other forms of suffering. Finally, it is
clear that Christ, the one who stands at the crossroads inviting all those who
suffer to come unto him, is and remains for Kierkegaard and Anti-Climacus
the paradigm of Christian suffering inasmuch as he embodies in himself the
qualitative contradiction of loftiness and lowliness that constitutes the inverted image of perfection for Christian strivers and presents the possibility
of offense to all those who accept his invitation to a life of suffering as well
as to those who do not.

Christ as the Paradigm of Suffering in *For Self-Examination* and *Judge for Yourself!*

Kierkegaard returns to the theme of Christ as the paradigm for Christian
suffering in *For Self-Examination* and its sequel, *Judge for Yourself!* with
emphasis being placed, as one might expect, on poverty, lowliness, abasement, and being forsaken by the world as constituting the narrow way of
Christ that the Christian striver must follow. In *For Self-Examination* this
is suggested as the appropriate (inverse) reflection for Ascension Day, the

day of Christ's triumph and victory (*FSE* 53–70). For the narrow way of Christ does not lead directly to victory but conversely becomes harder and harder, culminating in death and defeat before being transformed into triumph and glory. If it is not remembered that narrowness is the way right up to the end, then the Ascension will be taken in vain. Yet Kierkegaard also reminds us that it is not just the external conditions of poverty, lowliness, and so on, that determine the narrow way as the way of Christ. Many people are poor and lowly who are not Christians, and he underscores once again that the common human sufferings of life are not the narrow way of Christ. It is the factor of willingness that distinguishes the Christian's abased state from that of other unfortunate persons (*FSE* 67).

In these two works Kierkegaard's concern is no longer primarily directed, as it had been in the earlier Christian discourses, toward showing how Christians achieve an internal victory over suffering. Certainly suffering and abasement signify loftiness and exaltation for Christian strivers as they willingly choose and bear their suffering in life. But now the emphasis is placed upon coming to recognize and accept the fact that being a Christian means to remain in the world and to express overtly in it Christian qualities, values, actions, and so on. The inverse consequence that Christians must be prepared to face is that they will probably meet defeat rather than victory in the world. Thus they must be willing to venture with the recognition of, and in spite of, this probability. This presents the foremost difficulty in becoming a Christian, for the common human attitude is to avoid the danger and risk of being a Christian or to seek it only if it improves one's chances for success in the world. But Christians are required to renounce all and place sole reliance on God, knowing and expecting that this will literally spell temporal suffering and defeat.

As Kierkegaard sees it, this demand for an external expression of faith constitutes not only the second danger of self-denial and suffering but also a form of spiritual trial (*Anfægtelse*) that the Christian striver must undergo.[19] One's faith must be put to the test in real life and made recognizable in one's actions, and this test both poses a terror, from which one is tempted to flee if one but could, and bestows the courage with which to withstand that temptation. Insofar as suffering signifies glory and victory, this is something that is entirely inward and hidden, never directly recognizable but only inversely present in lowliness and abasement. Thus for the Christian striver, as it was for Christ,

> the Christian cross is not superficiality, externality, both-and, without depth, a decoration, a cross in a medal. No, seen from one side

it is quite literally, fearfully literally, a cross, and no eye sees the cross and the star combined in a higher unity, so that the radiance of the star is perhaps diminished but the suffering of the cross also becomes somewhat less excruciating. From the other side, conversely, the star is seen, but the star is not worn . . . alas, it is the cross that is carried . . . the badge of the order and the distinctive mark. (JFY 161)[20]

Kierkegaard sounds very Lutheran here in insisting that the *via crucis* rather than the *via gloriae* is the external mark of Christian existence, and he confirms this himself by claiming Luther as a proponent of the view that the Christian must suffer in the world:

> The highest is: unconditionally heterogeneous with the world by serving God alone, to remain in the world and in the middle of actuality before the eyes of all, to direct all attention to oneself—for then persecution is unavoidable. This is Christian piety: renouncing everything to serve God alone, to deny oneself in order to serve God alone—and then to have to suffer for it—to do good and then to have to suffer for it. It is this that the prototype expresses; it is also this, to mention a mere man, that Luther, the superb teacher of our Church, continually points out as belonging to true Christianity: to suffer for the doctrine, to do good and suffer for it, and that suffering in this world is inseparable from being a Christian in this world. (JFY 169)[21]

To exist in tension and conflict with the world, to will to suffer for the doctrine in the world, and to meet defeat at the hands of the world are what properly constitute the following of Christ and the highest expression of Christian existence. This is clearly a negative determination of what it means to be a Christian, but one that is inversely and indirectly a sign of the positive joy, blessedness, victory, and exaltation that also characterize the Christian life. In *Judge for Yourself!* Kierkegaard presents this stage as going beyond the expression of Christianity designated by Religiousness B in *Concluding Unscientific Postscript,* although both are rare among human beings.[22] While the psychical state of inwardness described in the latter text includes "the struggle of an anguished conscience, fear and trembling, furthermore, the deep and perilous collision of the essentially Christian, that the essentially Christian is an offense to the Jews and a foolishness to the

Greeks," it does not involve suffering for the doctrine as does following Christ in the stricter sense (*JFY* 201).

In his religious writings from 1847 through 1851, therefore, Kierkegaard exhibits a progressive development in perceiving and unfolding the distinctiveness and dialectic of Christian suffering and joy. The sense of Christianity's heterogeneity to the world, both in terms of values and actions, remains constant, but Kierkegaard's understanding of Christian existence undergoes considerable and significant expansion as he discovers and elucidates both the inward and outward forms and consequences of specifically Christian suffering. This is particularly true in comparison with the view of suffering advanced in *Concluding Unscientific Postscript* and even in comparison with the early Christian discourses, where the *inward inverse interpretation* rather than the *external inverse consequences* of suffering is emphasized. As Kierkegaard moves progressively in the writings of the second period toward the differentiation and definition of specifically Christian suffering, he gradually distinguishes its decisive form from other forms of suffering with which it had been confused (aesthetic suffering and unavoidable or ordinary human suffering, although the latter may be borne in a Christian way through an inversion of one's attitude toward such suffering) or with which it shares certain characteristics (religious suffering, ethical suffering, innocent suffering, guilty suffering, spiritual trial, inflicted suffering). In sum, Christian suffering is distinguished by its inverse dialectical relation to joy, by its voluntariness, by its having Christ as the prototype for suffering, by its being for the sake of the word, and by its inverse character and consequences. It is viewed as being both inward and outward in form, as both voluntary and inevitable, and as resulting from one's distance from the truth as well as from the hostility of the world. Suffering thus constitutes the most decisive negative expression of Christian existence and the inverse dialectic appropriate to it.

Consolation for Suffering

There is one other factor that is important to take into account in Kierkegaard's inverse dialectical understanding of Christian suffering. Just as there is joy to be found in suffering, so also there is consolation (*Trøst*) for suffering in Christian existence. The theme of consolation in Kierkegaard's writings is not as prominent as certain other positive factors such as faith, love, and joy, but there are references to it throughout the literature and journals of the second period of his authorship. It becomes particularly evident in the later journals of this period, where in light of the stringent view of Christianity Kierkegaard had developed by this time, he tries to show the correlative dialectical relation to consolation and mildness in which the rigor of Christian existence must be viewed. He avers that Christianity is pure consolation and mildness, but as usual he stresses that this is so only in an indirect manner. Christian consolation is always coupled with, or given in correspondence to, the rigorousness of Christianity contained in the requirement that a person must die to the world and endure the negative consequences of that act (JP 3:3749). Thus Christianity may be seen as consolation and mildness only as or after its rigor is imposed. Then the law becomes "the greater the rigorousness, the greater the consolation" (JP 3:3502). Christian consolation is primarily intended to relieve the Christian striver's anguished conscience over his or her sin, and as such it must be viewed as a corollary to or an aspect of forgiveness. Only secondarily does it have to do with common worldly sufferings. When consolation is extended for temporal distress, it is usually for the suffering the Christian encounters in the world as a result of his or her God-relation.

This dialectical correlation means that Christianity appears as both consolation and rigorousness, help and affliction, relief and a burden to the Christian striver. At the same time Christianity offers consolation for one's spiritual suffering it requires one to undergo a conversion in relation to sin and to die to the world, which in turn bring additional temporal suffering upon oneself. There is, then, a kind of inverse dialectic operative in consolation. One turns to Christianity for help to bear one's ordinary suffering in life and then discovers, first, that consolation is not offered for the kind of suffering for which one seeks comfort and relief; and second, that when one acquires a consciousness of sin and seeks Christianity's reassuring word about judgment, one has to suffer because of this comforting word. Thus the opposite of one's normal expectation occurs. The more one succeeds in meeting the requirements of Christianity, the more one has to suffer rather than be relieved from suffering. Instead of being one's comforter, God appears to be a deceiver (JP 2:1409). In return for its consolation, then, Christianity sets up a rigorous requirement that posits the possibility of offense and makes the offer of Christian consolation appear to human understanding as a deception and a terror rather than alleviation. While consolation is something one would ordinarily welcome in one's human struggles, the rigor attached to Christian consolation makes all one's worldly sufferings far preferable to being consoled in this manner (JP 4:4595). In *Christian*

Discourses Kierkegaard says that "from the worldly point of view Christian consolation is much more to despair over than the hardest earthly suffering and the greatest temporal misfortune" (*CD* 97). The misery of spiritual suffering over sin, dying to the world, and temporal suffering constitutes a misery that the natural person would altogether prefer to remain ignorant of and to avoid in life (*JP* 3:3502).

If Christian consolation brings suffering, the inversion also obtains that the sufferer is the one most qualified to bring consolation to others. Kierkegaard holds that it takes a sufferer, not a happy person, to comfort others and to be able to say to them that adversity is prosperity (*CD* 158). He notes that sufferers often say that if one were in their place, one would see that there is no consolation for their sorrows, and they complain of those who try to console them that these would-be comforters do not put themselves in the sufferer's place and thus have no idea what suffering is really like (*WA* 115). Not having suffered as the sufferer has, they are in no position to be able to offer true sympathy or consolation. Kierkegaard points out that only one person, Jesus Christ, is truly able to put himself in the sufferer's place, but he nevertheless holds up the offering of consolation to others as part of the Christian ideal for his followers (116–17). Christian strivers are not to seek consolation for their own suffering but, like Christ, should seek to console others in theirs (*JP* 1:472; 4:4652; *SKP* X³ A 167). Yet it is precisely in comforting others that one finds consolation for one's own sorrows. Christ is "the one of whom it is veritably true . . . that he unconditionally has no other comfort than to comfort others," but this holds true for his followers as well (*WA* 119). In this way suffering reaches its highest point but also its limit, "where everything turns around" (119). The sufferer becomes the comforter and finds his own consolation through this act.

To others this seeking to console rather than to be consoled, or of being consoled only through consoling others, will once again constitute the kind of situation and form of consolation contrary to what they desire, expect, or have been taught, and consequently it will be something they would gladly decline. Christian consolation is qualitatively different from the merely human conception of consolation. It is not mere compassion or human sympathy, a substitute for lost joy, an assurance that matters will be better soon, or an indulgence exempting one from the commandment to love others (*WL* 41–43, 64; *UDVS* 104, 145). These are all direct forms of consolation, whereas Christian consolation is indirect and inverse in character. Eternally viewed, it is joy itself, but Christianity's word of joy and consolation is expressed inversely in the assurance that adversity is prosperity, that one conquers eternally through lifelong suffering, that God remains faithful even when we are unfaithful, and that the command to love makes it possible and a duty to love others. Christianity thus begins where paganism ends (*JP* 4:4595). Where the world would despair over love and suffering and give up hope for alleviation or consolation, Christianity forbids despair, introduces the command and ability to love, and directs concern away from worldly suffering to a concern about sin and suffering in relation to God. This is where Christian consolation begins and everything is reversed. Worldly suffering then becomes inversely the result and sign of consolation rather than the cause or object of consolation. Consolation consists in consoling rather than being consoled and in loving rather than being loved.

As Kierkegaard prepared his attack on Christendom in his journals, one of the charges he brought against it was that it had preached Christianity undialectically as simply consolation and had represented its consolation in a direct and trivial manner as offering comfort for worldly suffering (*JP* 1:541). In *Judge for Yourself!* as well he accuses Christendom of trying "to sell Christianity as comfort in this way without life commitment" and equates this with the peddling of indulgences (*JFY* 132). He charges that the depiction of the inverse dialectic of consolation with its complementary relation to rigor and suffering is seldom or never heard in Christian sermons.[23] Consequently the general sermon in Christendom is not directed to true sufferers who stand in need of consolation, nor do they contain the degree of consolation that truly miserable persons need, for they do not acknowledge or consider the depth of suffering that constitutes true Christian suffering:

> Take any contemporary sermon you choose and hand it to someone who is really suffering, to someone suffering depression bordering on insanity, to someone with an obsession, or someone suffering for the sake of the truth—it sounds like mockery of him; it does not dare to console him because it never dares to think of his suffering.
>
> That there are sorrow and adversity and hardship, etc.—yes, even the happiest of people must surely be aware of them. The sermon does consider them but, mind you, on such a low key that the total impression in no way whatsoever disturbs the impression of a cozy, pleasurable life. And happy, prospering people, if they have a shred of human intelligence at all, like to hear this—and this is supposed to be Christianity! (*JP* 3:3501)

Kierkegaard indicts Bishop Mynster in particular of this kind of preaching, but he considers Mynster as representative of a general practice among the clergy.[24] Instead of preaching consolation to sufferers, the typical sermon in Christendom offers consolation to the fortunate (*SKP* X³ A 135). Kierkegaard admits that parishoners are given an "impression" of suffering and are encouraged to "sympathize" with sufferers. But this is not offered in any form that would disturb or prevent them from continuing to enjoy life. For it is suggested that matters are not really so bad for the unfortunate—there are examples, for instance, where the blind have "clearer" sight than those who have vision. Or it is suggested that the poor are far happier than the rich. They are "touchingly" depicted in their happiness and freedom from all the "burdens" of wealth. Once again Kierkegaard calls this mere mockery of true sufferers. They give the impression that the rich do not need to give the poor anything or much, since the poor are fundamentally happier than the wealthy and poverty has its "beautiful" side. Christendom thus consoles and supports those who do not need consolation by relieving them of the responsibility to help and console others and by transforming true consolation into a vapid kind of human sympathy that is really cruelty (*SKP* X³ A 179). The fortunate are called upon to "console" those who suffer by condescending to them without really having anything to do with them. They try to close their eyes to real suffering and keep sufferers at bay.

Those who are the recipients of such "human sympathy" are precisely the ones to whom Christianity offers true consolation. Whereas human sympathy is really cruelty, Christianity is really consolation for those who truly need it. Kierkegaard points out, however, that "the difficulty in Christianity is really to become so miserable that one really needs it—but if you are that, then truly it is also consolation" (*SKP* X³ A 179). The false, worldly form of consolation that Christendom extends to sufferers is the assurance that their plight is not so bad or that their situation will improve soon: "The consoling talk consoles with 'No doubt things will get better'— perhaps. It urges a little patience; it potters a little about the sufferer and says that by Sunday everything will be all right" (*UDVS* 115). But Christianity does not console worldly suffering in such a way or promise health, success, and happiness soon. It does not conceive misery as an illusory, temporary, or worldly state that will be overcome or compensated for by Christianity. Rather, it leads one beyond one's concern for ordinary worldly sufferings to a new kind of suffering for which consolation is given. It views one's worldly suffering as real and often unavoidable and as a fact of life that continues. Suffering even increases as one turns to God for consolation and alleviation, so that God even appears to be on the side of opposition, multiplying rather than relieving one's worldly suffering. When such suffering becomes inversely the sign of the God-relation, it is just then that consolation is most needed: "When the mark of the God-relationship is success, prosperity, earthly blessings, with a sprinkling of adversities at most, which no one avoids anyway—then there is no need for a Spirit who is the Comforter" (*JP* 2:1662). But when, in order to respond to God's mercy and love, one must constantly *work against oneself* in the world, losing rather than succeeding, becoming poor rather than rich, giving rather than receiving, loving rather than being loved, consoling rather than being consoled, and accepting new suffering rather than being relieved of the old, then one truly needs Christianity's consoling word, precisely in order to persevere in this strife.

God's Redoubling in the Strife of Suffering

There is one final point that needs to be brought out with regard to Kierkegaard's inverted dialectical understanding of Christian suffering in relation to joy and consolation, namely, that inverse dialectic applies not only to the individual's relation to God but also to God's relation to the individual in the strife of suffering.[25] That is, suffering is viewed as the inverse sign of God's love and grace. God loves an individual because that person is a sufferer, but it is also true that because an individual loves God, he or she must suffer (*JP* 4:4688). God's love is evident not in the fact that one enjoys happiness and good fortune in life but in the fact that one suffers as a result of one's love for God. In a journal entry from 1852 Kierkegaard distinguishes the gradations of a person's relation to God in accordance with the degree of recognition one has that suffering comes from God and is an inverse indication of God's love. Over against paganism and Judaism, in which the love of God is understood in a directly positive way as bringing happiness and prosperity with no or only a modicum of temporary suffering, "in Christianity being loved of God is suffering, continual suffering, the closer to God the more suffering, yet with the consolation of eternity and with the Spirit's testimony that this is God's love, this is what it is to dare to love God" (*JP* 2:1433).

Kierkegaard understands this inversion as constituting a kind of reduplication or *working against oneself* on the part of God in which the deity appears in converse form or works against the true nature of the divine by appearing in the first instance as cruel rather than loving. Because God is spirit and pure majesty and thus is qualitatively different from finite and lowly human beings, a redoubling on the part of the divine is required in order not to be misunderstood or taken directly in terms of a merely human conception of the divine. God's redoubling, Kierkegaard says, "consists precisely in this—that it is suffering which comes from him and that nevertheless this is to be the expression of love" (JP 2:1433). God is pure love—this is the "thesis of Christianity"—but the deity can express this positive nature only indirectly in the world (JP 2:1446). Thus God's love appears in the first instance as cruelty. But in Kierkegaard's estimation human beings are unable to bear such redoubling. They desire to understand God directly as love, to believe that only the good comes from God, and to expect that all will go well for them in the world as a result of God's love for them. Thus suffering, evil, misfortune, and unhappiness are sometimes interpreted as signs of God's disfavor, but never as a sign of God's love. On the contrary, more often than not they are seen as the work of the devil. In spite of the fact that Kierkegaard claims support from Luther in urging the necessity of suffering in Christian existence, he criticizes Luther for being undialectical and unchristian in attributing suffering to the devil rather than to God (JP 2:1447; see also 2:1449; 1:486).

Kierkegaard maintains that human beings do not naturally love God, although they may declare that they do. But when these declarations are probed, it turns out that the natural relation to God is really egoistic, that humans love God because they think God will send them worldly gifts or because God takes suffering away or can at least be expected to end it soon (JP 4:4690). Then when suffering persists they doubt God and come to the conclusion that God is not love. But, as we have seen, Kierkegaard denies that God's love is exemplified through the granting of worldly abundance and success or through the taking away of suffering and misfortune. If humans love God for these reasons, their love is false and is reciprocated with improper motives. But because humans have this direct, worldly, and insecure conception of God as love, it is necessary for God to cloak the divine expression of love to humans in a way that will teach them in what sense the deity is truly love. God requires humans to reciprocate that love on an unselfish basis, not extending love in exchange for worldly favors or regarding God's loving nature as a worldly indulgence toward humans. Thus, because God's conception of love and the true conception of God as love are not the human conception of love and because God must manifest divine love in a sinful world, God's love appears as cruelty, the opposite of the human conception, so as to negate and transform that conception (*JP* 1:489; see also 2:1409, 1410). God's love is not really cruel, nor is the apparent cruelty due to any duplicity in God's nature but rather to the fact that humans are sinners and live in a sinful world.

Kierkegaard admits that one must be very spiritually advanced in order to be able to understand suffering in this way. In fact, this apparent cruelty of God constitutes another form of spiritual trial (*Anfægtelse*) for the Christian striver. The temptation is to accuse God of being unloving and deceptive or to think that suffering is a sign of God's anger. The difficulty for advanced Christian strivers, therefore, is not so much in attributing their suffering to God as in understanding it as a sign of God's love. This is the *ultimate inversion* concerning suffering that Christians are required to make. In one sense, then, specifically Christian suffering is due to the opposition of an evil world against anyone who dares to express true Christianity in its midst, but in another sense Christians understand that this suffering is something that comes from God in exchange for salvation from another form of suffering far worse than any earthly suffering—the anguish of conscience over sin and the fear of judgment. Thus they view the new temporal suffering they must bear as a means of purification and sanctification, and they regard the experience of having to suffer like Christ a privilege rather than a cruel imposition by a vindictive and unloving God.

That Kierkegaard maintained the Christian thesis that God is love to the very end of his authorship and life is testified to by the publication of "The Changelessness of God" (originally written in 1851 and delivered at the Citadel Church later that year) in August, 1855, just about two and a half months before his death on November 11. In the prayer with which the discourse closes, he affirms once again that "whenever a person comes to you, at whatever age, at whatever time of day, in whatever condition—if he comes honestly, he will always find (like the spring's unchanged coolness) your love just as warm, you Changeless One!" (*TM* 281).

5

CHRISTIAN EXISTENCE WITHIN THE BROADER
DIALECTIC OF CHRISTIANITY

Kierkegaard's understanding of the basic qualifications of Christian existence is almost never simple or direct but complex, indirect, inverse, and dialectical, incorporating both positive and negative determinants that are related to one another in a complementary manner. This is the central feature of Kierkegaard's religious thought in the second period of his authorship. The failure to take cognizance of it accounts for much of the misunderstanding and misrepresentation of his views. Inverse dialectic constitutes Kierkegaard's hermeneutic, but this inverted method of interpretation also corresponds to, or casts into reflective form, the actual form of Christian reduplication and the existential qualifications for living Christianly as Kierkegaard understood them. The distinctiveness of Christianity and the qualifications of Christian existence are expressed in and through inverse dialectic. We have seen that the qualitative dialectic in Christian existence is informed at every turn by inversions, both with respect to the Christian qualifications themselves and with respect to the relation of Christianity to the aesthetic and ethical-religious spheres and life-forms.

Christian existence and its qualifications are defined both ideally and existentially in Kierkegaard's writings, but the existential definition predominates. The Christian ideals that constitute the positive qualitative criterion and goal for Christian strivers are inversely recognized in existence through the negative. The positive relation of Christian strivers to the ideals and their progress toward them are measured in terms of their sense of distance from the ideal, their encounter with the possibility of offense contained in Christianity and the Christian life-form, their voluntary self-denial and suffering, and their negative reception in the world as a consequence of attempting to give external expression to their inward passion. The ideal conception of the self as a synthesis before God finds its consummate expression in existence as the act of coming to oneself "in self-knowledge and before God as nothing before him, yet infinitely, unconditionally engaged" (*JFY* 104). As I pointed out earlier, in existence Christian strivers are never directly what they are but become so by being, or having been, precisely the opposite, only in such a way that their dialectical condition is no longer directly what it is either but has come to form for them an indirectly positive aid in becoming a self before God.

Thus the relation to Christianity is always indirect and has the opposite effect in life from what one would normally expect, for this religion, in the first instance at least, makes life unhappy rather than pleasant, difficult rather than easy, painful rather than simply carefree, repulsive rather than attractive. The need for repentance, the sense of sorrow and shame, the sacrifice and suffering, the lowliness and abasement, and the poverty, weakness, failure, and adversity that characterize Christian existence illustrate the negative makeup of such a life. It is a life that, humanly speaking, no person in his or her right mind would desire or choose to live. Yet these negative conditions are, from the Christian point of view, to be regarded inversely as aids toward willing the good and as a source of strength and deeper insight into the true nature of the eternal, life, love, hope, faith, and selfhood. The awareness that the negative conditions of Christian existence inversely signify new being, loftiness, riches, blessedness, possession of the eternal, closeness to God, and likeness to Christ converts the unhappiness, suffering, and rigor of life into joy and victory. The Christian is enabled to become essentially indifferent to external suffering and adversity and to find forgiveness and consolation in Christ.

Kierkegaard understands living Christianly as involving the transformation, qualification, and sanctification of human existence through the introduction of a transcendent criterion of what constitutes the human. This has the effect initially of setting the Christian life-form in opposition to the immediate and universal human forms of existence, but we have seen that ultimately Kierkegaard views Christianity as seeking to redefine and inform these dimensions in conformity with the Christian conception of what it means to be a human being. Thus he moves progressively in the literature toward the formulation of the decisive qualifications for living Christianly.

In the process of this development we have seen also that Kierkegaard comes to understand Christian existence as involving both inwardness and outwardness. The advanced Christian striver is not limited to a dialectic of personal inwardness, as in the ethical-religious or even the initial Christian expressions of pathos. When one ventures to express one's inwardness in one's relations to others, one encounters the double danger of having to deal with opposition not only within oneself but from the world as well. This double danger introduces the most decisive determinations and expressions of Christian existence in the forms of self-denial and suffering, thereby giving the qualitative dialectic of Christian existence an external as well as an internal dimension.

The perception of the external dimension of Christian existence enabled Kierkegaard to arrive at a more balanced, if also more stringent, view of Christianity. Kierkegaard himself recognized the significance of this development in his understanding and regarded it as the primary distinguishing factor between the earlier and later literature:

> To be a Christian involves a double danger.
> First, all the intense internal suffering involved in becoming a Christian, this losing human reason and being crucified on the paradox.—This is the issue *Concluding Unscientific Postscript* presents as ideally as possible.
> Then the danger of the Christian's having to live in the world of secularity and here express that he is a Christian. Here belongs all the later productivity. (*JP* 1:493)

Kierkegaard credited his conflict with *The Corsair,* a local satirical-political periodical, as the factor that led him to discover or understand more fully what is involved in being a Christian.[1] Without it, he states, "I would have escaped completely the *double*-danger connected with the essentially Christian. I would have gone on thinking of the difficulties involved with Christianity as being purely interior to the self" (*JP* 6:6548). Thus he concludes that "as author I have gotten a new string in my instrument, have been enabled to hit notes I never would have dreamed of otherwise" (*JP* 6:6548).

Kierkegaard's discovery of the external dimension of Christian existence also meant that in his mature view Christian existence acquires an indirect, paradoxical, converse recognizability through the opposition the Christian striver encounters in the world: "To the degree that my being a Christian has more truth, to the same degree would this be recognizable by the greater opposition" (*PC* 212). This means that being a Christian is neither directly recognizable through external acts and appearances, as generally believed in the world, nor simply a matter of hidden inwardness, as expressed in Christendom in distorted form and in Religiousness A and B through subjective pathos.

Viewed together, the individual productions of Kierkegaard's second pe-

riod of authorship and the complementary qualifications for living Christianly elucidated in them suggest that the Christian qualifications must be
understood finally within an even broader complementary dialectical framework that is characteristic of Christianity. As Kierkegaard understood it,
Christianity incorporates both gospel and law, grace and works, mildness
and rigor, and presents Jesus Christ as the Christian striver's redeemer and
prototype for living Christianly. We have seen that while Kierkegaard is frequently interpreted as advancing in his later works only the demanding,
negative, and severe side of Christianity, he emphasized this dimension only
as a corrective of medieval and contemporary distortions of Christianity.
Ultimately his view is that Christianity is entirely positive—all gentleness,
love, and grace—but in accordance with the formula operative in the determination of everything Christian, the positive is defined according to, or on
the other side of, a dialectic in which "every qualification of the essentially
Christian is first of all its opposite" (JFY 98). Only when this dialectic has
been brought to bear is it true that Christianity is all gentleness, love, and
grace.

This broader dialectical framework that informs Christianity and the individual's relation to it becomes most apparent in Kierkegaard's later writings and journals of the second period. It is almost as if, realizing that he
had incorporated seemingly disparate points of view in the individual productions of the period, Kierkegaard consciously sought to piece them together, to show how one implies and serves the other, and to demonstrate
how they are interrelated. Thus he explains that the rigor of Christianity is
intended to protect and give impetus toward its ultimate leniency and mildness:

> In my representation rigorousness is a dialectical factor in Chris-
> tianity, but clemency is just as strongly represented: the former is
> represented poetically by pseudonyms, the other personally by my-
> self. This is the need of the present age, which has taken Christian-
> ity in vain. But it is something entirely different if a despairing
> person has nothing to say about Christianity except that it is the
> cruelest self-torment. In order to put an end to playing fast and
> loose, I had to introduce rigorousness—and introduced it simply to
> provide movement into Christianity's clemency. This is my under-
> standing of Christianity and my task. If I had understood only its
> frightful rigorousness—I would have kept silent. This is what Jo-
> hannes de Silentio has already called attention to, that in such cir-

cumstances one must be silent and at least demonstrate that he loves other human beings—by being silent, because merely negative outcomes, at least dreadfully negative outcomes, are not to be communicated. Such a thing is not communication, no, it is an assault, a betrayal, a character deficiency, which is determined at least to have the deplorable satisfaction of making others just as unhappy and confused as one is himself. (*JP* 6:6590, translation slightly amended)

Thus the Christian formula is: "first of all rigorousness, the rigorousness of the ideal, then mildness" (*JP* 6:6275).[2] When the dialectical side of rigor is done away with, the conception of Christianity as mildness becomes untrue, for Christianity is not mildness in the sense that it requires nothing of human beings. It is only "mildness in severity" (*JP* 3:2873). The severity or rigor, Kierkegaard says, shall indeed become abrogated or turned into mildness, but it must first be present and in force before it becomes abrogated.

The fact that rigorous requirements condition the correct understanding of Christianity as mildness means also that the understanding of Christianity as a gospel of grace must include a relation to works and the law.[3] One cannot have a true conception of the magnitude of grace if one does not have a true conception of the magnitude of the Christian requirements (*JP* 2:1497). Kierkegaard asserts that Christianity is gospel, but he also takes seriously Christ's command to love and his declaration that he came not to abolish the law but to fulfill it. "When this is disregarded," Kierkegaard says, "the gospel and grace are taken in vain" (*JP* 2:1484). Christ not only fulfills the law but makes it more rigorous in the process; or it could be stated conversely that grace is more rigorous than the law (*JP* 2:1484). Christianity is gospel, but it is also the Absolute which says, "You shall." While the Atonement is "everything" in relation to a person's salvation, so that it makes no difference in that regard what a person does to secure it, Christians are still not permitted to be indolent by the fact that Christ does all. The requirement remains and is even sharpened under grace, since it demands imitation of Christ, forsaking and dying to the world, and as a consequence of this, having to suffer for one's self-denial.

Because Christianity is the Absolute, its requirements are so high that no human being can fulfill them, but precisely in and through this highness they serve to humble Christian strivers and to establish a feeling in them of the need for grace. The requirement is not imposed in order to crush Christian strivers but, on the contrary, to lift them up. If it falls upon one crushingly, this is a sign that one is incorrectly related to it (*JFY* 153). The correct relation is the *inverse* one, that one sees exaltation in one's humiliation, loftiness in one's lowliness, and views the unconditional requirement not as a weight that one must lift but as the means whereby one is to be lifted up in faith and worship.

While the absoluteness of the Christian requirement makes it impossible to fulfill and therefore necessitates grace, the converse is also true that grace makes fulfillment of the law possible for the first time. Kierkegaard explains that

> under the law my salvation is linked to the condition of fulfilling the requirement of the law. Under grace I am freed from this concern, which at its maximum must bring me to despair and make me utterly incapable of fulfilling even the least of the law's requirements—but the requirement is the same.
>
> The law's requirement is a tightening. To be sure, tightening such as the tightening of a bowstring creates motion, but one can tighten a bowstring to the breaking point. This is precisely what the law as such does. Yet it is not the requirement of the law which breaks, but that which is added—the fact that your eternal salvation depends upon your fulfillment of the requirement. No human being can endure this. Indeed, the more earnest he is, the more certain is his simultaneous despair, and it becomes completely impossible for him even to begin to fulfill the law.
>
> Then comes "grace." Naturally, it knows very well what the trouble is, where the shoe pinches. It takes away this concern, the appendage of the fulfilling of the law, which is precisely what made the fulfilling of the law impossible. "Grace" takes away this concern and says: Only believe—then eternal salvation is assured to you. But no more, not the slightest abatement of the law's demand; now you are to begin to realize precisely this. But there will be rest and peace in your soul, for your eternal salvation is assured to you if only you believe. (*JP* 2:1475)

With relief from the strain and anxiety incurred by the dependence of salvation upon works, Christianity assumes that it is now possible for one to fulfill the law (*JP* 2:1489). Therefore, no excuses are acceptable, and God begins to require real earnestness on the part of the individual. It is as if,

Kierkegaard says, a new teacher has come to replace the old one (*JP* 2:1475). Where the former teacher, being an old man, admonished and punished, yet let matters slide, the new, young teacher enters with a gentleness that rejuvenates the school and then resumes the requirement of work, keeping a sharp eye and becoming more inflexible than the old one about getting the work done. Rather than exempting persons from striving, grace enables them to strive and aids them on the way.

The formula of the relation of law and gospel is thus *law—grace— renewed earnestness,* although grace is operative throughout the process of striving. It comes first in response to the humble admission of one's distance from the requirement. But precisely because a reprieve or indulgence is granted, one is required to exert oneself all the more. Yet "soon or immediately this striving, too, comes to need grace—and again grace—because after having received grace it is so imperfect" (*JP* 2:1482). The effect of this is a continually deepening understanding of how one stands in need of grace. Kierkegaard understands Christian striving, not as a gradual achievement of perfection directly understood as a progressive movement forward, but indirectly and inversely as a retrogression in the deepening recognition of the imperfection of one's striving: "Every step forward toward the ideal is a backward step, for the progress consists precisely in my discovering increasingly the perfection of the ideal—and consequently my greater distance from it" (*JP* 2:1789). If one is actually striving, however, the emphasis falls not so much on actually fulfilling the ideal as on getting an impression of the requirement in all its infinitude, so that one is humbled by it and learns to rely on grace (*JP* 1:993). Paradoxically, this increasing recognition of the imperfection of one's striving is precisely what constitutes Christian perfection (*JP* 2:1482). Thus the requirements of the law serve to affirm the gospel of grace rather than to negate it. The whole point of the law both before and after grace is to drive a person to grace and to underscore its sufficiency for salvation (*JP* 2:1491).

In Kierkegaard's estimation, it is not works themselves but the notion of merit so easily attached to their performance that leads to a misconception of the role of the law and its place under grace. Kierkegaard distinguishes his concept of law and works from the medieval view precisely on the basis of their differing attitudes toward merit (*FSE* 15, 17). Whereas in his view the medieval monastic movement collapsed grace into law, making good works everything, Kierkegaard sees grace as becoming everything through the absoluteness of the law. Thus both law and grace are affirmed. The difficulty is that "in every human being there is an inclination *either* to want to be meritorious when it comes to works *or,* when faith and grace are to be emphasized, also to want to be free from works as far as possible" (16). A person can adjust to either works or grace, but not both: "If it is to be works and nevertheless grace, that is indeed foolishness" (17). Kierkegaard interprets Luther's protest against the medieval order in conformity with his own as an attempt to take meritoriousness away from works, not to do away with works as well. However, the world was quick to take Luther's declaration that persons are saved by faith alone and twist it to mean that they are liberated from all works. That this happened was an indication to Kierkegaard that Luther had not been sufficiently dialectical in his presentation of the relation of grace and works: "Ah, but Luther was not a dialectician; he did not see the enormous danger involved in making something else supreme, something which relates to and presupposes a first and for which there is no test whatsoever. He did not understand that he had provided the corrective and that he ought to turn off the tap with extreme caution lest people automatically make him into a paradigm" (*JP* 3:2521). In the margin of this journal entry Kierkegaard continues:

> No wonder Luther very quickly got such great support! The secular mentality understood immediately that here was a break. That this was true of Luther was beside the point to them; they understood at once how with a little lying this could be used to great profit. They invented the assurance, they assured that in their deep inwardness they were willing to give everything to the poor, etc., but since it was not the highest, they did not do it, kept every penny and grinned in their beards at our Lord, the New Testament, Luther—especially at Luther, that chosen instrument of God who had helped men so splendidly to make a fool of God. (*JP* 3:2522)

Grace, therefore, had been pushed into an entirely wrong position and used to slough off the requirement of the law. By contrast, the Christian view, according to Kierkegaard, is that one must do everything and then understand that one is nevertheless saved by grace, that grace pertains to one's unworthiness rather than to one's worthiness.

This whole relationship of mildness and strictness, works and grace, law and gospel, in Christianity as it applies to Christian existence is further clarified in Kierkegaard's understanding of the dual role of Jesus Christ as the Christian striver's redeemer and prototype for living Christianly.[4] The works of the second period offer little direct explanation of the complementary relation of these dual roles, although both are emphasized in the course of the authorship. *Judge for Yourself!* for example, contains a section on Christ as the prototype, while the communion discourses emphasize Christ's grace and atonement for the contrite sinner. Kierkegaard notes in his journals that even in the Bible there are differences of emphasis in the individual books: the epistles stress Christ as redeemer, while in the gospels the prototype is more prominent (*JP* 2:1920). In a reflection on Luther's distinction between Christ as pattern and Christ as gift, Kierkegaard admits that he himself has steered in the direction of Christ as pattern, but in a manner that incorporates rather than excludes Christ as gift (*JP* 3:2503). Properly understood, the doctrine of the prototype "encompasses everything," for the other side of the prototype is that Christ is the redeemer and compassionate one (*JP* 2:1432, 1857). As in the case of works and grace, Kierkegaard accuses the Middle Ages of having chosen only Christ as the prototype and his own age Christ as the redeemer, only in such a way as to "steal" grace (*JP* 2:1917). Consequently, he concludes: "It is entirely clear that it is Christ as the prototype [*Forbilledet*] which must now be stressed dialectically, for the very reason that the dialectical (Christ as gift), which Luther stressed, has been taken completely in vain, so that the 'imitator' [*Efterfølgeren*] in no way resembles the prototype but is absolutely undifferentiated, and then grace is merely slipped in" (*JP* 2:1862).

Kierkegaard affirms both roles of Christ by maintaining that the function of the prototype is to teach us how greatly we stand in need of grace (*JP* 2:1432, 1857, 1922). The Middle Ages assumed that humans could actually achieve the ideal of resembling Christ; thus they held up Christ literally and directly as a prototype for Christians. But Kierkegaard regards this as a childish, naïve, and unrealistic view of human ability (*JP* 1:693; 2:1432, 1857). The more one achieves religious maturity, the more one realizes how infinitely far one is from resembling the ideal and how qualitatively different the prototype is from the merely human. Then one does not dare to try to resemble him directly but instead becomes humbled by the ideal (*JP* 2:1135, 1432). It is just then that Christ becomes the gift, bestowing pure compassion and grace in relation to one's imperfect striving. The role of Christ thus alternates: "When we are striving, then he is the prototype, and when we stumble, lose courage, etc., then he is the love which helps us up, and then he is the prototype again" (*JP* 1:334; see also 349, 692; 2:1863).

For Kierkegaard, then, Christ *is* the prototype for Christian strivers, but not simply or directly a prototype. With respect to his role as redeemer, he is not an object for imitation at all, and in being the fulfillment of the ideal he stands at such an infinite distance from all human striving that all direct efforts at resemblance fall infinitely short and are reduced to nothing. But insofar as Christ is the prototype for Christian strivers, he requires them to strive toward a likeness to himself, since as the prototype he "constitutes the eternal strenuousness in what it means to be a human being" and expresses in his life everything essential to the Christian life (*JP* 2:1847, 1848). This striving toward reduplication in imitation once again has the consequence of *working against oneself,* for the more one strives to be like Christ, the further from being like him one seems to oneself, and the more aware one becomes of Christ's heterogeneity, the more one must come to rely on grace rather than on one's own efforts. From a Christian perspective, then, reduplication does not signify in the first instance the achievement of likeness to Christ, but a growing realization of one's unlikeness to him. Only through Christ's help can one come to resemble him at all. But in order to arrive at a point where one needs, wants, and can accept this help, one must attain a sense of one's own impotence and nothingness before God. This is what Christ as the prototype in the first instance is intended to accomplish. Imitation is thus used dialectically in Christianity to train Christian strivers in the need for grace so that they may effectively flee to it in faith and not use it in vain (*JP* 1:692; 2:1785, 1905, 1906). The prototype represents the ideal for Christians, not as something they can directly and realistically expect to fulfill on their own, but rather as that which they cannot fulfill. If Christ did not then appear in his other role as a redeemer, he would fall upon Christian strivers crushingly as the prototype and be the infliction of cruelty pure and simple upon them as well as the occasion of despair in requiring them to become something they could not (*JFY* 153). Thus Christ never appears simply as the prototype but incorporates in himself the grace whereby real imitation is made possible. While the role of prototype initially occupies first place, then, that position is ultimately given over to Christ as gift (*JP* 2:1135). In like manner, the requirement of imitation yields to the primacy of faith as the expression of the Christian striver's respect for the qualitative difference between his or her striving and the ideal.

The primacy of faith and Christ as gift does not mean that the prototype and imitation are thereby dispensed with, however, for "the prototype remains with his demand that there be a striving to be like him" (*JP* 2:1432). At the same time Christ is at once the atoner for the past and the prototype for the future (*JP* 2:1919). Similarly, there is a reciprocal relation between faith and imitation: imitation leads dialectically to faith, but faith is succeeded by imitation. Imitation comes after grace, by grace, as the fruit of gratitude and faith (*JP* 2:1884, 1886, 1892, 1908). The prototype appears before grace as a source of humiliation but after grace as the model for imitation. Kierkegaard lamented that he himself was incapable of using the prototype in this second way (*JP* 2:1899). But insofar as every person continually falls short of the ideal in his or her striving, the dialectical alternation of Christ between the roles of prototype and redeemer is continually necessitated for every Christian striver.

There is a difference, however, in how the requirement and imitation are to be regarded before and after grace. As the prototype, Christ belongs to the proclamation of the law, only in him the law is raised to an even higher level, requiring Christian strivers to be like him (*JP* 2:1863). Because Christ fulfills the law, he can require the absolute of human beings; but by fulfilling the law, Christ also destroys it. Through his fulfillment of the law he ransoms humanity from law to grace by presenting himself as the prototype who dialectically causes persons to flee to grace. Thus he enables one to "die to the prototype," the law, and the works righteousness that require individuals to resemble the prototype by their own effort (*JP* 1:349). When the requirement of imitation is then reintroduced after grace, it comes not as a requirement of the law but as an expression of gratitude enabled by grace. The continued role of Christ as prototype and the requirement of imitation after grace thus do not signify to Kierkegaard a reintroduction of the law or any new form of the law and works righteousness. Next to faith, *gratitude* is what Christ expects from his followers, and in the disciple in the stricter sense that gratitude takes the form of imitation. If imitation does not come as the glad fruit of gratitude, it is not imitation (*Efterfølgelse*), for "fearfully extorted discipleship is rather a perverted mimicking [*Efterabelse*]" (*JP* 2:1892). Imitation is a sign or witness to the fact that one's relation to grace is true, that one has been helped by it, and that it is by grace that one is able to follow Christ (*JP* 2:1877). Thus, while imitation after grace constitutes the most rigorous and paradoxical form of being a Christian, involving as it does the double danger of Christian existence, it is not divorced from grace nor is it independent of grace but rather is a testimony to how Christianity combines both gospel and law, grace and works, mildness and rigor, through a relation to Jesus Christ as the Christian striver's redeemer and prototype for living Christianly.

In conclusion, this study suggests that if the works of any period may be regarded as normative for the interpretation of Kierkegaard's understanding of Christianity and Christian existence, those of the second period of his authorship surely should serve in that capacity. For it is in this body of literature that Kierkegaard specifically undertakes the conceptual definition and clarification of the qualifications of Christian existence and achieves his most fully developed and balanced view of Christianity. According to the pseudonym Johannes Climacus, the earlier pseudonymous writings move in the direction of depicting the decisive expression of religious existence but all fall short of actually achieving it (*CUP* 1:268–69). The transitional works, *Concluding Unscientific Postscript* and *The Book on Adler,* differentiate Christian subjectivity from other forms of existential pathos and appropriation and prepare the way for the conceptual definition and clarification of the specifically Christian qualifications in the later literature, but they do not provide a final or full description of Christian subjectivity and Christian existence.

To declare the centrality of the later literature and its inverse dialectical perspective for understanding Kierkegaard, however, is not to overlook the fact that he does not always succeed in sustaining the dialectical position attained in these writings. Even within the later journals and writings of the second period he shows signs of moving toward an undialectical posture of unqualified opposition to the world and any positive form of participation in it. Numerous interpreters have found Kierkegaard's attitude in his last writings to be radically negative and world-denying. In light of the inverse dialectic that informs his perspective in the second period, however, such a culmination would represent not the logical conclusion of his central vision but rather an abrogation of it. For in the writings of the second period Kierkegaard generally affirms both the positive and the negative, not allowing either to define "the essentially Christian" without reference to the other. This complementary inverse dialectical stance is the distinguishing feature of his thought in that period. For were it not for the operation of inverse dialectic, even these writings would appear to be advancing a directly negative conception of living Christianly, as indeed many interpreters have understood them to do. It is essential, therefore, that one recognize the operation of inverse dialectic in Kierkegaard's thought; otherwise his perspective will be distorted or given an entirely wrong representation. His foremost intent was to assert the positive in and through the negative, not to advance a purely negative characterization of Christian existence. One may not be willing to accept this interpretation of living Christianly or be convinced that it preserves the positive in any way other than a purely theoretical manner, but it at least should be recognized as affirming both the positive and the negative. The unique feature in Kierkegaard's dialectical conception and formulation of these dimensions in Christian existence is how they are interpreted and correlated through inverse dialectic.

It is questionable, however, whether Kierkegaard achieves quite as much as he thinks through this dialectical method. The qualifications elucidated through inverse dialectic may be characteristic of Christian existence but are not altogether unique to it. Kierkegaard's intent, however, was precisely to bring out the distinctiveness of Christian inwardness and its qualifications, to show how Christian existence is made qualitatively different from, and even the opposite of, other forms of existence, both the aesthetic and the ethical-religious, through its basic qualifications and the operation of inverse dialectic in them. But the fact that he initially interprets the whole range of existential pathos via this form of dialectic presents some difficulty in using it in the later literature to establish the distinctiveness of Christianity. Kierkegaard attempts to get around this by depicting Christian existence as involving a greater degree of inversion than the ethical-religious as well as some forms of inversion that are peculiar to the Christian life or qualitatively different from their corresponding ethical-religious expressions of inversion. The first measure establishes only a quantitative difference— something Kierkegaard himself always rejected as a sufficient measure of differentiation between Christian subjectivity and other forms of pathos. With regard to the second measure, the forms of inversion that are peculiar to Christianity and distinguish Christian existence more decisively are perhaps advanced at the expense of not sufficiently appreciating corresponding qualifications in other religious traditions.

For example, although Judaism affirms transcendent categories in common with Christianity, Kierkegaard generally manifests a negative or lukewarm attitude toward this religion. He apparently envisions it as falling within the sphere of the ethical-religious, in spite of the fact that he views this sphere as being characterized by immanence. He tends to represent Judaism as maintaining essentially a directly positive attitude toward life in this world, although he recognizes that it also incorporates self-denial and suffering. But in his estimation, self-denial in Judaism is not voluntary as it is in Christianity and suffering is regarded as only a temporary ingredient of life. Kierkegaard does not consider the importance of the consciousness of sin as an expression of faith in Judaism, nor does he regard Judaism as in any way presenting the possibility of offense. Kierkegaard's understanding of Judaism and its existential determinants thus warrants further investigation before his view of the distinctiveness of Christian existence may be allowed to stand without qualification. The same may be said with regard to his understanding of paganism.

With respect to the Christian tradition itself, however, Kierkegaard's critique of Christendom and the secular, merely human mentality it reflects undoubtedly constitutes the most penetrating and most devastating assessment of church and society of his time and is equally applicable to the present age, if not more so. For the tendency to turn religion into a feel-good form of aesthetic entertainment that reflects and reinforces the basic values and goals of secular society rather than critiquing them from the standpoint of a higher spiritual ideal is perhaps even greater and more predominant now than in Kierkegaard's time. In suggesting that the Christian way of life, like the way of Christ, is constantly to *work against oneself* in the world by becoming lowly rather than exalted, poor rather than rich, giving rather than receiving, losing rather than succeeding, loving rather than seeking to be loved, consoling rather than being consoled, and accepting new suffering rather than being relieved of the old, Kierkegaard undoubtedly presents a demanding and difficult Christian ethic that runs counter to ordinary human desires, values, and goals in life. But it is not for that reason any less true or binding upon those who would be followers of Christ. Nor should it be forgotten that this ethic itself is informed by inverse dialectic inasmuch as one becomes exalted in being lowly, receives consolation in consoling others, finds joy and alleviation in and through the strife of suffering, and so on. Even though no one is capable of fully embodying the ideality of Christian existence in the inverse manner described by Kierkegaard, there is still a need for a higher standard or ideal by which to measure ourselves and the societies in which we live and toward which we may strive as individuals in gratitude and grace before God.

In its strong emphasis on a contrite or anguished consciousness of sin and a sense of distance from the divine as constituting the proper posture of faith before God, in its reintroduction of the possibility of offense as a means of protecting Christian faith and existence from being entered into blithely and in vain, in its affirmation of the spiritual equality of all human beings in love of the neighbor through the double danger of self-denial, in its view of joy and consolation as being inextricably bound up with internal and external suffering for the sake of the Word, and in its uncompromising requirement of rigorous striving and works of love as requisite for a true understanding and experience of the ultimate mildness, leniency, and grace of Christianity and Christ, Kierkegaard's poetic portrayal of living Christianly offers a profound as well as provocative understanding of what true Christianity is all about. I doubt that the Christian life has ever been described with more precision and perspicuity than he has presented it—and that is so precisely because he has brought inverse dialectic to bear in casting Christianity into reflection and in setting forth its uncompromising ideals. The originality and uniqueness of Kierkegaard's understanding of Christian existence are thus to be found chiefly in his conception and use of inverse dialectic in interpreting and correlating its basic and most decisive qualifications.

This is not to say that Kierkegaard has presented a perfect likeness or picture of the Christian, for by his own testimony a perfect representation of that ideality is possible only existentially through reduplication. Moreover, various aspects of his portrayal may be questioned or contested, as has been done at various points in this study as well as in other assessments of his thought. On the whole, however, Kierkegaard may be judged to have succeeded in capturing the essence of living Christianly in his poetic presentation of the complementary qualifications of Christian existence. In my estimation, he has succeeded where others have failed precisely because he has understood and presented the Christian life dialectically rather than one-dimensionally. His dialectical portrayal of the essentially Christian thus stands as both a corrective and a challenge to modern as well as postmodern optimism and pessimism, asserting that life, in particular living Christianly, is neither simply positive nor wholly negative, but positive as well as negative, and that the former is experienced in existence precisely in and through the latter in its inverse role as an indirect expression of spiritual ideals.

NOTES

Introduction

1. See, for example, David J. Gouwens, *Kierkegaard as Religious Thinker* (Cambridge: Cambridge University Press, 1996), which focuses to a large extent on Kierkegaard's views on becoming a Christian but ranges more widely than the present study in discussing Kierkegaard as a religious thinker in a broader context and in terms of the earlier pseudonymous works as well as the later religious writings. See also Per Lønning, "Kierkegaard as a Christian Thinker," in *Kierkegaard's View of Christianity*, ed. Niels Thulstrup and Marie Mikulová Thulstrup, Bibliotheca Kierkegaardiana 1 (Copenhagen: C. A. Reitzels Boghandel, 1978), 163–79, and Vernard Eller, *Kierkegaard and Radical Discipleship: A New Perspective* (Princeton: Princeton University Press, 1968).

2. For a good summary of other approaches to Kierkegaard and their limitations, see Gouwens, *Kierkegaard as Religious Thinker*, 3–12. See also George Pattison, *Kierkegaard's Upbuilding Discourses: Philosophy, Theology, Literature* (London: Routledge, 2002), which focuses on Kierkegaard's early upbuilding discourses rather than the pseudonymous works but also interprets Kierkegaard "within the general horizons of a philosophical or humanistic approach" (3; cf. also 32–33).

3. For other studies that place their focus on the later religious and specifically Christian writings, see Arnold Come, *Kierkegaard as Theologian: Recovering My Self* (Montreal: McGill-Queen's University Press, 1997); John Elrod, *Kierkegaard and Christendom* (Princeton: Princeton University Press, 1981); Bruce H. Kirmmse, *Kierkegaard in Golden Age Denmark* (Bloomington: Indiana University Press, 1990); Bradley R. Dewey, *The New Obedience: Kierkegaard on Imitating Christ* (Washington, D.C.: Corpus Books, 1968); and Eller, *Kierkegaard and Radical Discipleship*. Elrod and Kirmmse concentrate on the social and political dimensions of Kierkegaard's later writings, particularly his critique of Christendom. Come focuses primarily on the concept of the self, Dewey on the imitation of Christ, and Eller on Kierkegaard's sectarian understanding of Christianity.

4. *The Book on Adler*, drafted in 1846 and copiously revised in subsequent years, is not included here except for the section "The Difference Between a Genius and an Apostle," which was excerpted and published by Kierkegaard as part of *Two Ethical-Religious Essays* in 1849. Delineating Christian subjectivity on two levels, first from the standpoint of the special individual whose experience is qualified by the fact of having received a revelation, and then on an ordinary level as an emotion (*grebethed*) that is qualitatively different from more universal forms of religious experience, *The Book on Adler* really belongs with the *Concluding Unscientific Postscript* inasmuch as it provides a test case or actual example of the lack of categorical definition of Christian concepts and the confusion of Christian inwardness with other kinds of inwardness that the *Postscript* seeks to point out.

5. Although "that little article," as Kierkegaard affectionately called this short piece of aesthetic criticism (*JP* 6:6238, 6242), focuses on two modes of dramatic development or metamorphosis in the life of an actress as represented by two prominent Danish actresses of the time, Luise Heiberg and Anna Nielsen, Kierkegaard regarded it as providing a dialectical balance in the development of the authorship. Just as the early pseudonymous works were accompanied by upbuilding discourses, so the aesthetic was brought back in the period of the later religious writings to signify that the writer was not an aesthetic writer who later became religious, but from the first a religious writer who employed the aesthetic for religious purposes. For a good discussion of this little aesthetic work, see Janne Risum, "Towards Transparency: Søren Kierkegaard on Danish Actresses," in *Kierkegaard and His Contemporaries: The Culture of Golden Age Denmark*, ed. Jon Stewart, Kierkegaard Studies Monograph Series 10 (Berlin: Walter de Gruyter, 2003), 330–42.

6. Recent deconstructive efforts to undermine and discredit Kierkegaard's own account of his authorship by questioning his motives in writing are not very convincing. See Walsh, "Reading Kierkegaard With Kierkegaard Against Garff," *Søren Kierkegaard Newsletter* 38 (July 1999): 4–8, which is a critique of Joakim Garff's article, "The Eyes of Argus: The Point of View and Points of View with Respect to Kierkegaard's 'Activity as an Author,'" *Kierkegaardiana* 15 (1991): 29–54, reprinted in *Kierkegaard: A Critical Reader*, ed. Jonathan Rée and Jane Chamberlain (Oxford: Basil Blackwell, 1998), 75–102. See also Garff's reply to my critique, "Rereading Oneself," in the same issue of *Søren Kierkegaard Newsletter*, 9–14, and his book *"Den Søvnløse": Kierkegaard læst æstetisk/biografisk* (Copenhagen: C. A. Reitzels Forlag, 1995), 298–330.

7. On Kierkegaard's role as a "poet of the religious" and more specifically as a "Christian poet and thinker" (*JP* 6:6511, 6521, 6391), see Walsh, *Living Poetically: Kierkegaard's Existential Aesthetics* (University Park: The Pennsylvania State University Press, 1994), chap. 8. The present volume begins where that book leaves off and thus forms a companion volume of sorts inasmuch as it explores in greater depth and length Kierkegaard's "poet-communication" of the Christian ideals in the later literature, which is only briefly discussed in the previous book, since it ranges over the whole course of Kierkegaard's authorship.

8. On the need for conceptual clarity with regard to the conceptual definitions of Christianity, see *BA* 113–15.

9. For a recent study that argues Kierkegaard was primarily a theologian, albeit "of a very peculiar kind," see Come, *Kierkegaard as Theologian*. Gouwens, in *Kierkegaard as Religious Thinker*, also describes him as "a kind of theologian" or a "theologian with a difference" (12), and David R. Law, in *Kierkegaard as Negative Theologian* (Oxford: Clarendon Press, 1993), regards him as an "apophatic" theologian in the tradition of Dionysius the Areopagite. See also Michael Plekon, "Kierkegaard the Theologian: The Roots of His Theology in *Works of Love*," in *Foundations of Kierkegaard's Vision of Community: Religion, Ethics, and Politics in Kierkegaard*, ed. George B. Connell and C. Stephen Evans (Atlantic Highlands, N.J.: Humanities Press, 1992), 2–17, and Louis Dupré, *Kierkegaard as Theologian: The Dialectic of Christian Existence* (New York: Sheed and Ward, 1963).

10. On the role of dialectic in Kierkegaard's thought, see also Law, *Kierkegaard as Negative Theologian*, 35–70; Gregor Malantschuk, *Kierkegaard's Thought*, ed. and trans. Howard V. Hong and Edna H. Hong (Princeton: Princeton University Press, 1971); Stephen N. Dunning, *Kierkegaard's Dialectic of Inwardness: A Structural Analysis of the Theory of Stages* (Princeton: Princeton University Press, 1985); Hermann Diem, *Kierkegaard's Dialectic of Existence*, trans. Harold Knight (Edinburgh: Oliver and Boyd, 1959); and Eller, *Kierkegaard and Radical Discipleship*, 144–45.

11. On the difference between Socratic and Platonic dialectic as Kierkegaard understood them, see Walsh, "Ironic Love: An Amorist Interpretation of Socratic Eros," in *International*

Kierkegaard Commentary: "The Concept of Irony," vol. 2, ed. Robert L. Perkins (Macon: Mercer University Press, 2001), 123–40, and *The Concept of Irony* itself (*CI* 32–33, 36–37, 121–26). In Kierkegaard's view, Socratic dialectic consists in dialogue, the art of conversing or asking questions, that is perpetually negative or inconclusive and thus ironic or lacking any positive content, whereas Platonic dialectic, like Hegelian dialectic, is speculative in character, namely, it begins with an abstract idea and seeks to give positive, concrete content or definition to it through the dialectical process. On Hegelian dialectic and Kierkegaard's critique of it, see Law, *Kierkegaard as Negative Theologian,* 39–50, and Jon Stewart, *Kierkegaard's Relations to Hegel Reconsidered* (New York: Cambridge University Press, 2003), 397–411, 573–78. See also Theodor W. Adorno, *Negative Dialectics,* trans. E. B. Ashton (New York: Continuum, 1973), for a critique and rejection of "the dialectics of identity" or positivity in Hegel's philosophy in favor of an understanding of dialectical contradiction that is "insolubly nonidentical" or negative in character (145–48, 158–60). Adorno regards the paradoxicality of Kierkegaard's dialectic as a "decaying form of dialectics" inasmuch as it appeals to an extrasocial Being (God) rather than to critical reflection itself to resolve the paradoxes of thought; indeed, Adorno even entertains the statement, "we can think against our thought," as a possible definition of dialectic (141). In rejecting the principle of identity in Hegelian dialectic, however, Adorno is closer to Kierkegaard than he thinks.

12. Malantschuk, *Kierkegaard's Thought,* 305.

13. On the complementary character of Kierkegaardian dialectic, see also Eller, *Kierkegaard and Radical Discipleship,* 145.

14. On the dialectic of communication in Kierkegaard's thought, see Lars Bejerholm, *"Meddelelsens Dialektik": Studier i Søren Kierkegaards teorier om språk, kommunikation och pseudonymitet* (Copenhagen: Munksgaard, 1962). On Kierkegaard's understanding of communication more generally, see Poul Houe and Gordon D. Marino, eds., *Søren Kierkegaard and the Word(s): Essays on Hermeneutics and Communication* (Copenhagen: C. A. Reitzel, 2003), and Roger Poole, *Kierkegaard: The Indirect Communication* (Charlottesville: University Press of Virginia, 1993).

15. See, for example, *JP* 1:760; 3:2525, 3329, 3349; 4:4289, 4666, 4680, 4696, 4782; 5:5997; and 6:6593, and *WA* 67. For previous brief discussions of inverse dialectic in Kierkegaard's thought (elements of which have been incorporated in this study), see Sylvia Walsh Utterback, "Kierkegaard's Inverse Dialectic," *Kierkegaardiana* 11 (1980): 34–54; Sylvia Walsh, "Kierkegaard: Poet of the Religious," in *Kierkegaard on Art and Communication,* ed. George Pattison (New York: St. Martin's Press, 1992), 1–22; and Walsh, *Living Poetically,* 227–28. So far as I am aware, only Gouwens, in *Kierkegaard as Religious Thinker,* has appropriated the terminology of inverse dialectic in discussing Kierkegaard's views on becoming a Christian, but only in a few instances and primarily with regard to the role of the imagination. Jolita Pons, in "On Imitating the Inimitable: Example, Comparison, and Prototype," in *International Kierkegaard Commentary: "Upbuilding Discourses in Various Spirits,"* vol. 15, ed. Robert L. Perkins (Macon: Mercer University Press, 2005), notes Kierkegaard's use of inverse dialectic with respect to indirect communication in part 2 of *Upbuilding Discourses in Various Spirits.*

16. Michael Theunissen, in "Kierkegaard's Negativistic Method," trans. Charlotte Baumann, in *Kierkegaard's Truth: The Disclosure of the Self,* ed. Joseph H. Smith, Psychiatry and the Humanities 5 (New Haven: Yale University Press, 1981), 381–423, has noted the negative character of Kierkegaard's method in his discussion of the relation between despair and the self in *The Sickness unto Death,* but he misses the indirectly positive character of the negative in that work. Defining "negativity" in a direct manner as "a deficiency in human life," Theunissen maintains that "Kierkegaard . . . begins with negative phenomena . . . in order to reveal successful human existence [health, faith, selfhood] through them," but this positive conception

of the self is inferred through the analysis of despair and is presupposed by it only in a preliminary or anticipatory way. In other words, Theunissen views Kierkegaard as taking a Marxist/ Heideggerian approach that moves from the material to ideology rather than vice versa, although he does concede that despair and the self are interdependent concepts in Kierkegaard's thought. But the material element is preponderant in defining the self. In inverse dialectic the positive is not a product of the negative; rather, the negative is an indirect sign of the positive. Theunissen adopts (his understanding of) Kierkegaard's negative procedure in working out his own "negative theology" and theory of communicative freedom. For a brief discussion of these features in Theunissen's thought, see Jürgen Habermas, "Communicative Freedom and Negative Theology," translated with notes by Martin J. Matuštík and Patricia J. Huntington, in *Kierkegaard in Post/Modernity*, ed. Martin J. Matuštík and Merold Westphal (Bloomington: Indiana University Press, 1995), 182–98. See also Michael Theunissen, *Das Selbst auf dem Grund der Verzweiflung. Kierkegaards negativistische Methode* (Frankfurt am Main: Suhrkamp, 1991). In a similar vein, Arne Grøn, in *Subjektivitet og Negativitet: Kierkegaard* (Copenhagen: Gyldendalske Boghandel, 1997), examines the negative phenomena of anxiety, despair, spiritlessness, and indeterminateness and their significance for understanding the self in *The Concept of Anxiety* and *The Sickness unto Death*.

17. For fuller discussions of these negative expressions of existential pathos in the *Postscript*, see David R. Law, "Resignation, Suffering and Guilt in Kierkegaard's *Concluding Unscientific Postscript to 'Philosophical Fragments,'*" in *International Kierkegaard Commentary: "Concluding Unscientific Postscript to 'Philosophical Fragments,'"* vol. 12, ed. Robert L. Perkins (Macon: Mercer University Press, 1997), 263–89; Merold Westphal, *Becoming a Self: A Reading of Kierkegaard's "Concluding Unscientific Postscript"* (West Lafayette: Purdue University Press, 1996), chap. 11; and C. Stephen Evans, *Kierkegaard's "Fragments" and "Postscript": The Religious Philosophy of Johannes Climacus* (Atlantic Highlands, N.J.: Humanities Press, 1983), chap. 9.

18. One of the forms of inwardness from which Climacus seeks to differentiate true inwardness or subjectivity, including Christian inwardness, is "momentary inwardness" or "feminine inwardness," which he associates specifically with the external "blather" and "feminine screaming" or "momentary feminine squealing" of women in contrast to true inwardness, which is inward, hidden, and characteristic of men (*CUP* 1:236–37; 239–40; 291). For a critique of this sexist feature of the text, see Walsh, "Subjectivity versus Objectivity: Kierkegaard's *Postscript* and Feminist Epistemology," in Perkins, *International Kierkegaard Commentary: "Concluding Unscientific Postscript to 'Philosophical Fragments,'"* 11–31; reprinted in Céline Léon and Sylvia Walsh, eds., *Feminist Interpretations of Søren Kierkegaard* (University Park: The Pennsylvania State University Press, 1997), 267–85.

19. For a fuller account of this dialectical factor, see Lee C. Barrett III, "Subjectivity Is (Un)Truth: Climacus's Dialectically Sharpened Pathos," in Perkins, *International Kierkegaard Commentary: "Concluding Unscientific Postscript to 'Philosophical Fragments,'"* 291–306.

20. On the relation of reduplication to redoubling, see Martin Andic, "Love's Redoubling and the Eternal Like for Like," and Andrew J. Burgess, "Kierkegaard's Concept of Redoubling and Luther's 'Simul Justus,'" in *International Kierkegaard Commentary: "Works of Love,"* vol. 16, ed. Robert L. Perkins (Macon: Mercer University Press, 1999), 9–38 and 39–55. See also Gregor Malantschuk, "Begrebet Fordoblelse hos Søren Kierkegaard," *Kierkegaardiana* 2 (1957): 42–53. On the importance of reduplication in Kierkegaard's later writings, see Poole, *Kierkegaard: The Indirect Communication*, 254–57, 270.

21. Even here, however, immediacy per se is not totally excluded inasmuch as in his journals Kierkegaard frequently defines Christian faith as constituting a new or second immediacy (*JP* 1:9, 49, 235, 972, 1032; 2:1101, 1123, 1215, 1335, 1942, 1943; 5:6135).

22. For a range of feminist critiques of Kierkegaard, see Léon and Walsh, *Feminist Inter-*

pretations of Søren Kierkegaard. On Kierkegaard's emphasis on our common humanity, see Walsh, "If the Lily Could Speak: On the Contentment and Glory of Being Human," in Perkins, *International Kierkegaard Commentary: "Upbuilding Discourses in Various Spirits."* On the spiritual (but not social) equality of all human beings in Kierkegaard's thought, see Walsh, "When 'That Single Individual' Is a Woman," in *Kierkegaard Studies Yearbook 2000,* ed. Niels Jørgen Cappelørn, Hermann Deuser, Jon Stewart, and Christian Fink Tolstrup (Berlin: Walter de Gruyter, 2000), 1–18; reprinted in *International Kierkegaard Commentary: "Eighteen Upbuilding Discourses,"* vol. 5, ed. Robert L. Perkins (Macon: Mercer University Press, 2003), 31–50.

Chapter 1

1. Climacus tends to identify the religious stage proper with Christianity, as the previous quotation illustrates. Religiousness A, in spite of its designation as a form of religiousness, is more closely associated with the ethical stage and should be regarded as ethical-religious in character. The primary distinctions in the *Postscript* are between the aesthetic, the ethical-religious, and the Christian religious.

2. See, for example, *JP* 1:67; 2:1215, 1216; 3:2466; 4:4011, 4013; 5:6050, 6092.

3. See also *JP* 4:4012, where Kierkegaard associates this phrase explicitly with Bishop Mynster, who preaches that "sin is the human being's corruption" on Sunday but on Monday acts as if everything is in order and the whole country is Christian.

4. See John J. Davenport, "Towards an Existential Virtue Ethics: Kierkegaard and MacIntyre," in *Kierkegaard After MacIntyre: Essays on Freedom, Narrative, and Virtue,* ed. John J. Davenport and Anthony Rudd (Chicago: Open Court, 2001), 265–323; Robert C. Roberts, in "Dialectical Emotions and the Virtue of Faith," in Perkins, *International Kierkegaard Commentary: "Concluding Unscientific Postscript to 'Philosophical Fragments,'"* 73–93, and "Existence, Emotion, and Virtue: Classical Themes in Kierkegaard," in *The Cambridge Companion to Kierkegaard,* ed. Alastair Hannay and Gordon D. Marino (Cambridge: Cambridge University Press, 1998), 177–206; and Gouwens in *Kierkegaard as Religious Thinker,* 94–95, 138, 141, for studies that characterize Kierkegaard as a virtue ethicist. Presumably, however, they understand by that designation something different from what Kierkegaard rejects here, namely, the notion of virtue as a moral quality acquired autonomously, inasmuch as for them virtue is a human excellence acquired through dependence on God. But it must not be forgotten that for Kierkegaard the Christian life is governed throughout by an inverted dialectic that measures progress toward and closeness to the eternal or Christian ideals not by a gradual achievement of perfection through the cultivation of virtues but by a deepening sense of one's imperfection and distance from the ideal. As Kierkegaard states it in his journals: "Every step forward toward the ideal is a backward step, for the progress consists precisely in my discovering increasingly the perfection of the ideal—and consequently my greater distance from it" (*JP* 2:1789).

5. For a range of essays focusing on various aspects of Anti-Climacus's analysis of despair, see Niels Jørgen Cappelørn and Hermann Deuser, eds., *Kierkegaard Studies Yearbook 1996* (Berlin: Walter de Gruyter, 1996), and Robert L. Perkins, ed., *International Kierkegaard Commentary: "The Sickness unto Death,"* vol. 19 (Macon: Mercer University Press, 1987). See also Come, *Kierkegaard as Theologian,* 191–245, and Alastair Hannay, "Kierkegaard and the Variety of Despair," in Hannay and Marino, *Cambridge Companion to Kierkegaard,* 329–48.

6. See *SUD* 47. The Danish term used here connotes a subjective or concrete awareness,

impression, representation, or notion of despair rather than an objective, abstract concept (*Begreb*) of it.

7. Gerhard Ebeling, *Luther: An Introduction to His Thought*, trans. R. A. Wilson (Philadelphia: Fortress Press, 1964), 194.

8. On Anti-Climacus's critique of the Danish speculative theologians, especially Martensen, in *The Sickness unto Death*, see also Stewart, *Kierkegaard's Relations to Hegel Reconsidered*, 550–95. See also Darío González, "Sin, Absolute Difference," in *Kierkegaard Studies Yearbook 2003*, ed. Niels Jørgen Cappelørn, Hermann Deuser, Jon Stewart, and Christian Fink Tolstrup (Berlin: Walter de Gruyter, 2003), 373–83, on Kierkegaard's opposition to the speculative dogmatics of his time and the tension between the psychological description of despair and the dogmatic presupposition of sin in his thought.

9. The Hongs translate the first clause of the last sentence of the note on page 61 as: "The condition for healing is always this repenting *of . . .*" But the Danish text states: "Betingelsen for Helbredelsen er altid denne Omvendelse" (*SV₁* 11:173n). It is a turning around or an about-face, not repentance, that is called for here, although certainly repentance is part and parcel of that movement.

10. See Harold V. Martin, *The Wings of Faith* (New York: Philosophical Library, 1951), 95–96, for a brief comparison of Kierkegaard with William James on the will to believe. But James affirms the will to believe because it is, in his opinion, more consonant with the practical needs of life than disbelief is, whereas Kierkegaard views faith as arising out of the tension of longing for salvation while denying its possibility in the consciousness of sin. One believes because one is passionately driven to believe, not because it is practical to do so. See also Steven M. Emmanuel, *Kierkegaard and the Concept of Revelation* (Albany: The State University of New York Press, 1996), who like Martin thinks that Kierkegaard's view of faith bears a strong resemblance to that of James (51–60), and Klaus-M. Kodalle, "The Utilitarian Self and the 'Useless' Passion of Faith," in Hannay and Marino, *Cambridge Companion to Kierkegaard*, 397–410, who sees the movement of faith as running counter to utilitarianism.

11. Considerable discussion on the role of the will in the transition to faith has been generated among recent Kierkegaard scholars by M. Jamie Ferreira's book, *Transforming Vision: Imagination and Will in Kierkegaardian Faith* (Oxford: Clarendon Press, 1991). Emphasizing the central place of the imagination (as opposed to thought, feeling, and will) in Kierkegaard's pseudonymous literature, Ferreira argues for a nonvolitional, imaginative transition to faith based on a broadened concept of the will as being tied to imagination and involving more than deliberate decision on the part of an individual. As she sees it, the moment of transition is a moment of imaginative revisioning or a shift in perspective which itself constitutes faith understood as a qualitatively new way of seeing God. While I agree wholeheartedly with Ferreira's emphasis on the importance of imagination in Kierkegaard's writings, I do not think she does justice to the factor of conscious decision in the transition to faith, especially in *The Sickness unto Death*, which for all its emphasis on the role of imagination in becoming a self envisions the transition as occurring through an inversion of the will and faith as involving the will to believe against the understanding.

12. Dupré, *Kierkegaard as Theologian*, 81.

13. Adi Shmuëli, *Kierkegaard and Consciousness*, trans. Naomi Handelman (Princeton: Princeton University Press, 1971), 5.

14. Emanuel Skjoldager, *Søren Kierkegaards Syn på Samvittigheden* (Copenhagen: Munksgaard, 1967), 36.

15. For a range of interpretive essays on this book, see Perkins, *International Kierkegaard Commentary: "Upbuilding Discourses in Various Spirits."*

16. See also "On the Occasion of a Confession," in *Three Discourses on Imagined Occasions* (1845), which anticipates the emphasis in the later literature on sorrow, repentance, and

confession of sins. On the occasion of confession in "An Occasional Discourse," see also Sheridan Hough, "'Halting Is Movement': The Paradoxical Pause of Confession in 'An Occasional Discourse,'" in Perkins, *International Kierkegaard Commentary: "Upbuilding Discourses in Various Spirits."*

17. See Eller, *Kierkegaard and Radical Discipleship,* 104–5, for an illuminating word study of *den Enkelte* ("the individual"). According to Eller, what Kierkegaard meant by the term was "that a person needs to become *individuum*, undivided, at one with himself . . . and not that he should cut himself off from the race." Thus Eller takes issue with Buber's characterization of the individual in Kierkegaard's thought as being primarily solitary and isolated. See also George Connell, *To Be One Thing: Personal Unity in Kierkegaard's Thought* (Macon: Mercer University Press, 1985), on the importance of achieving a unified selfhood in Kierkegaard's thought. For Connell's further reflections on this issue, see "Postmodern Readings of Kierkegaard and the Requirement of Oneness," in Perkins, *International Kierkegaard Commentary: "Upbuilding Discourses in Various Spirits."*

18. On the concept of vocation in "An Occasional Discourse," see Christopher A.P. Nelson, "Kierkegaard's Concept of Vocation in 'An Occasional Discourse,'" in Perkins, *International Kierkegaard Commentary: "Upbuilding Discourses in Various Spirits."*

19. In his journals Kierkegaard makes it clear that Christian discourses are different from both upbuilding discourses and sermons (*JP* 1:638; cf. also *CUP* 1:256–57, 273). While they distinguish Christian categories from the universally human, which is the focus of the upbuilding discourses, they deal with Christianity without the authority assumed by a sermon from an ordained priest. Thus they can be delivered by a layperson and are associated to a certain extent with the problem of doubt. In the preface to these discourses Kierkegaard expresses the hope of aiding the single sufferer "who perhaps is also going astray in many thoughts" (*UDVS* 215). Although Kierkegaard in his role as author claimed no authority, the problem of doubt in these discourses is nevertheless countered with authority, but it is the authority of the Bible, not that of reflection. In the earlier upbuilding discourses Kierkegaard could not invoke biblical authority so strongly, for upbuilding discourses persuade by the help of thought and are, as Johannes Climacus calls them, "speculative," even though they develop religious themes (*JP* 1:207; *CUP* 1:273; cf. *SKP* VIII A 21).

20. On the relation between the consciousness of sin and forgiveness in Kierkegaard's thought, see also Ettore Rocca, "The Threefold Revelation of Sin," trans. Domenico Pacitti, in Cappelørn, Deuser, Stewart, and Tolstrup, *Kierkegaard Studies Yearbook 2003,* 384–94. As Rocca sees it, these are one and the same inasmuch as, in his view, "the revelation of sin *presupposes* and *is founded on* the revelation of forgiveness" (391). But certainly the two may be distinguished in Kierkegaard's thought, and even Rocca recognizes that the unity may be broken through the intensification of sin in sin against the Holy Spirit.

21. Michael Plekon, in "Kierkegaard and the Eucharist," *Studia Liturgica* 22 (1992): 214–36, has pointed out that Kierkegaard published a thirteenth discourse on communion in *Practice in Christianity.* But only twelve were published under that title; the other one was published as the first discourse of No. III in *Practice in Christianity* (*PC* 151–56).

22. On the centrality of these discourses in Kierkegaard's theology, see also Emanuel Skjoldager, *Den egentlige Kierkegaard: Søren Kierkegaards syn på kirke og de kirkelige handlinger* (Copenhagen: C. A. Reitzels Forlag, 1982), 96–116.

23. On Kierkegaard as "a poet who flies to grace," see Walsh, *Living Poetically,* 239–42.

24. In Denmark during Kierkegaard's lifetime, confession (*skiftemål*) was a separate, public service that preceded communion (*altergang*). General confession was made to a priest who delivered a brief penitential sermon (*skriftetale*) and gave absolution or assurance of the pardoning of sins before the participants went to communion, which was offered on Fridays, Sundays, and holy days. It is clear that Kierkegaard's communion discourses were intended for the

second service, not for the confessionals, as several of them mention that confession has already been made. Three of these discourses were actually delivered by Kierkegaard at Our Lady's Church (*Vor Frue Kirke*), the Lutheran cathedral in Copenhagen. See Plekon, "Kierkegaard and the Eucharist," 215–18; Niels Jørgen Cappelørn, "Die ursprüngliche Unterbrechung. Søren Kierkegaard beim Abendmahl im Freitagsgottesdienst der Kopenhagener Frauenkirche," trans. Krista-Maria Deuser, in Cappelørn and Deuser, *Kierkegaard Studies Yearbook 1996*, 315–88, which gives a detailed account of confessional and communion practices in Denmark before and during Kierkegaard's time; and Niels Thulstrup, *Kierkegaard and the Church in Denmark*, Bibliotheca Kierkegaardiana 13 (Copenhagen: C. A. Reitzels Forlag, 1984), 147–52.

25. Cappelørn, in "Die ursprüngliche Unterbrechung," maintains that despite Kierkegaard's claim to the contrary, the communion discourses correspond to *kommunionsprædikener* or *altergangsprædikener,* communion sermons that were preached by priests or theological candidates at the altar before communion was served, and they were advertised as such in the local newspapers, including the ones Kierkegaard delivered at Our Lady's Church. Plekon, in "Kierkegaard and the Eucharist," concurs that they were actually homilies or sermons (216–17).

26. On Kierkegaard's own habit of attending communion on Fridays, see Plekon, "Kierkegaard and the Eucharist," who relies on the archival research of Grethe Kjær and Julia Watkin (218). See also Cappelørn, "Die ursprüngliche Unterbrechung," who reports that, according to church records, Kierkegaard took communion forty-one times during his lifetime, almost always on Fridays. Between 1800 and 1855, the average number of times parishoners took communion during a year was twice. Kierkegaard's family generally went to communion on Fridays together, but after the death of his parents he always went alone.

27. See Poole, *Kierkegaard: The Indirect Communication*, 233–61, for an insightful account of references in Kierkegaard's "Discourses at the Communion on Fridays" to the marble statue of Christ and his apostles by the Danish neoclassical sculptor, Bertel Thorvaldsen, that overlooks the altar of Our Lady's Church in Copenhagen, where Kierkegaard took communion and delivered several of his communion discourses. On Thorvaldsen's artistry, see Else Kai Sass, "Thorvaldsen: An Introduction to his Work," in Stewart, *Kierkegaard and His Contemporaries,* 375–405. Unfortunately, however, she does not discuss his statue of Christ.

28. J. Preston Cole, "Kierkegaard's Doctrine of the Atonement," *Religion in Life* 23 (1964): 599.

29. Ibid., 592.

30. This positive association of a woman with piety or true religiosity contrasts sharply with the misogyny that characterizes much of Kierkegaard's writings. See, for example, Walsh, "Issues That Divide: Interpreting Kierkegaard on Woman and Gender," in *Kierkegaard Revisited,* ed. Niels Jørgen Cappelørn and Jon Stewart, Kierkegaard Studies Monograph Series 1 (Berlin: Walter de Gruyter, 1997), 191–205, and the essays in Léon and Walsh, *Feminist Interpretations of Søren Kierkegaard,* especially the essay by Wanda Warren Berry, "The Silent Woman in Kierkegaard's Later Religious Writings" (287–306). For an excellent article on the role of the "female sinner" and other women as apostolic paradigms of faith and the inverse dialectic (although this phrase is not used) that characterizes their piety in Kierkegaard's writings, see Mark Lloyd Taylor, "Practice in Authority: The Apostolic Women of Søren Kierkegaard's Writings," in *Anthropology and Authority: Essays on Søren Kierkegaard,* ed. Poul Houe, Gordon D. Marino, and Sven Hakon Rossel (Amsterdam: Rodopi, 2000), 85–98. See also Louise Carroll Keeley, "Silence, Domesticity, and Joy: The Spiritual Life of Women in Kierkegaard's *For Self-Examination,*" in *International Kierkegaard Commentary: "For Self-Examination" and "Judge For Yourself!"* vol. 21, ed. Robert L. Perkins (Macon: Mercer University Press, 2002), 223–57, which, like Taylor and contra Berry (on some points), casts the spirituality of women in Kierkegaard's later religious thought in a more positive light.

31. See Chapter 4 for a discussion of this inversion.

Chapter 2

1. The Hongs translate "Plage" as "nuisance," which it certainly can mean, but I think that term considerably waters down the connotation Kierkegaard has in mind here; thus I prefer Lowrie's stronger rendition in Søren Kierkegaard, *Training in Christianity*, trans. Walter Lowrie (Princeton: Princeton University Press, 1944), 66.

2. See, for example, the essays on reason and faith in Jerry Gill, ed., *Essays on Kierkegaard* (Minneapolis: Burgess, 1969), part 2; C. Stephen Evans, *Passionate Reason: Making Sense of Kierkegaard's "Philosophical Fragments"* (Bloomington: Indiana University Press, 1992), and "Is Kierkegaard an Irrationalist? Reason, Paradox, and Faith," *Religious Studies* 25 (1989): 347–62; Karen L. Carr and Philip J. Ivanhoe, *The Sense of Antirationalism: The Religious Thought of Zhuangzi and Kierkegaard* (New York: Seven Bridges Press, 2000); Louis J. Pojman, *The Logic of Subjectivity* (Tuscaloosa: University of Alabama Press, 1984); and Emmanuel, *Kierkegaard and the Concept of Revelation*. For a good critical discussion of romantic, idealist, and empirical approaches to the issue, see Murray Rae, *Kierkegaard's Vision of the Incarnation: By Faith Transformed* (Oxford: Clarendon Press, 1997), who sees Kierkegaardian faith as being secured through a process of conversion construed in terms of the New Testament concept of *metanoia*, which involves a transformation of the whole person, including the understanding, and thus makes possible a whole new way of understanding the world that resembles, in some ways and in other contexts, Rae thinks, notions of transformation in Ludwig Wittgenstein, Thomas Kuhn, and Peter Berger.

3. See also N. H. Søe, "Kierkegaard's Doctrine of the Paradox," in *A Kierkegaard Critique*, ed. Howard A. Johnson and Niels Thulstrup (New York: Harper & Brothers, 1962), 207–27, for another treatment of Kierkegaard's response to this text.

4. The title of the book, published in 1850, is *Is Faith a Paradox and "by Virtue of the Absurd," a Question Prompted by 'Fear and Trembling' by Johannes de Silentio, Answered with the Help of the Confidential Communications of a Knight of Faith, for the Mutual Edification of Jews, Christians, and Moslems, by the Above-mentioned Knight of Faith's Brother, Theophilus Nicolaus.*

5. Arnold Come has rightly pointed out in *Kierkegaard as Theologian* that "the Danish *Menneske* is the term for that humanity which is held as common by both man (male) and woman (female)" and that "in contrast to English, Danish conveniently has the term *Mand* to indicate the male human being" (22). Accordingly, Come translates *Gud-Menneske* as "God-humanbeing," which is conceptually more precise than "God-man" but runs together two words in English that are usually separated. Hence my slight modification. While "God–human being" is less felicitous in English than the traditional "God-man," it is a more accurate translation of the term and, moreover, redeems Kierkegaard from the charge of being sexist with regard to the Incarnation. Since English has only one term, "man," to cover both the male sex and generic humanity, it is an ambiguous term that is best not used with respect to Christ. The issue is not whether Christ was a male or not but whether he embodies a fundamental humanity that is shared by both males and females. As Come points out, the Danish is quite clear on that matter, as it uses the more inclusive term, "menneske," rather than the explicitly masculine term, "mand," to refer to Christ.

6. For another account of offense in Anti-Climacus's writings, see Niels Jørgen Cappelørn, "The Movements of Offense Toward, Away From, and Within Faith: 'Blessed Is He Who Is Not Offended Me,'" trans. K. Brian Söderquist, in *International Kierkegaard Commentary: "Practice in Christianity,"* vol. 20, ed. Robert L. Perkins (Macon: Mercer University Press, 2004), 95–124. Cappelørn conducts his analysis of offense toward and within faith primarily through a consideration of the various biblical passages Anti-Climacus cites to illustrate

the possibility of offense, while the present study focuses on the inverse character of the possibility of offense in relation to Christ and Christian existence.

7. The nature of the contradiction that characterizes the absolute paradox in *Philosophical Fragments* and *Concluding Unscientific Postscript* and the God–human being as a paradox in *Practice in Christianity* is an issue that has been much debated in Kierkegaard studies. Scholars have tended to treat the paradox in a logical context, arguing variously that it entails a logical or formal contradiction, that it is only an apparent contradiction, that it is not a logical impossibility, and even that it is not a contradiction at all but a limit of thought that merely has the form of a logical contradiction. For a good discussion of the issue, see C. Stephen Evans, *Kierkegaard's "Fragments" and "Postscript,"* who takes the position that it is an apparent contradiction (212–32). My intent here, however, is to shift consideration of this issue away from treating it in a logical context to a focus on how Anti-Climacus actually describes the paradox, which is to say that it is a qualitative contradiction, not a logical or formal contradiction. Insofar as logical claims can be made about the paradox, however, Evans is right in saying that it is an apparent contradiction, for the reasons given in his discussion and in mine below. This view complements my reading in the first part of this chapter, where I emphasize that the earlier pseudonymous treatments of the paradox as the absurd present only the first form or obverse side of the truth.

8. Ibid., 214–15.

9. See Søren Holm, *Søren Kierkegaards Historiefilosofi* (Copenhagen: Bianco Lunos Bogtrykkeri, 1952), for a "fictionalist" interpretation of Kierkegaard (112, 116). See also Søe, "Kierkegaard's Doctrine of the Paradox," 207–27, for a refutation of that argument.

Chapter 3

1. "Self-denial" is spelled in two different ways in the Danish editions of Kierkegaard's collected writings. These terms have been translated into English variously as self-denial, self-renunciation, and self-abnegation; and as Valter Lindström has shown, Kierkegaard's concept of self-denial is closely related to his concept of self-annihilation, or the recognition that before God one is nothing or can do nothing by oneself. See Lindström, "A Contribution to the Interpretation of Kierkegaard's Book *The Works of Love,*" *Studia Theologica* 6 (1953): 1–29, and "Kierkegaards Tolkning Av Självförnekelsen såsom Kristendomens Livsform," *Svensk teologisk Kvartalskrift* 26 (1950): 326–34.

2. Gene Outka, *Agape: An Ethical Analysis* (New Haven: Yale University Press, 1972), 19.

3. For refutations of such characterizations of Kierkegaard's thought, see M. Jamie Ferreira, *Love's Grateful Striving: A Commentary on Kierkegaard's "Works of Love,"* (Oxford: Oxford University Press, 2001), and Lee C. Barrett III, "The Neighbor's Material and Social Well-Being in Kierkegaard's *Works of Love:* Does It Matter?" in Perkins, *International Kierkegaard Commentary: "Works of Love,"* 137–65. However, Ferreira fails to include self-denial among the "six crucial elements" she identifies as comprising Kierkegaard's model of neighbor love (256), although she does discuss it at various points in her commentary.

4. See, for example, Louis Mackey, "The Poetry of Inwardness," in *Kierkegaard: A Collection of Critical Essays,* ed. Josiah Thompson (Garden City, N.Y.: Doubleday Anchor Books, 1972), 1–102. Mackey characterizes Kierkegaard's view of the Christian as a happy and contented man who attends to his work, delights in his wife, brings up children, loves his neighbors, and enjoys life (86). While Kierkegaard certainly affirms that the Christian life contains love, joy, and happiness, these qualities are understood and experienced inversely through self-denial and suffering.

5. On the theme of death in *For Self-Examination*, see David Cain, "Death Comes in Between: Reflections on Kierkegaard's *For Self-Examination*," *Kierkegaardiana* 15 (1991): 69–81. See also Stephen N. Dunning, "Love Is Not Enough: A Kierkegaardian Phenomenology of Religious Experience," *Faith and Philosophy* 12, no. 1 (1995): 22–39, on the importance of "dying to" in *For Self-Examination* as a precondition for and constant demand in Christian religious experience. On the rather neglected role of the Holy Spirit in Kierkegaard's religious thought, see Paul Martens, "The Emergence of the Holy Spirit in Kierkegaard's Thought: Critical Theological Developments," in Perkins, *International Kierkegaard Commentary: "For Self-Examination" and "Judge for Yourself!"* 199–222, and Matthew J. Frawley, "The Essential Role of the Holy Spirit in Kierkegaard's Biblical Hermeneutic," in Houe and Marino, *Søren Kierkegaard and the Word(s)*, 93–104.

6. The *Dansk Ordbog*, ed. Christian Molbech (Copenhagen: Gyldendalske Boghandling, 1859), points out that whenever *af* is added to a noun, adjective, or verb as a prefix it indicates an act whereby something is abandoned, left behind, put aside, or gone away from. But since the Hong translations of Kierkegaard's writings use "to die to," I am adopting their rendition of the term here.

7. See, for example, *Eighteen Upbuilding Discourses*, where Kierkegaard discusses certain aspects of Christian love (*EUD* 55–78). No clear distinction between Christianity and the religious stage in general had yet been drawn in these discourses, but Kierkegaard already contrasts Christian love to both pagan and Jewish conceptions of love. In another discourse he holds up the self-denying character of John the Baptist as an example for persons to follow "in lesser situations" of life, and he claims, in anticipation of the later development of his thought, that the fulfillment of joy in life is to be found in "the incorruptible apparel of self-denial" (288). For an examination of the theme of love in this work, see Pattison, *Kierkegaard's Upbuilding Discourses*.

8. See, for example, Arnold B. Come, *Kierkegaard as Humanist: Discovering My Self* (Montreal: McGill-Queen's University Press, 1995); Gouwens, *Kierkegaard as Religious Thinker;* Anthony Rudd, *Kierkegaard and the Limits of the Ethical* (Oxford: Clarendon Press, 1993); C. Stephen Evans, "Authority and Transcendence in *Works of Love*," in *Kierkegaard Studies Yearbook 1998*, ed. Niels Jørgen Cappelørn, Hermann Deuser, Jon Stewart, and Christian Fink Tolstrup (Berlin: Walter de Gruyter, 1998), 23–40; and Johannes Sløk, *Kierkegaard—humanismens tænker* (Copenhagen: Hans Reitzel, 1978).

9. C. Stephen Evans and Jan Evans, "Translator's Preface and Introduction," in Paul Müller, *Kierkegaard's "Works of Love": Christian Ethics and the Maieutic Ideal*, trans. and ed. Evans and Evans (Copenhagen: C. A. Reitzel, 1993), ix.

10. For other recent analyses of this concept, see especially Law, "Resignation, Suffering, and Guilt," 263–89, and Evans, *Kierkegaard's "Fragments" and "Postscript,"* 161–84.

11. See Torsten Bohlin, *Kierkegaards Tro och andra Kierkegaardstudier* (Stockholm: Svenska Kyrkans Diakonistyrelses Bokförlag, 1944) and *Sören Kierkegaards etiska åskådning med särskild hänsyn till begreppet den enskilde* (Stockholm: Svenska Kyrkans Diakonistyrelses Bokförlag, 1918), and Valter Lindström, *Stadiernas Teologi: En Kierkegaard-studie* (Lund: C.W.K. Gleerup, 1943) and *Efterföljelsens Teologi hos Sören Kierkegaard* (Stockholm: Svenska Kyrkans Diakonistyrelses Bokförlag, 1956).

12. Aage Henriksen, *Methods and Results of Kierkegaard Studies in Scandinavia: A Historical and Critical Survey* (Copenhagen: Ejnar Munksgaard, 1951), 141.

13. Bohlin, *Kierkegaards Tro*, 145ff.

14. Lindström, *Efterföljelsens Teologi*, 134.

15. Lindström, *Stadiernas Teologi*, 340.

16. Bohlin, *Sören Kierkegaards etiska åskådning*, 268, 308. For similar, more recent assessments, see Rudd, *Kierkegaard and the Limits of the Ethical*, 165; Come, *Kierkegaard as Theologian*, 213–14; and Dupré, *Kierkegaard as Theologian*, 46 n. 8.

17. Henriksen, *Methods and Results*, 141.

18. Ibid., 148, 146–52.

19. Neither critic, however, is sufficiently sensitive to the problem of pseudonymity in Kierkegaard's authorship, tending to identify Kierkegaard's views with those of the pseudonyms on the issue of consistency or inconsistency in relation to a particular concept and in the authorship as a whole. On the need to be attentive to this problem, see Walsh, *Living Poetically*, 10–15; M. Holmes Hartshorne, *Kierkegaard, Godly Deceiver: The Nature and Meaning of His Pseudonymous Writings* (New York: Columbia University Press, 1990); Evans, *Kierkegaard's "Fragments" and "Postscript"*; and Poole, *Kierkegaard: The Indirect Communication*.

20. On the question of the otherworldly character of Kierkegaard's religious thought, especially in *Works of Love*, see M. Jamie Ferreira, "Other-Worldliness in Kierkegaard's *Works of Love*," *Philosophical Investigations* 22, no. 1 (1999): 65–79, and my response, "Other-Worldliness in Kierkegaard's *Works of Love*—A Response," in the same issue, 80–85. See also Rudd, *Kierkegaard and the Limits of the Ethical*, 166–67.

21. Lindström, "Contribution," 20 n. 2.

22. For a range of recent critical essays on *Works of Love*, see Perkins, *International Kierkegaard Commentary: "Works of Love,"* and Cappelørn, Deuser, Stewart, and Tolstrup, *Kierkegaard Studies Yearbook 1998*. Unfortunately, none of the essays in these collections focuses on the concepts of dying to the world and self-denial, although the essay by Stacey Ake, "'And yet a braver thence doth spring': The Heuristic Values of *Works of Love*," in the latter volume does touch on self-renunciation in the discussion of the Virgin Mary (93–112). See also Ferreira, *Love's Grateful Striving*; Amy Laura Hall, *Kierkegaard and the Treachery of Love* (Cambridge: Cambridge University Press, 2002), 11–50; Pia Søltoft, *Svimmelhedens Etik—om forholdet mellem den enkelte og den anden hos Buber, Levinas og især Kierkegaard* (Copenhagen: Gads Forlag, 2000), 277–323; Sylvia Walsh Perkins, "Kierkegaard's Philosophy of Love," in *The Nature and Pursuit of Love: The Philosophy of Irving Singer*, ed. David Goicoechea (Amherst, N.Y.: Prometheus Books, 1995), 167–79, and Sylvia Walsh, "Forming the Heart: The Role of Love in Kierkegaard's Thought," in *The Grammar of the Heart: New Essays in Moral Philosophy and Theology*, ed. Richard Bell (New York: Harper & Row, 1988), 234–56.

23. See, for example, Lindström, *Efterföljelsens Teologi*, 102, 104.

24. On the problematic character of Kierkegaard's claim that natural love lacks any ability to love unselfishly, see Walsh, "Forming the Heart," 248.

25. On the concept of redoubling in *Works of Love*, see also Andic, "Love's Redoubling," 9–38, and Burgess, "Kierkegaard's Concept of Redoubling,'" 39–55, in Perkins, *International Kierkegaard Commentary: "Works of Love."* See also Malantschuk, "Begrebet Fordoblelse hos Søren Kierkegaard," 42–53.

26. Theodor W. Adorno, "On Kierkegaard's Doctrine of Love," *Studies in Philosophy and Social Science* 8 (1940): 416. For other critiques of Adorno's interpretation of *Works of Love*, see Ferreira, *Love's Grateful Striving*, 188–89, and Louise Carroll Keeley, "Loving 'No One,' Loving Everyone: The Work of Love in Recollecting One Dead in Kierkegaard's *Works of Love*," in Perkins, *International Kierkegaard Commentary: "Works of Love,"* 211–48. Like Adorno, Outka in *Agape* also interprets Kierkegaard in a simplistically negative fashion in suggesting that Kierkegaard sees only an incompatibility between love and friendship while Karl Barth, in his view, offers a more satisfactory view because "he does not just oppose them as Kierkegaard is inclined to do" (210; see also, 18–19, 34–38). For a more nuanced discussion of the relation between Barth and Kierkegaard on love, see Gouwens, *Kierkegaard as Religious Thinker*, 188–97.

27. On this point, see also Ferreira's critique of K. E. Løgstrup in *Love's Grateful Striving*, 76–77.

28. On the socioeconomic implications of Kierkegaard's views on love and human equal-

ity, see also Ferreira, *Love's Grateful Striving*, 57–64 and 94–98, and Barrett, "The Neighbor's Material and Social Well-Being," 137–65. Both Ferreira and Barrett argue that Kierkegaard is not indifferent to the concrete material conditions and needs of others, which is certainly true, and Ferreira further claims that "his recommendation to ignore distinctions does not preclude a basis for programs of socioeconomic change" (63). While that is true, I am suggesting that Kierkegaard understands social transformation in a radically different way than is usually advocated in attempts to bring about socioeconomic changes in society. Kierkegaard does not advocate any form of social equality, as for example in the case of women, who are to remain subservient to their husbands (*WL* 138), although the egalitarian nature of his social ethic would seemingly bring about a change in the patriarchal structure of marriage and male-female relations more generally. On Kierkegaard's views of social equality for women, see Walsh, "When 'That Single Individual' Is a Woman." For a highly negative critique of the (presumed) "underdeveloped" and "politically naïve" communal dimension of *Works of Love*, whose conception of neighbor love is deemed to be "unscriptural and ultimately unchristian," see David R. Law, "Cheap Grace and the Cost of Discipleship in Kierkegaard's *For Self-Examination*," in Perkins, *International Kierkegaard Commentary: "For Self-Examination" and "Judge for Yourself!"* 111–42. For an examination of Kierkegaard's biblical hermeneutic that takes quite a different view of it than Law, see Timothy Houston Polk, *The Biblical Kierkegaard: Reading by the Rule of Faith* (Macon: Mercer University Press, 1997).

29. In *Love's Grateful Striving*, Ferreria argues that opposition from the world is neither a *necessary* nor *sufficient* condition of Christian love and thus is *not inevitable* (75, 128, 164). But one must be careful not to tone down the element of opposition in this work. To say that opposition is not inevitable, or as Kierkegaard puts it, that "opposition can perhaps come but also perhaps not arise," is, in his view, "totally un-Christian" (*WL* 194).

30. See Lindström, *Efterföljelsens Teologi*, 136–62, and "Contribution," 16.

31. For examples of the first form of self-denial, see *CD* 72, 146, 155, 170, 171–72, 178–79, 184, 186, 227; *FSE* 77–79, 82, 83–84, 122, 135; and *PC* 129–30. For examples of the second form, see *CD* 222–33; *PC* 213, 138–39, 222, 225; *JFY* 116, 135, 205; and *JP* 2:1962 and 4:4661.

32. Marie Mikulová Thulstrup, "Kierkegaards 'onde verden,'" *Kierkegaardiana* 1 (1955): 42–54.

33. See Merold Westphal, "Kierkegaard's Teleological Suspension of Religiousness B," in Connell and Evans, *Foundations of Kierkegaard's Vision of Community*, 110–29 (henceforth cited parenthetically in the text).In his more recent work, *Becoming a Self*, Westphal continues to characterize Kierkegaard's understanding of Christianity in his later works as Religiousness C but offers no additional justification for it (197–98).

34. For other discussions of Kierkegaard's views in his last years, see Julia Watkin, "The Logic of Kierkegaard's Misogyny, 1854–55," *Kierkegaardiana* 15 (1991): 79–93, reprinted in Léon and Walsh, *Feminist Interpretations of Søren Kierkegaard*, 69–82, and Rudd, *Kierkegaard and the Limits of the Ethical*, 168–69. Watkin argues that Kierkegaard's negative remarks about women, sex, and marriage in the late journals do not signify a radical change or distortion in his thought but rather reflect "metaphysical assumptions about God and creation, the eternal and the temporal, that make it difficult, if not impossible, for him to reconcile marriage and procreation with an ideal likeness to God that demands total self-renunciation" (88/76). Rudd, by contrast, reads the late journals as reflecting a radical dualism that is at odds with orthodox Christianity and is thus heretical: "A hatred of the physical world, and the desire to escape from it, are hardly compatible with a belief in its divine creation, and must therefore appear heretical on Jewish, Christian, or Islamic standards" (168). Rudd further claims that in the late journals Kierkegaard abandons the doctrine of salvation by divine grace in favor of a radical doctrine of human autonomy and salvation by one's own striving (168–69). For

a refutation of the latter claim, see Chapter 5, in which I examine the relation of grace and works.

Chapter 4

1. In making passing reference to the "remarkable blend of suffering and joy" in Kierkegaard's thought, Paul Sponheim, in *Kierkegaard on Christ and Christian Coherence* (London: SCM Press, 1968), rightly cautions that "one may criticize Kierkegaard's comments on suffering as freely as one likes, but one ought not to seek to claim that this is all there is to be found in Kierkegaard's characterization of Christian existence" (170). For an example of just that sort of negative approach, see John J. Ansbro, in "Kierkegaard's Gospel of Suffering," *Philosophical Studies* (Maynooth, Ireland) 16 (1967): 182–92.

2. See, for example, Edward John Carnell, *The Burden of Søren Kierkegaard* (Grand Rapids, Mich.: Eerdmans, 1965), 134–47; Dewey, *New Obedience*, 144–51; Knud Ejler Løgstrup, *Opgør med Kierkegaard* (Copenhagen: Gyldendalske Boghandel, 1967), 40–47; Dupré, *Kierkegaard as Theologian*, 173–79; Marie Mikulová Thulstrup, "Lidelsens problematik hos Kierkegaard og Mystikerne," *Kierkegaardiana* 3 (1959): 48–72; and Arild Christensen, "Romantismens og Søren Kierkegaards Opfattelse af Lidelse," *Kierkegaardiana* 1 (1955): 16–41.

3. Other interpreters have also noted a development in Kierkegaard's thought on suffering from *Concluding Unscientific Postscript* to the later religious writings, but they have not traced that development in detail or in terms of its inverse dialectical relation to joy and consolation. See, for example, Come, *Kierkegaard as Theologian*, 214–18, 289–93, 336–37 n. 163; Gouwens, *Kierkegaard as Religious Thinker*, 162–79; Merold Westphal, "Kierkegaard's Phenomenology of Faith as Suffering," in *Writing the Politics of Difference*, ed. Hugh J. Silverman, Selected Studies in Phenomenology and Existential Philosophy 14 (Albany: The State University of New York Press, 1991), 55–71; John William Elrod, "Climacus, Anti-Climacus and the Problem of Suffering," *Thought: A Review of Culture and Idea* 55 (September 1980): 306–19; and Marie Mikulová Thulstrup, "Suffering," in *Kierkegaard and Human Values*, ed. Niels Thulstrup and Marie Mikulová Thulstrup, Bibliotheca Kierkegaardiana 7 (Copenhagen: C. A. Reitzels Boghandel, 1980), 135–62. See also Abrahim H. Khan, "The Treatment of the Theme of Suffering in Kierkegaard's Works" (Ph.D. diss., McGill University, 1973).

4. For an insightful study of the Lutheran christological heritage that informs Kierkegaard's view of Christ and the problem of suffering in this set of discourses, see Lee C. Barrett III, "The Joy in the Cross: Kierkegaard's Appropriation of Lutheran Christology in 'The Gospel of Sufferings,'" in Perkins, *International Kierkegaard Commentary: "Upbuilding Discourses in Various Spirits."*

5. Whether innocent children should be considered guilty before God as well is not discussed here, but presumably they are, potentially at least, by virtue of original sin.

6. For stimulating discussions of the implications for theodicy in "The Gospel of Sufferings," see David R. Law, "Wrongness, Guilt, and Innocent Suffering in Kierkegaard's *Either/Or*, Part Two, and *Upbuilding Discourses in Various Spirits*," in Perkins, *Internatiional Kierkegaard Commentary: "Upbuilding Discourses in Various Spirits*," and David J. Kangas, "The Very Opposite of Beginning with Nothing: Guilt Consciousness in Kierkegaard's 'The Gospel of Sufferings' IV," in the same volume. Law makes use of insights from Lévi-Strauss to explicate Kierkegaard's binary perspective of being wrong as opposed to being guilty before God, while Kangas uses Levinas to illumine the phenomenological differences between them.

7. Kierkegaard deprecates such expectation as "sensate" and "frivolous" Jewish misunderstanding, reflecting here as elsewhere in his writings a negative, simplistic, and unjustified attitude toward Judaism, despite his regard for Abraham as a knight of faith. For a more de-

tailed discussion of Kierkegaard's attitude toward Judaism, see Bruce H. Kirmmse, "Kierke-gaard, Jødedommen og Jøderne," *Kirkehistoriske Samlinger* (1992): 77–107, or its condensed version in English, "Kierkegaard, Jews, and Judaism," *Kierkegaardiana* 17 (1994): 83–97. See also K. Bruun Andersen, "Kierkegaard og jøderne," *Kierkegaardiana* 1 (1955): 84–87, for a defense of Kierkegaard against charges that he was anti-Semitic.

8. I prefer Lowrie's rendition of *Stemninger* in Søren Kierkegaard, *Christian Discourses*, trans. Walter Lowrie (London: Oxford University Press, 1939), 97, to the Hongs' translation of it as "States of Mind," which in my view does not adequately express the more emotional than mental connotation of the term and its association with music through being derived from the Danish word *stemme*, which means "voice," especially "singing voice."

9. In *Two Ethical-Religious Essays*, published in 1848, Kierkegaard considers precisely this possibility and concludes that no one has the right to do what Christ did in this respect because no one possesses absolute truth as he did and thus has no right to place oneself in opposition to other human beings as Christ did. Furthermore, an ordinary person has no right to provoke others to put him or her to death, because that person has made them guilty without having the power to atone for or forgive their deed. Kierkegaard is able to justify an exception in the case of the apostles, however, on the basis that the opposition which resulted in their deaths was between Christianity and non-Christianity. Over against the non-Christian world, the Christian may be said to be in possession of the absolute truth, and thus death may be justified. But in relation to other Christians, no Christian dares to claim such absolute possession of the truth in opposition to them. Between Christian and Christian there is only a relative difference. No Christian would be justified in permitting one's brothers and sisters to become guilty of one's death when one is not able to bring an absolute expression of the truth against them (*WA* 55–89). On the concept of martyrdom in Kierkegaard's thought, see also Marie Mikulová Thulstrup, "Søren Kierkegaard's Martyrbegreb," *Dansk teologisk Tidskrift* 27 (1964): 100–114. Thulstrup claims that while Kierkegaard in the beginning understood martyrdom in terms of physical death, he later defined it in terms of dying to the world, self-denial, asceticism, and "bloodless" suffering for Christ's sake. She further points out that "the concept of a Christian is . . . according to Kierkegaard neither identical with martyrdom nor with sacrifice but with the witness to the truth." While "the concept of a witness to the truth contains [blood] martyrdom as the highest form of testimony," witnessing is done not only by martyrdom but with one's whole life.

10. I have amended the Hongs' translation of this phrase as "the natural man" (*PC* 117), which like the term "God-man" is imprecise and seemingly sexist in a manner that Kierkegaard is not guilty of, at least not in this instance. As pointed out earlier, *menneske* connotes the generic term "human being," while *mand* is the specific Danish term for a man or member of the male sex. Given the ambiguity or duplicity involved in using a single word to refer to both the human race and the male sex in the English language, in my opinion it is better to avoid the appearance of sexism in the translation of Kierkegaard's texts, especially when it is not warranted.

11. For discussions of the charge of misogyny in Kierkegaard's authorship, see Léon and Walsh, *Feminist Interpretations of Søren Kierkegaard*, especially the introduction and the essays by Berry, Bertung, Watkin, and Perkins.

12. See Watkin, "The Logic of Søren Kierkegaard's Misogyny."

13. On the role of the imagination in this text as well as others in the authorship, see especially David J. Gouwens, *Kierkegaard's Dialectic of the Imagination* (New York: Peter Lang, 1989), and Ferreira, *Transforming Vision*. See also Walsh, *Living Poetically*, 229–32.

14. On the importance of the will in Anti-Climacus's writings, see also Come, *Kierkegaard as Theologian*, 321–30, and Chapter 1 of this study.

15. The Danish term for "youth" generally refers to a young man. Certainly the Hongs

understand the term as having that connotation, since they translate it as "young man" at least twice and consistently use masculine pronouns to refer to the two youths in the English text, as does Kierkegaard in the Danish text (*PC* 188, 194). Apparently, then, Kierkegaard has only young men in mind in these examples, although the process he describes them undergoing is (or should be) equally applicable to young women.

16. Another Kierkegaardian figure, Judge William, argues similarly in *Either/Or*, part 2, that the imagination is unable to depict internal history, or the development of those qualities such as marital love, humility, patience, faithfulness, and long-suffering, whose ideality consists in continuous realization over the years. The judge states: "Everything I am talking about here certainly can be portrayed esthetically, but not in poetic reproduction, but only by living it, by realizing it in the life of actuality" (*EO* 2:137). For a discussion of the judge's "existential aesthetics," see Walsh, *Living Poetically*, chap. 4.

17. Malantschuk, in *Kierkegaard's Thought*, claims that in making "Christ's visible degradation the measure of the Christian life," Kierkegaard moves from qualitative dialectic, which "directs all its attention to man's inner actuality," to quantitative dialectic, "in which external characteristics come to play a significant role" (367–68, 371). But just as outward works of love are no sure sign or proof that one is a Christian, so the same must be said with respect to suffering. Externally, it is never clear whether the outer is commensurate with the inner. And given the Christian striver's own increasing inner sense of imperfection and distance from the ideal, external suffering could never provide a direct measure of Christian sanctification. Ultimately, then, Christianity and Christian existence are still essentially inwardness for Kierkegaard.

18. Come, in *Kierkegaard as Theologian*, criticizes the view of Christian suffering that emerges in Kierkegaard's later writings, regarding it as overemphasizing external suffering and signifying a shift from what he, among others, regards as a more positive perspective in Kierkegaard's earlier religious writings of the period, for example, *Works of Love*, to the increasingly negative mood of darkness, pessimism, and world-weariness of his last years (337 n. 163). See also Rudd, *Kierkegaard and the Limits of the Ethical*, 164–69, and the views of Bohlin, Lindström, M. Thulstrup, and Westphal discussed in the previous chapter.

19. On the concept of spiritual trial in Kierkegaard's thought, see Niels Thulstrup, "Trial, Test, Tribulation, Temptation," in *Some of Kierkegaard's Main Categories*, ed. Niels Thulstrup and Marie Mikulová Thulstrup, Bibliotheca Kierkegaardiana 16 (Copenhagen: C. A. Reitzels Forlag, 1988), 105–19, and Gregor Malantschuk, *Nøglebegreber i Søren Kierkegaards tænkning*, ed. Grethe Kjær and Paul Müller (Copenhagen: C. A. Reitzels Forlag, 1993), 18–20.

20. For an insightful interpretation of this passage, see also David Cain, "A Star in a Cross: Getting the Dialectic Right," in Perkins, *International Kierkegaard Commentary: "For Self-Examination" and "Judge For Yourself!"* 315–34.

21. On Kierkegaard's relation to Luther, see Craig Q. Hinkson, "Luther and Kierkegaard: Theologians of the Cross," *International Journal of Systematic Theology* 3, no. 1 (2001): 27–45, and "Will the Real Martin Luther Please Stand Up! Kierkegaard's View of Luther vs. the Evolving Perceptions of the Tradition," in Perkins, *International Kierkegaard Commentary: "For Self-Examination" and " Judge For Yourself!"* 37–76. See also Tim Rose, *Kierkegaard's Christocentric Theology* (Aldershot: Ashgate, 2001), 114–17, and Daphne Hampson, *Christian Contradictions: The Structures of Lutheran and Catholic Thought* (Cambridge: Cambridge University Press, 2001), 249–84.

22. As noted in Chapter 3, Marie Thulstrup and Merold Westphal designate this stricter expression of Christianity in the later literature as "Religiousness C," whereas I have argued that Kierkegaard understands Christianity as combining both inwardness and outwardness throughout the writings of the second period, although certainly the external dimension is accentuated in the later writings. But inwardness is not negated or relegated in favor of outwardness; rather, both are essential to a full definition and expression of Christian existence.

23. Kierkegaard was certainly critical of the content of the sermons preached in Christendom, but it is a gross exaggeration to suggest, as Michael Strawser does in *Both/And: Reading Kierkegaard from Irony to Edification* (New York: Fordham Univeristy Press, 1997), that "Kierkegaard did not think that anyone had the authority to preach or teach regarding matters existential or Christian" and that "the effect of his work in the field of edification is the abolition of the sermon as an acceptable form of Christian communication" (187).

24. On Kierkegaard's critique of Mynster, see Christian Fink Tolstrup, " 'Playing a Profane Game with Holy Things': Understanding Kierkegaard's Critical Encounter with Bishop Mynster," in Perkins, *International Kierkegaard Commentary: "Practice in Christianity,"* 245–74. See also John Saxbee, "The Golden Age in an Earthen Vessel: The Life and Times of Bishop J. P. Mynster," in Stewart, *Kierkegaard and His Contemporaries,* 149–63.

25. Here, in order to complete the analysis of this important topic, I shall venture beyond the self-imposed limit of the present study a bit by citing some journal entries after 1851.

Chapter 5

1. For a range of essays focusing on Kierkegaard's encounter with the scandalous periodical *The Corsair,* see *International Kierkegaard Commentary: "The 'Corsair' Affair,"* vol. 13, ed. Robert L. Perkins (Macon: Mercer University Press, 1990).

2. On the increasing importance of rigor in Kierkegaard's writings in the second period of his authorship, see also David Possen, "The Voice of Rigor," in Perkins, *International Kierkegaard Commentary: "Practice in Christianity,"* 161–85.

3. On Kierkegaard's understanding of the relation of law and gospel, grace and works, see also Lee C. Barrett III, "Faith, Works, and the Uses of the Law: Kierkegaard's Appropriation of Lutheran Doctrine," in Perkins, *International Kierkegaard Commentary: "For Self-Examination" and "Judge For Yourself!"* 77–109, and Murray Rae, "Kierkegaard, Barth, and Bonhoeffer: Conceptions of the Relation Between Grace and Works," in the same volume, 143–67. See also Hall, *Kierkegaard and the Treachery of Love,* 16–50, and Rudd, *Kierkegaard and the Limits of the Ethical,* 164–73, who makes the astonishing claim that in his later thought Kierkegaard abandons "the doctrine of salvation by divine grace" in favor of a "radical doctrine of human autonomy" (168). Rudd bases this claim on a misreading of Kierkegaard's comments on Augustine and Luther in a journal entry from 1854 (*JP* 3:2551), in which Kierkegaard states that he *stands by* the Lutheran principle of salvation by grace, although, as Rudd rightly points out, he does chide Luther for reducing Christianity to grace as a way to avoid despair over our inability to win salvation through our own striving. But that does not equate to an abandonment of the doctrine of salvation by grace; rather, Kierkegaard's concern is that Luther's rationale is argued "from the human side" rather than from the standpoint of Christianity's "unconditional sovereignty," which requires a bold and forthright admission that one cannot fulfill the Christian requirements, not a watering down of them because "otherwise we must despair." Kierkegaard states that "Luther should have made the true connection known." In another journal entry from 1854 (*JP* 3:2554), Kierkegaard also takes Luther to task for (presumably) separating law and gospel, thereby turning Christianity into "an optimism anticipating that we are to have an easy life in this world," which in Kierkegaard's opinion changes Christianity into Judaism.

4. On Christ as prototype, see also Walsh, *Living Poetically,* 237–38, on which the present discussion is based but considerably expanded.

WORKS CONSULTED

Adorno, Theodor W. *Negative Dialectics.* Translated by E. B. Ashton. New York: Continuum, 1973.

———. "On Kierkegaard's Doctrine of Love." *Studies in Philosophy and Social Science* 8 (1940): 413–29.

Ake, Stacey. "'And yet a braver thence doth spring': The Heuristic Values of *Works of Love.*" In Cappelørn, Deuser, Stewart, and Tolstrup, *Kierkegaard Studies Yearbook 1998,* 93–112.

Andersen, K. Bruun. "Kierkegaard og jøderne." *Kierkegaardiana* 1 (1955): 84–87.

Andic, Martin. "Love's Redoubling and the Eternal Like for Like." In Perkins, *International Kierkegaard Commentary: "Works of Love,"* 9–38.

Ansbro, John J. "Kierkegaard's Gospel of Suffering." *Philosophical Studies* (Maynooth, Ireland) 16 (1967): 182–92.

Barrett, Lee C., III. "Faith, Works, and the Uses of the Law: Kierkegaard's Appropriation of Lutheran Doctrine." In Perkins, *International Kierkegaard Commentary: "For Self-Examination" and "Judge For Yourself!"* 77–109.

———. "The Joy in the Cross: Kierkegaard's Appropriation of Lutheran Christology in 'The Gospel of Sufferings.'" In Perkins, *International Kierkegaard Commentary: "Upbuilding Discourses in Various Spirits."*

———. "The Neighbor's Material and Social Well-Being in Kierkegaard's *Works of Love:* Does It Matter?" In Perkins, *International Kierkegaard Commentary: "Works of Love,"* 137–65.

———. "Subjectivity Is (Un)Truth: Climacus's Dialectically Sharpened Pathos." In Perkins, *International Kierkegaard Commentary: "Concluding Unscientific Postscript to 'Philosophical Fragments,'"* 291–306.

Bejerholm, Lars. *"Meddelelsens Dialektik": Studier i Søren Kierkegaards teorier om språk, kommunikation och pseudonymitet.* Copenhagen: Munksgaard, 1962.

Bell, Richard, ed. *The Grammar of the Heart: New Essays in Moral Philosophy and Theology.* New York: Harper & Row, 1988.

Berry, Wanda Warren. "The Silent Woman in Kierkegaard's Later Religious Writings." In Léon and Walsh, *Feminist Interpretations of Søren Kierkegaard,* 287–306.

Bohlen, Torsten. *Kierkegaards dogmatiska åskådning i dess historiska sammanhang.* Stockholm: Svenska Kyrkans Diakonistyrelses Bokförlag, 1925.

————. *Kierkegaards Tro och andra Kierkegaardstudier.* Stockholm: Svenska Kyrkans Diakonistyrelses Bokförlag, 1944.

————. *Sören Kierkegaards etiska åskådning med särskild hänsyn till begreppet den enskilde.* Stockholm: Svenska Kyrkans Diakonistyrelses Bokförlag, 1918.

Burgess, Andrew J. "Kierkegaard's Concept of Redoubling and Luther's 'Simul Justus.'" In Perkins, *International Kierkegaard Commentary: "Works of Love,"* 39–55.

Cain, David. "Death Comes in Between: Reflections on Kierkegaard's *For Self-Examination.*" *Kierkegaardiana* 15 (1991): 69–81.

————. "A Star in a Cross: Getting the Dialectic Right." In Perkins, *International Kierkegaard Commentary: "For Self-Examination" and "Judge For Yourself!"* 315–34.

Cappelørn, Niels Jørgen. "Die ursprüngliche Unterbrechung. Søren Kierkegaard beim Abendmahl im Freitagsgottesdienst der Kopenhagener Frauenkirche." Translated by Krista-Maria Deuser. In Cappelørn and Deuser, *Kierkegaard Studies Yearbook 1996,* 315–88.

————. "The Movements of Offense Toward, Away From, and Within Faith: 'Blessed Is He Who Is Not Offended by Me.'" Translated by K. Brian Söderquist. In Perkins, *International Kierkegaard Commentary: "Practice in Christianity,"* 95–124.

Cappelørn, Niels Jørgen, and Hermann Deuser, eds. *Kierkegaard Studies Yearbook 1996.* Berlin: Walter de Gruyter, 1996.

Cappelørn, Niels Jørgen, and Jon Stewart, eds. *Kierkegaard Revisited.* Kierkegaard Studies Monograph Series 1. Berlin: Walter de Gruyter, 1997.

Cappelørn, Niels Jørgen, Hermann Deuser, Jon Stewart, and Christian Fink Tolstrup, eds. *Kierkegaard Studies Yearbook 1998.* Berlin: Walter de Gruyter, 1998.

————. *Kierkegaard Studies Yearbook 2000.* Berlin: Walter de Gruyter, 2000.

————. *Kierkegaard Studies Yearbook 2003.* Berlin: Walter de Gruyter, 2003.

Carnell, Edward John. *The Burden of Søren Kierkegaard.* Grand Rapids, Mich.: Eerdmans, 1965.

Carr, Karen L., and Philip J. Ivanhoe. *The Sense of Antirationalism: The Religious Thought of Zhuangzi and Kierkegaard.* New York: Seven Bridges Press, 2000.

Christensen, Arild. "Romantismens og Søren Kierkegaards Opfattelse af Lidelse." *Kierkegaardiana* 1 (1955): 16–41.

Cole, Preston J. "Kierkegaard's Doctrine of the Atonement." *Religion in Life* 23 (1964): 592–601.

Come, Arnold. *Kierkegaard as Humanist: Discovering My Self.* Montreal: McGill-Queen's University Press, 1995.

————. *Kierkegaard as Theologian: Recovering My Self.* Montreal: McGill-Queen's University Press, 1997.

Connell, George. "Postmodern Readings of Kierkegaard and the Requirement of Oneness." In Perkins, *International Kierkegaard Commentary: "Upbuilding Discourses in Various Spirits."*

————. *To Be One Thing: Personal Unity in Kierkegaard's Thought.* Macon: Mercer University Press, 1985.

Connell, George B., and C. Stephen Evans, eds. *Foundations of Kierkegaard's Vision of Community: Religion, Ethics, and Politics in Kierkegaard.* Atlantic Highlands, N.J.: Humanities Press, 1992.

Davenport, John J. "Towards an Existential Virtue Ethics: Kierkegaard and MacIntyre." In Davenport and Rudd, *Kierkegaard After MacIntyre,* 265–323.

Davenport, John J., and Anthony Rudd, eds. *Kierkegaard After MacIntyre: Essays on Freedom, Narrative, and Virtue.* Chicago: Open Court, 2001.

Deuser, Hermann. "Religious Dialectics and Christology." In Hannay and Marino, *Cambridge Companion to Kierkegaard,* 376–96.

Dewey, Bradley. *The New Obedience: Kierkegaard on Imitating Christ.* Washington, D.C.: Corpus Books, 1968.

Diem, Hermann. *Kierkegaard's Dialectic of Existence.* Translated by Harold Knight. Edinburgh: Oliver and Boyd, 1959.

Dunning, Stephen N. *Kierkegaard's Dialectic of Inwardness: A Structural Analysis of the Theory of Stages.* Princeton: Princeton University Press, 1985.

———. "Love Is Not Enough: A Kierkegaardian Phenomenology of Religious Experience." *Faith and Philosophy* 12, no. 1 (1995): 22–39.

Dupré, Louis. *Kierkegaard as Theologian: The Dialectic of Christian Existence.* New York: Sheed and Ward, 1963.

Ebeling, Gerhard. *Luther: An Introduction to His Thought.* Translated by R. A. Wilson. Philadelphia: Fortress Press, 1964.

Eller, Vernard. *Kierkegaard and Radical Discipleship: A New Perspective.* Princeton: Princeton University Press, 1968.

Elrod, John. "Climacus, Anti-Climacus and the Problem of Suffering." *Thought: A Review of Culture and Idea* 55 (September 1980): 306–19.

———. *Kierkegaard and Christendom.* Princeton: Princeton University Press, 1981.

Emmanuel, Steven M. *Kierkegaard and the Concept of Revelation.* Albany: The State University of New York Press, 1996.

Evans, C. Stephen. "Authority and Transcendence in *Works of Love.*" In Cappelørn, Deuser, Stewart, and Tolstrup, *Kierkegaard Studies Yearbook 1998,* 23–40.

———. "Is Kierkegaard an Irrationalist? Reason, Paradox, and Faith." *Religious Studies* 25 (1989): 347–62.

———. *Kierkegaard's "Fragments" and "Postscript": The Religious Philosophy of Johannes Climacus.* Atlantic Highlands, N.J.: Humanities Press, 1983.

———. *Passionate Reason: Making Sense of Kierkegaard's "Philosophical Fragments."* Bloomington: Indiana University Press, 1992.

Evans, C. Stephen, and Jan Evans. "Translator's Preface and Introduction." In Müller, *Kierkegaard's "Works of Love,"* vii–xi.

Ferreira, M. Jamie. *Love's Grateful Striving: A Commentary on Kierkegaard's "Works of Love."* Oxford: Oxford University Press, 2001.

———. "Other-Worldliness in Kierkegaard's *Works of Love.*" *Philosophical Investigations* 22, no. 1 (1999): 65–79.

———. *Transforming Vision: Imagination and Will in Kierkegaardian Faith.* Oxford: Clarendon Press, 1991.

Frawley, Matthew J. "The Essential Role of the Holy Spirit in Kierkegaard's Biblical Hermeneutic." In Houe and Marino, *Søren Kierkegaard and the Word(s),* 93–104.

Garff, Joakim. *"Den Søvnløse": Kierkegaard læst æstetisk/biografisk.* Copenhagen: C. A. Reitzels Forlag, 1995.

———. "The Eyes of Argus: The Point of View and Points of View with Respect to Kierkegaard's 'Activity as an Author.'" *Kierkegaardiana* 15 (1991): 29–54. Reprinted in Rée and Chamberlain, *Kierkegaard: A Critical Reader,* 75–102.

———. "Rereading Oneself." *Søren Kierkegaard Newsletter* 38 (July 1999): 9–14.

Gill, Jerry H., ed. *Essays on Kierkegaard.* Minneapolis: Burgess Publishing, 1969.

Goicoechea, David, ed. *The Nature and Pursuit of Love: The Philosophy of Irving Singer.* Amherst, N.Y.: Prometheus Books, 1995.

González, Darío. "Sin, Absolute Difference." In Cappelørn, Deuser, Stewart, and Tolstrup, *Kierkegaard Studies Yearbook 2003,* 373–83.

Gouwens, David J. *Kierkegaard as Religious Thinker.* Cambridge: Cambridge University Press, 1996.

———. *Kierkegaard's Dialectic of the Imagination.* New York: Peter Lang, 1989.

Grøn, Arne. *Subjektivitet og Negativitet: Kierkegaard.* Copenhagen: Gyldendalske Boghandel, 1997.

Habermas, Jürgen. "Communicative Freedom and Negative Theology." Translated with notes by Martin J. Matuštík and Patricia J. Huntington. In Matuštík and Westphal, *Kierkegaard in Post/Modernity,* 182–98.

Hamilton, Christopher. "Kierkegaard on Truth as Subjectivity: Christianity, Ethics, and Asceticism." *Religious Studies* 34 (1998): 61–79.

Hamilton, Kenneth. "Kierkegaard on Sin." *Scottish Journal of Theology* 17 (1964): 289–302.

Hampson, Daphne. *Christian Contradictions: The Structures of Lutheran and Catholic Thought.* Cambridge: Cambridge University Press, 2001.

Hall, Amy Laura. *Kierkegaard and the Treachery of Love.* Cambridge: Cambridge University Press, 2002.

Hannay, Alastair. *Kierkegaard.* London: Routledge & Kegan Paul, 1982.

———. *Kierkegaard: A Biography.* Cambridge: Cambridge University Press, 2001.

———. "Kierkegaard and the Variety of Despair." In Hannay and Marino, *Cambridge Companion to Kierkegaard,* 329–48.

Hannay, Alastair, and Gordon D. Marino, eds. *The Cambridge Companion to Kierkegaard.* Cambridge: Cambridge University Press, 1998.

Hartshorne, M. Holmes. *Kierkegaard, Godly Deceiver: The Nature and Meaning of His Pseudonymous Writings.* New York: Columbia University Press, 1990.

Henriksen, Aage. *Methods and Results of Kierkegaard Studies in Scandinavia: A Historical and Critical Survey.* Copenhagen: Ejnar Munksgaard, 1951.

Hinkson, Craig Q. "Luther and Kierkegaard: Theologians of the Cross." *International Journal of Systematic Theology* 3, no. 1 (2001): 27–45.

———. "Will the Real Martin Luther Please Stand Up! Kierkegaard's View of Luther vs. the Evolving Perceptions of the Tradition." In Perkins, *International Kierkegaard Commentary: "For Self-Examination" and "Judge For Yourself!"* 37–76.

Holm, Søren. *Søren Kierkegaards Historiefilosofi.* Copenhagen: Bianco Lunos Bogtrykkeri, 1952.

Houe, Poul, and Gordon D. Marino, eds. *Søren Kierkegaard and the Word(s): Essays on Hermeneutics and Communication.* Copenhagen: C. A. Reitzel, 2003.

Houe, Paul, Gordon D. Marino and Sven Hakon Rossel, eds. *Anthropology and Authority: Essays on Søren Kierkegaard.* Amsterdam: Rodopi, 2000.

Hough, Sheridan. "'Halting Is Movement': The Paradoxical Pause of Confession in 'An Occasional Discourse.'" In Perkins, *International Kierkegaard Commentary: "Upbuilding Discourses in Various Spirits."*

Johnson, Howard A., and Niels Thulstrup, eds. *A Kierkegaard Critique.* New York: Harper & Brothers, 1962.

Kangas, David J. "The Very Opposite of Beginning with Nothing: Guilt Consciousness in Kierkegaard's 'The Gospel of Sufferings' IV." In Perkins, *International Kierkegaard Commentary: "Upbuilding Discourses in Various Spirits."*

Keeley, Louise Carroll. "Loving 'No One,' Loving Everyone: The Work of Love in Recollecting One Dead in Kierkegaard's *Works of Love.*" In Perkins, *International Kierkegaard Commentary: "Works of Love,"* 211–48.

———. "Silence, Domesticity, and Joy: The Spiritual Life of Women in Kierkegaard's *For Self-Examination.*" In Perkins, *International Kierkegaard Commentary: "For Self-Examination" and "Judge For Yourself!"* 223–57.

Khan, Abrahim H. "The Treatment of the Theme of Suffering in Kierkegaard's Works." Ph.D. diss., McGill University, 1973.

Kierkegaard, Søren. *Christian Discourses.* Translated by Walter Lowrie. London: Oxford University Press, 1939.

———. *Training in Christianity.* Translated by Walter Lowrie. Princeton: Princeton University Press, 1944.

Kirmmse, Bruce H. *Kierkegaard in Golden Age Denmark.* Bloomington: Indiana University Press, 1990.

———. "Kierkegaard, Jews, and Judaism." *Kierkegaardiana* 17 (1994): 83–97 (condensed English version).

———. "Kierkegaard, Jødedommen og Jøderne." *Kirkehistoriske Samlinger* (1992): 77–107 (longer Danish version).

Kodalle, Klaus-M. "The Utilitarian Self and the 'Useless' Passion of Faith." In Hannay and Marino, *Cambridge Companion to Kierkegaard,* 397–410.

Law, David R. "Cheap Grace and the Cost of Discipleship in Kierkegaard's *For Self-Examination.*" In Perkins, *International Kierkegaard Commentary: "For Self-Examination" and "Judge For Yourself!"* 111–42.

———. *Kierkegaard as Negative Theologian.* Oxford: Clarendon Press, 1993.

———. "Resignation, Suffering, and Guilt in Kierkegaard's *Concluding Unscientific Postscript to 'Philosophical Fragments.'*" In Perkins, *International Kierkegaard Commentary: "Concluding Unscientific Postscript to 'Philosophical Fragments,'"* 263–89.

———. "Wrongness, Guilt, and Innocent Suffering in Kierkegaard's *Either/Or,* Part Two, and *Upbuilding Discourses in Various Spirits.*" In Perkins, *International Kierkegaard Commentary: "Upbuilding Discourses in Various Spirits."*

Léon, Céline, and Sylvia Walsh, eds. *Feminist Interpretations of Søren Kierkegaard.* University Park: The Pennsylvania State University Press, 1997.

Lindström, Valter. "A Contribution to the Interpretation of Kierkegaard's Book *The Works of Love*." *Studia Theologica* 6 (1953): 1–29.

———. *Efterföljelsens Teologi hos Sören Kierkegaard*. Stockholm: Svenska Kyrkans Diakonistyrelses Bokförlag, 1956.

———. "Eros och agape i Kierkegaards åskådning." *Kierkegaardiana* 1 (1955): 102–12.

———. "Kierkegaards Tolkning Av Självförnekelsen såsom Kristendomens Livsform." *Svensk telologisk Kvartalskrift* 26 (1950): 326–34.

———. *Stadiernas Teologi: En Kierkegaard-studie*. Lund: C.W.K. Gleerup, 1943.

Løgstrup, Knud Ejler. *Opgør med Kierkegaard*. Copenhagen: Gyldendalske Boghandel, 1967.

———. *The Ethical Demand*. Translated by Theodor Jensen, Eric Watkins, and Gary Puckering with an introduction by Hans Fink and Alasdair MacIntyre. Notre Dame: Notre Dame University Press, 1997.

Lønning, Per. "Kierkegaard as a Christian Thinker." In Thulstrup and Thulstrup, *Kierkegaard's View of Christianity*, 163–79.

———. *Samtidighedens Situation: en studie i Sören Kierkegaards Kristendomsforståelse*. Oslo: Forlaget Land og Kirke, 1954.

Mackey, Louis. "The Poetry of Inwardness." In Thompson, *Kierkegaard: A Collection of Critical Essays*, 1–102.

Malantschuk, Gregor. "Begrebet Fordoblelse hos Søren Kierkegaard." *Kierkegaardiana* 2 (1957): 42–53.

———. *Kierkegaard's Thought*. Edited and translated by Howard V. Hong and Edna H. Hong. Princeton: Princeton University Press, 1971.

———. *Nøglebegreber i Søren Kierkegaards tænkning*. Edited by Grethe Kjær and Paul Müller. Copenhagen: C. A. Reitzels Forlag, 1993.

Martin, Harold V. *The Wings of Faith*. New York: Philosophical Library, 1951.

Martens, Paul. "The Emergence of the Holy Spirit in Kierkegaard's Thought: Critical Theological Developments." In Perkins, *International Kierkegaard Commentary: "For Self-Examination" and "Judge For Yourself!"* 199–222.

Matuštík, Martin J., and Merold Westphal, eds. *Kierkegaard in Post/Modernity*. Bloomington: Indiana University Press, 1995.

Molbech, Christian, ed. *Dansk Ordbog*. 2 vols. Copenhagen: Gyldendalske Boghandling, 1859.

Müller, Paul. *Kierkegaard's "Works of Love": Christian Ethics and the Maieutic Ideal*. Translated and edited by C. Stephen and Jan Evans. Copenhagen: C. A. Reitzel, 1993.

Nelson, Christopher A.P. "Kierkegaard's Concept of Vocation in 'An Occasional Discourse.'" In Perkins, *International Kierkegaard Commentary: "Upbuilding Discourses in Various Spirits."*

Outka, Gene. *Agape: An Ethical Analysis*. New Haven: Yale University Press, 1972.

Pattison, George. *Kierkegaard's Upbuilding Discourses: Philosophy, Theology, Literature*. London: Routledge, 2002.

———, ed. *Kierkegaard on Art and Communication*. New York: St. Martin's Press, 1992.

Perkins, Robert L. "Anti-Climacus in His Social and Political Environment." In Perkins, *International Kierkegaard Commentary: "Practice in Christianity,"* 275–302.

———, ed. *International Kierkegaard Commentary: "The Concept of Irony,"* vol. 2. Macon: Mercer University Press, 2001.

———. *International Kierkegaard Commentary: "Concluding Unscientific Postscript to 'Philosophical Fragments,'"* vol. 12. Macon: Mercer University Press, 1997.

———. *International Kierkegaard Commentary: "The 'Corsair' Affair,"* vol. 13. Macon: Mercer University Press, 1990.

———. *International Kierkegaard Commentary: "Eighteen Upbuilding Discourses,"* vol. 5. Macon: Mercer University Press, 2003.

———. *International Kierkegaard Commentary: "For Self-Examination"* and *"Judge For Yourself!"* vol. 21. Macon: Mercer University Press, 2002.

———. *International Kierkegaard Commentary: "Practice in Christianity,"* vol. 20. Macon: Mercer University Press, 2004.

———. *International Kierkegaard Commentary: "The Sickness unto Death,"* vol. 19. Macon: Mercer University Press, 1987.

———. *International Kierkegaard Commentary: "Upbuilding Discourses in Various Spirits,"* vol. 15. Macon: Mercer University Press, 2005.

———. *International Kierkegaard Commentary: "Works of Love,"* vol. 16. Macon: Mercer University Press, 1999.

Perkins, Sylvia Walsh. "Kierkegaard's Philosophy of Love." In Goicoechea, *Nature and Pursuit of Love,* 167–79.

Plekon, Michael. "Kierkegaard and the Eucharist." *Studia Liturgica* 22 (1992): 214–36.

———. "Kierkegaard the Theologian: The Roots of His Theology in *Works of Love.*" In Connell and Evans, *Foundations of Kierkegaard's Vision of Community,* 2–17.

Pojman, Louis J. *The Logic of Subjectivity.* Tuscaloosa: University of Alabama Press, 1984.

Polk, Timothy Houston. *The Biblical Kierkegaard: Reading by the Rule of Faith.* Macon: Mercer University Press, 1997.

Pons, Jolita. "On Imitating the Inimitable: Example, Comparison, and Prototype." In Perkins, *International Kierkegaard Commentary: "Upbuilding Discourses in Various Spirits."*

Poole, Roger. *Kierkegaard: The Indirect Communication.* Charlottesville: University Press of Virginia, 1993.

Possen, David. "The Voice of Rigor." In Perkins, *International Kierkegaard Commentary: "Practice in Christianity,"* 161–85.

Quinn, Philip L. "Kierkegaard's Christian Ethics." In Hannay and Marino, *Cambridge Companion to Kierkegaard,* 349–75.

Rae, Murray. "Kierkegaard, Barth, and Bonhoeffer: Conceptions of the Relation Between Grace and Works." In Perkins, *International Kierkegaard Commentary: "For Self-Examination"* and *"Judge For Yourself!"* 143–67.

———. *Kierkegaard's Vision of the Incarnation: By Faith Transformed.* Oxford: Clarendon Press, 1997.

Rée, Jonathan, and Jane Chamberlain, eds. *Kierkegaard: A Critical Reader.* Oxford: Basil Blackwell, 1998.

Risum, Janne. "Towards Transparency: Søren Kierkegaard on Danish Actresses." In Stewart, *Kierkegaard and His Contemporaries*, 330–42.

Roberts, Robert C. "Dialectical Emotions and the Virtue of Faith." In Perkins, *International Kierkegaard Commentary: "Concluding Unscientific Postscript to 'Philosophical Fragments,'"* 73–93.

———. "Existence, Emotion, and Virtue: Classical Themes in Kierkegaard." In Hannay and Marino, *Cambridge Companion to Kierkegaard,* 177–206.

Rocca, Ettore. "The Threefold Revelation of Sin." Translated by Domenico Pacitti. In Cappelørn, Deuser, Stewart, and Tolstrup, *Kierkegaard Studies Yearbook 2003,* 384–94.

Rose, Tim. *Kierkegaard's Christocentric Theology.* Aldershot: Ashgate, 2001.

Rudd, Anthony. *Kierkegaard and the Limits of the Ethical.* Oxford: Clarendon Press, 1993.

Sass, Else Kai. "Thorvaldsen: An Introduction to His Work." In Stewart, *Kierkegaard and His Contemporaries,* 375–405.

Saxbee, John. "The Golden Age in an Earthen Vessel: The Life and Times of Bishop J. P. Mynster." In Stewart, *Kierkegaard and His Contemporaries,* 149–63.

Shmuëli, Adi. *Kierkegaard and Consciousness.* Translated by Naomi Handelman. Princeton: Princeton University Press, 1971.

Silverman, Hugh J., ed. *Writing the Politics of Difference.* Selected Studies in Phenomenology and Existential Philosophy 14. Albany: The State University of New York Press, 1991.

Skjoldager, Emanuel. *Den egentlige Kierkegaard: Søren Kierkegaards syn på kirke og de kirkelige handlinger.* Copenhagen: C. A. Reitzels Forlag, 1982.

———. *Søren Kierkegaards Syn på Samvittigheden.* Copenhagen: Munksgaard, 1967.

Sløk, Johannes. *Kierkegaard—humanismens tænker.* Copenhagen: Hans Reitzel, 1978.

Smith, Joseph H., ed. *Kierkegaard's Truth: The Disclosure of the Self.* Psychiatry and the Humanities 5. New Haven: Yale University Press, 1981.

Søe, N. H. "Kierkegaard's Doctrine of the Paradox." In Johnson and Thulstrup, *Kierkegaard Critique,* 207–27.

Søltoft, Pia. *Svimmelhedens Etik—om forholdet mellem den enkelte og den anden hos Buber, Levinas og især Kierkegaard.* Copenhagen: Gads Forlag, 2000.

Sponheim, Paul. "Kierkegaard and the Suffering of the Christian Man." *Dialog* 3 (1964): 199–206.

———. *Kierkegaard on Christ and Christian Coherence.* London: SCM Press, 1968.

Stewart, Jon. *Kierkegaard's Relations to Hegel Reconsidered.* New York: Cambridge University Press, 2003.

———, ed. *Kierkegaard and His Contemporaries: The Culture of Golden Age Denmark.* Kierkegaard Studies Monograph Series 10. Berlin: Walter de Gruyter, 2003.

Strawser, Michael. *Both/And: Reading Kierkegaard from Irony to Edification.* New York: Fordham University Press, 1997.

Taylor, Mark Lloyd. "Practice in Authority: The Apostolic Women of Søren Kierke-gaard's Writings." In Houe, Marino, and Rossel, *Anthropology and Author-ity*, 85–98.

Theunissen, Michael. *Das Selbst auf dem Grund der Verzweiflung. Kierkegaards negativistische Methode*. Frankfurt am Main: Suhrkamp, 1991.

———. "Kierkegaard's Negativistic Method." Translated by Charlotte Baumann. In Smith, *Kierkegaard's Truth*, 381–423.

Thomas, J. Heywood. *Subjectivity and Paradox*. Oxford: Basil Blackwell, 1957.

Thompson, Josiah, ed. *Kierkegaard: A Collection of Critical Essays*. Garden City, N.Y.: Doubleday Anchor Books, 1972.

Thulstrup, Marie Mikulová. "Efterfølgelsens dialektik hos Søren Kierkegaard." *Dansk Teologisk Tidskrift* 21 (1958): 193–209.

———. "Kierkegaards 'onde verden.'" *Kierkegaardiana* 1 (1955): 42–54.

———. "Lidelsens problematik hos Kierkegaard og Mystikerne." *Kierkegaardiana* 3 (1959): 48–72.

———. "Søren Kierkegaards Martyrbegreb." *Dansk teologisk Tidskrift* 27 (1964): 100–114.

———. "Suffering." In Thulstrup and Thulstrup, *Kierkegaard and Human Values*, 135–62.

Thulstrup, Niels. *Kierkegaard and the Church in Denmark*. Bibliotheca Kierke-gaardiana 13. Copenhagen: C. A. Reitzels Forlag, 1984.

———. "Trial, Test, Tribulation, Temptation." In Thulstrup and Thulstrup, *Some of Kierkegaard's Main Categories*, 105–19.

Thulstrup, Niels, and Marie Mikulová Thulstrup, eds. *Kierkegaard and Human Val-ues*. Bibliotheca Kierkegaardiana 7. Copenhagen: C. A. Reitzels Boghandel, 1980.

———. *Kierkegaard and the Church in Denmark*. Bibliotheca Kierkegaardiana 13. Copenhagen: C. A. Reitzels Forlag, 1984.

———. *Kierkegaard's View of Christianity*. Bibliotheca Kierkegaardiana 1. Copen-hagen: C. A. Reitzels Boghandel, 1978.

———. *Some of Kierkegaard's Main Categories*. Bibliotheca Kierkegaardiana 16. Copenhagen: C. A. Reitzels Forlag, 1988.

Tolstrup, Christian Fink. "'Playing a Profane Game with Holy Things': Understand-ing Kierkegaard's Critical Encounter with Bishop Mynster." In Perkins, *Inter-national Kierkegaard Commentary: "Practice in Christianity,"* 245–74.

Utterback, Sylvia Walsh. "Kierkegaard's Inverse Dialectic." *Kierkegaardiana* 11 (1980): 34–54.

Walsh, Sylvia. "Forming the Heart: The Role of Love in Kierkegaard's Thought." In Bell, *Grammar of the Heart*, 234–56.

———. "If the Lily Could Speak: On the Contentment and Glory of Being Human." In Perkins, *International Kierkegaard Commentary: "Upbuilding Discourses in Various Spirits."*

———. "Ironic Love: An Amorist Interpretation of Socratic Eros." In Perkins, *In-ternational Kierkegaard Commentary: "The Concept of Irony,"* 123–40.

———. "Issues That Divide: Interpreting Kierkegaard on Woman and Gender." In Cappelørn and Stewart, *Kierkegaard Revisited*, 191–205.

———. "Kierkegaard: Poet of the Religious." In Pattison, *Kierkegaard on Art and Communication*, 1–22.

———. *Living Poetically: Kierkegaard's Existential Aesthetics*. University Park: The Pennsylvania State University Press, 1994.

———. "Other-Worldliness in Kierkegaard's *Works of Love*—A Response." *Philosophical Investigations* 22, no. 1 (1999): 80–85.

———. "Reading Kierkegaard With Kierkegaard Against Garff." *Søren Kierkegaard Newsletter* 38 (July 1999): 4–8.

———. "Subjectivity versus Objectivity: Kierkegaard's *Postscript* and Feminist Epistemology." In Perkins, *International Kierkegaard Commentary: "Concluding Unscientific Postscript to 'Philosophical Fragments,'"* 11–31. Reprinted in Léon and Walsh, *Feminist Interpretations of Søren Kierkegaard*, 267–85.

———. "When 'That Single Individual' Is a Woman." In Cappelørn, Deuser, Stewart, and Tolstrup, *Kierkegaard Studies Yearbook 2000*, 1–18. Reprinted in Perkins, *International Kierkegaard Commentary: "Eighteen Upbuilding Discourses,"* 31–50.

Watkin, Julia. "The Logic of Kierkegaard's Misogyny, 1854–55." *Kierkegaardiana* 15 (1991): 79–93. Reprinted in Léon and Walsh, *Feminist Interpretations of Søren Kierkegaard*, 69–82.

Westphal, Merold. *Becoming a Self: A Reading of Kierkegaard's "Concluding Unscientific Postscript."* West Lafayette: Purdue University Press, 1996.

———. "Kierkegaard's Phenomenology of Faith as Suffering." In Silverman, *Writing the Politics of Difference*, 55–71.

———. "Kierkegaard's Teleological Suspension of Religiousness B." In Connell and Evans, *Foundations of Kierkegaard's Vision of Community*, 110–29.

INDEX

abasement, 133–34, 136
Abraham, 60, 126, 178 n. 7
absolute paradox, 9, 54–63, 68–69, 174 n. 7
absurd, the, 54–62, 77
acoustical illusion, 55–56, 62
Adorno, T. W., 97, 167 n. 11, 176 n. 26
adversity versus prosperity, 125–26, 129, 143
Ake, Stacey, 176 n. 22
Andersen, K. Bruun, 179 n. 7
Andic, Martin, 168 n. 20, 176 n. 25
Ansbro, John J., 178 n. 1
Anti-Climacus, 20–21
asceticism, 87–88
atonement, 18, 26, 44, 153, 172 nn. 28–29
Aufhebung, Hegelian concept of, 107
Augustine, Saint, 181 n. 3
Barrett, Lee C., III, 168 n. 19, 174 n. 3, 177
    n. 28, 178 n. 4, 181 n. 3

Barth, Karl, 176 n. 26
Beelzebul, 29
Bejerholm, Lars, 167 n. 14
Berger, Peter, 173 n. 2
Berry, Wanda Warren, 172 n. 30, 179 n. 11
Bertung, Birgit, 179 n. 11
Bible
    authority of, 171 n. 19
    New Testament, 116, 156; Gospel of Luke,
        39, 41, 45; Gospel of Matthew, 29
    Old Testament, 126
Bohlin, Torsten, 86–89, 175 nn. 11, 13, 16,
    176 n. 19, 180 n. 18
Buber, Martin, 171 n. 17
Burgess, Andrew J., 168 n. 20, 176 n. 25

Cain, David, 175 n. 5, 180 n. 20
Cappelørn, Niels Jørgen, 169 n. 5, 172 nn.
    24–26, 173 n. 6, 176 n. 22
Carnell, Edward John, 178 n. 2
Carr, Karen L., 173 n. 2

Christ
    ascension of, 138–39
    communion with, 44–45
    compassion of, 71, 73, 132
    consequences of his life, 70–71
    as criterion of human beings, 27, 63, 150
    as fulfillment of the law, 159
    as *Gud-Menneske*, 63, 173 n. 5
    imitation of, 121, 133, 157–59, 165 n. 3
    as individual human being, 65–66
    invitation of, 64–65, 73, 130, 138
    as leniency and love, 131
    loftiness and lowliness of, 65–66, 70–74,
        108, 134–36, 138
    as occasion for offense, 65–66, 74
    as prototype and redeemer, 14, 93, 152,
        156–59, 181 n. 4
    self-denial of, 93
    as sign of contradiction, 66, 71–72
    as sign of offense and object of faith,
        65–66
    suffering of, 44, 132–33, 139–40
Christendom, 2, 4, 14, 48, 53, 65, 76, 109,
    127, 137, 145, 162, 165 n. 3
Christensen, Arild, 178 n. 2
Christian
    discipleship, 92–93, 121–22, 138, 140,
        159
    ideal picture of, 4, 163
    inverted recognizability of, 137, 151
    point of view, 10
    simplicity, 2–3
    strivers and striving, 11–15, 30, 32, 36, 75,
        77, 89, 101, 120, 133, 138–39, 149–50,
        153–55, 157–59, 162
Christian existence
    dialectic of, 5–6, 36, 82, 152
    double danger of, 101–3, 106, 111,
        137–38, 150–51, 159, 162
    ideally versus existentially defined, 13,
        149–50, 162

Christian existence (*continued*)
  inverseness of, 76–77, 120
  as new form of life and hope, 14, 79–81,
    90, 94, 111–12
  qualifications of, 5, 10, 13–15, 20, 86, 110,
    113, 140, 149, 152
Christianity
  contradictoriness, absoluteness, and
    heterogeneity of, 54, 77, 82, 93, 130,
    141, 153–54
  as existence-communication, 3, 10
  first form of, 52, 62, 81
  gospel and law in, 14, 152–56, 181 n. 3
  grace and works in, 14, 152–56, 158–59,
    162, 177 n. 34, 181 n. 3
  ideality of, 3, 5
  as inwardness, 18
  as leniency and love, 131
  medieval view of, 109, 155
  mildness and rigor in, 14, 47, 131, 142,
    152–53, 162, 181 n. 2
  misanthropic, misogynous, and
    misogamous appearance of, 130–31
  relation to world, 9–10, 12, 82, 86, 91,
    103, 119
  as source of comfort for temporal
    suffering, 48–49
Church triumphant versus Church militant,
  137
Cole, J. Preston, 44, 172 nn. 28–29
Come, Arnold B., 165 n. 3, 166 n. 9, 169
  n. 5, 173 n. 5, 175 nn. 8, 16, 178 n. 3,
  179 n. 14, 180 n. 18
communication, 167 n. 14
  Christian, 7, 181 n. 23
  dialectic of, 7, 167 n. 14
  direct versus indirect, 7, 71
  ethical and ethical-religious, 7
  poet-communication, 16, 166 n. 7
communion, 171 n. 24, 172 nn. 25–26
compassion, divine versus human, 73
confession, 33–35, 37–38, 45, 120, 170
  n. 16, 171–72 n. 24
Connell, George, 171 n. 17
conscience, 33–34, 43, 170 n. 14
  anguished, 33, 46–47, 50, 142, 148, 162
consciousness, structure of, 33
consolation, 14, 113–14, 121, 141–46, 150,
  162
contradiction, logical versus qualitative,
  66–67, 138, 174 n.7

conversion, 31, 142, 173 n. 2
The Corsair, 151, 181 n. 1

Davenport, John J., 169 n. 4
death, 80–81, 111, 175 n. 5
defiance, 28
despair, 168 n. 16
  choice of self through, 94
  consciousness of, 21, 30
  as double-mindedness, 34
  as first factor in faith, 30–31
  forms of, 21
  of forgiveness, 27–28
  over sin, 27–28
  as sin, 22–23
Deuser, Hermann, 169 n. 5, 176 n. 22
Dewey, Bradley R., 165 n. 3, 178 n. 2
dialectic, dialectical, 5–14, 166 n. 10, 167
  n. 13
  of consciousness of sin and forgiveness,
    32–45
  Hegelian, Platonic, and Socratic forms of,
    6, 166–67 n. 11
  inverse, 7–9, 11–13, 32, 35, 47–48, 80, 82,
    93, 100, 113–14, 123–26, 138, 141–42,
    144, 146, 149, 152, 160–63, 167 n. 15,
    168 n. 16, 169 n. 4, 172 n. 30, 178 n. 3
  method, 11, 161, 167 n. 16
  qualitative (existential) versus quantitative
    (conceptual), 6–7, 25–26, 149, 151, 180
    n. 17
Diem, Hermann, 166 n. 10
discourses
  Christian versus upbuilding, 171 n. 19
  communion or confessional, 37–38, 43,
    45, 171 nn. 21–22, 172 nn. 24–25, 27
double-mindedness, 34, 92, 117
Dunning, Stephen N., 166 n. 10, 175 n. 5
Dupré, Louis, 33, 166 n. 9, 170 n. 12, 175
  n. 16, 178 n. 2
dying to, 81, 107, 175 nn. 5–6
  ethical-religious conception of, 92
  immanence, 90–91
  immediacy, 82, 84–87, 89, 90, 94, 115,
    119
  the prototype, 159
  relation to self-denial, 82, 91–92
  selfishness, 86–88, 90–92, 103
  the world or worldliness, 14, 81–83,
    87–88, 90–92, 103, 106–7, 111, 126,
    176 n. 22

Ebeling, Gerhard, 22, 170 n. 7
Eller, Vernard, 165 n. 1, 166 n. 10, 167 n. 13,
    171 n. 17
Elrod, John, 165 n. 3, 178 n. 3
Emmanuel, Steven M., 170 n. 10, 173 n. 2
equality, spiritual versus social, 16, 98, 162,
    169 n. 22, 176–77 n. 28
established order
    Christ as threat to, 108
    deification of, 74–75
eternal, the, 8, 13, 35, 117–19
    gaining, 124–25
    in time, 9, 63, 67, 90
ethic, Kierkegaard's, 162
    social, 87, 100–101, 176–77 n. 28
    of transformation, 82, 100–101
ethical-religious, the 12–13, 82–83, 89,
    93–94, 116, 161
Evans, C. Stephen, 67, 83, 168 n. 17, 173
    n. 2, 174 nn. 7–8, 175 nn. 8–10, 176
    n. 19
Evans, Jan, 83, 175 n. 9

faith, 9, 14, 17, 19, 32, 41, 139, 173 n. 2
    the absurd as negative sign of, 59–60
    as belief in possibility, 49–50, 76–77
    double vision of, 60, 77
    existential versus ideal definition of, 31, 51
    as letting go of probability, 76
    primacy of, 158
    relation to possibility of offense, 51, 77
    relation to reason, 59, 61–62, 151, 173
    n. 2
    as second immediacy, 88, 168 n. 21
    as will to believe, 31, 77, 170 n. 10
Ferreira, M. Jamie, 170 n. 11, 174 n. 3, 176
    nn. 20, 22, 26–27, 177 nn. 28–29, 179
    n. 13
forgiveness, 14, 17–18, 20, 36–39, 41–42,
    45, 48–49, 63–64, 142, 150
    consciousness of, 32, 36, 122, 171 n. 20
    need for, 43, 63
Frawley, Matthew J., 175 n. 5

Garff, Joakim, 166 n. 6
Gill, Jerry, 173 n. 2
God
    conception of, 24, 27
    infinite qualitative difference from human
    beings, 63, 66, 68, 147

as love, 79, 135, 146–48
    as middle term in love, 99
    relation to, 9, 36, 39–40, 63, 99, 128,
    162
González, Darío, 170 n. 8
good, the, 34, 92, 117, 119
goods, spiritual versus worldly, 123–24
Gouwens, David J., 165 nn. 1–2, 166 n. 9,
    167 n. 15, 169 n. 4, 175 n. 8, 176 n. 26,
    178 n. 3, 179 n. 13
grace, 110, 127, 153–59, 162, 177 n. 34, 181
    n. 3
gratitude, 159, 162
Grøn, Arne, 168 n. 16
guilt, consciousness of, 8, 35–36, 38, 45, 85,
    168 n. 17, 178 n. 6

Habermas, Jürgen, 168 n. 16
Hall, Amy Laura, 176 n. 22, 181 n. 3
Hampson, Daphne, 180 n. 21
Hannay, Alastair, 169 n. 5
happiness, eternal, 83–86, 90, 115–16
Hartshorne, M. Holmes, 176 n. 19
Henriksen, Aage, 175 n. 12, 176 nn. 17–18
Hegel, G. W. F., 67
Heiberg, Luise, 166 n. 5
Hinkson, Craig Q., 180 n. 21
Holm, Søren, 174 n. 9
Holy Communion, 37, 44, 171 n. 21
Holy Spirit, 43, 80–81, 175 n. 5
    as Comforter, 142, 146
    sin against, 29, 171 n. 20
Hong, Howard V., and Edna H., 170 n. 9,
    173 n. 1, 175 n. 6, 179 nn. 8, 10, 15
honor, 128
hope versus hopelessness, 14, 79–80,
    111–12, 123
Houe, Poul, 167 n. 14
Hough, Sheridan, 171 n. 16
human
    Christian, 89–90, 94
    natural, 86, 88–91, 94, 130–31, 143, 179
    n. 10
    universal human, 89–91, 94
humility, 39–40

imagination, 134–35, 170 n. 11, 179 n. 13,
    180 n. 16
immanence, 13, 82, 85, 88–89, 94, 137, 161

32, 84–89, 89,

, 108, 158

124,

93, 95,
4, 168 n. 18,
180 nn. 17, 22
hidden, 95, 109, 132–33, 137, 151
inversion(s), 47, 149, 154, 161
relating to Christ, 64, 131
relating to Christian suffering, 120–26,
129, 131, 133, 143, 148
relating to confession, 38–39
of vision, 35
Isaac, 126
Ivanhoe, Philip J., 173 n. 2

James, William, 170 n. 10
Job, 126
John the Baptist, 175 n. 7
joy, 14, 119, 143, 162
Judaism, 74, 120, 127, 146, 161, 175 n. 7,
178–79 n. 7, 181 n. 3
Judge William, 94, 180 n. 16
justice, 42

Kangas, David J., 178 n. 6
Keeley, Louise Carroll, 172 n. 30, 176 n. 26
Khan, Abrahim, 178 n. 3
Kierkegaard
as Christian author, poet, and thinker, 1–3,
83, 151, 162–63, 166 n. 7, 171 n. 23
early pseudonymous authorship of, 3, 37,
82, 93–94, 97, 160, 165 n. 1, 176 n. 19
as humanist or Christian humanist, 83,
165 n. 2, 175 n. 8
personal relation to Christianity, 15–16,
20–21, 37
second period of authorship, 1–3, 18–19,
37, 63, 82, 86, 91–92, 109–10, 113,
149, 152, 159–60, 166 n. 5, 178 n. 3,
180 n. 22
as theologian, 5, 166 n. 9
as virtue ethicist, 169 n. 4
WRITINGS
An Occasional Discourse (Purity of
Heart), 12

An Open Letter, 2
An Upbuilding Discourse, 2
Armed Neutrality, 2, 4, 6
Christian Discourses, 2, 18, 21, 37, 48,
104, 107, 114, 138, 143
Concluding Unscientific Postscript, 1, 3, 8,
12, 17, 54, 58–59, 62, 68–69, 82–88,
91, 94–95, 108, 114–16, 119, 136–38,
140–41, 160, 165 n. 4, 169 n. 1, 178
n. 3
Eighteen Upbuilding Discourses, 175 n. 7
Either/Or, 7, 37, 94, 180 n. 16
Fear and Trembling, 59
For Self-Examination, 2, 11, 37, 91,
106–7, 111, 114, 138–39, 175 n. 5
Journals & Papers, 167 n. 15, 169 nn. 2–3,
181 n. 3
Judge for Yourself!, 2, 10, 102, 107, 114,
138–41, 144, 157
On My Work as an Author, 2, 11
Philosophical Fragments, 54–59, 61–62,
67–69
Practice in Christianity, 2, 45–47, 51, 60,
63–64, 69, 107–8, 114, 129–38, 171
n. 21
The Book on Adler, 160, 165 n. 4, 166 n. 8
The Changelessness of God, 2, 148
The Concept of Anxiety, 66, 168 n. 16
The Concept of Irony, 167 n. 11
The Crisis and a Crisis in the Life of an
Actress, 2, 166 n. 5
The Lily in the Field and the Bird of the
Air: Three Devotional Discourses, 2
The Moment, 2, 87, 107
The Point of View for My Work as an
Author, 2
The Sickness unto Death, 2, 20–32, 37, 44,
63, 134, 167–68 n. 16, 169 n. 6, 170
n. 11
"The Single Individual": Two "Notes"
Concerning My Work as an Author, 2
Three Discourses at the Communion on
Fridays, 2
Three Discourses on Imagined Occasions,
170 n. 16
Two Discourses at the Communion on
Fridays, 2
Two Ethical-Religious Essays, 2, 165 n. 4,
179 n. 9
Upbuilding Discourses in Various Spirits,

2, 33–35, 45, 92–93, 109, 114, 117–22, 138, 170 n. 15, 171 nn. 16, 18
Without Authority, 167 n. 15
Works of Love, 2, 18, 79, 93–106, 137, 176 nn. 20, 22, 26, 177 n. 28, 180 n. 18
Kirmmse, Bruce H., 165 n. 3, 179 n. 7
Kjær, Grethe, 172 n. 26
Kodalle, Klaus-M., 170 n. 10
Kuhn, Thomas, 173 n. 2

language, 16, 100
Law, David R., 166 nn. 9–10, 167 n. 11, 168 n. 17, 175 n. 10, 177 n. 28, 178 n. 6
Leibniz, Gottfried, 61–62
Léon, Céline, 168 n. 22, 172 n. 30
Lévi-Strauss, Claude, 178 n. 6
Levinas, Emmanuel, 178 n. 6
Lindström, Valter, 86–89, 104–6, 109–10, 174 n. 1, 175 nn. 11, 14–15, 176 nn. 19, 21, 23, 177 n. 30, 180 n. 18
love
  of Christ, 40–42
  Christian or spiritual, 79–80, 94–101, 175 n. 7, 177 n. 29
  continuity of, 96
  distinctions in, 98
  divine, 79
  of God, 79, 99, 147
  as "hate," 101–2
  natural, pagan, and merely human forms of, 94–97, 175 n. 7, 176 n. 24
  of neighbor, 79, 97–99, 162, 177 n. 28
  recognizability of, 95
  of self, 79, 96–97, 99
  self-denying or sacrificial, 79–80, 82, 93, 99, 102–3, 110
  as sign of being a Christian, 79
  special relations in, 97–98
  works of, 95, 162
Lowrie, Walter, 173 n. 1, 179 n. 8
Luther, Martin, 6, 22, 33, 91–92, 140, 147, 156–57, 180 n. 21, 181 n. 3
Løgstrup, Knud Ejler, 176 n. 27, 178 n. 2
Lønning, Per, 165 n. 1

Mackey, Louis, 174 n. 4
Malantschuk, Gregor, 166 n. 10, 167 n. 12, 168 n. 20, 176 n. 25, 180 nn. 17, 19
Marino, Gordon D., 167 n. 14
marriage, 107, 109, 130–31

Martens, Paul, 175 n. 5
Martensen, Hans Lassen, 25, 170 n. 8
Martin, Harold V., 170 n. 10
martyrdom, 128, 179 n. 9
meritoriousness, 41, 155–56
Molbech, Christian, 175 n. 6
Mynster, Bishop, 145, 169 n. 3, 181 n. 24

negative, the, 8–9, 13–14, 25, 32, 51, 76, 79–80, 93, 109–11, 113, 119, 121, 138, 141, 149–50, 160, 163, 167 n. 16
Nelson, Christopher A. P., 171 n. 18
Nicolaus, Theophilus (Magnus Eiriksson), 58–60, 173 n. 4
Nielsen, Anna, 166 n. 5

objectivity, 107–8
offense
  as despair of forgiveness, 28
  passive or suffering character of, 54–55
  pertaining to Christ, 65–66, 69, 108, 132
  pertaining to the Christian life, 75–76, 107–8
  possibility of, 8–9, 14, 51–77, 108, 130, 162, 173–74, n. 6
  as sin, 27–29
  as stumbling block, 54
otherworldliness, 176 n. 20
Outka, Gene, 174 n. 2, 176 n. 26
outwardness, 74, 83, 93, 95, 102, 108–10, 150–51, 180 n. 22

paganism, 29, 96, 120, 127, 144, 146
pathos, existential or ethical versus aesthetic, 83–84, 90, 114, 116
Pattison, George, 165 n. 2, 175 n. 7
penitence, 38
perfection, 121, 134–36, 138, 155, 169 n. 4
Perkins, Robert L., 169 n. 5, 170 n. 15, 176 n. 22, 179 n. 11
Perkins, Sylvia Walsh, 176 n. 22
Plekon, Michael, 166 n. 9, 171 n. 21, 172 nn. 24–26
Pojman, Louis, 173 n. 2
Polk, Timothy, 177 n. 28
Pons, Jolita, 167 n. 15
Poole, Roger, 167 n. 14, 168 n. 20, 172 n. 27
positive, the, 8, 13–14, 25–26, 47, 76, 79–80, 93, 109–10, 111, 113–14, 121, 134, 149, 152, 160, 163
Possen, David, 181 n. 2

Rae, Murray, 173 n. 2, 181 n. 3
redoubling, 11, 96–97, 168 n. 20, 176 n. 25
  of divine love, 114, 146–48
reduplication
  Christian, 10–11, 14–15, 149, 158, 163
  in general, 10–11, 168 n. 20
reflection, 2–3, 26
Religiousness A, 8, 84–86, 89, 95, 108, 136–37, 151, 169 n. 1
Religiousness B, 84–86, 107–8, 136–37, 140, 151
Religiousness C, 107–9, 177 n. 33, 180 n. 22
repentance, 26, 33–36, 38, 150, 170 n. 9
resignation, 8, 49–50, 82–85, 168 n. 17
Risum, Jane, 166, n. 5
Roberts, Robert C., 169 n. 4
Rocca, Ettore, 171 n. 20
Rose, Tim, 180 n. 21
Rudd, Anthony, 175 n. 16, 176 n. 20, 177 n. 34, 180 n. 18, 181 n. 3

Sass, Else Kai, 172 n. 27
Saxbee, John, 181 n. 24
self, the, 21, 165 n. 3, 168 n. 16
  coram Deo (before God), 22–23
  criterion of, 23, 27–28
  ideal versus actual, 27–28, 63, 149–50
  theological, 23, 27–28
  transformation of, 49, 85, 89–90, 93–94, 99–100, 114, 135–37, 173 n. 2
  unity of, 34, 171 n. 17
self-denial or self-renunciation, 14, 79, 84, 91, 97, 101, 174 nn. 1, 3, 175 n. 7, 176 n. 22
  Christian, 82–83, 86–88, 91–94, 101–6, 109–11, 126, 128, 137–38, 162, 177 n. 31
  ethical-religious or merely human, 91, 94, 102–6
  medieval practice of, 102, 110–11
selfishness, 10, 79, 86, 88, 96–97, 102, 147
sermons
  Christian, 48, 103, 144–45, 171 n. 19, 181 n. 23
  communion, 172 n. 25
Shmuëli, Adi, 33, 170 n. 13
sin
  actuality of, 26
  alleviation of, 47–50
  confession of, 42–43, 171 n. 24

consciousness of, 8, 14, 17–50, 85, 122, 171 n. 20
continuity or consistency of, 26–27, 41–42
definition of, 19–32
as despair, 22
as dialectical, 19, 29–32
forgiveness of, 27–28, 31, 63
as ignorance, 24, 26
knowledge of, 24
as lack of love, 42
as offense, 29
as paradox, 26
Plotinian/Augustinian understanding of, 25
as a position, 25–26
relation to faith, 19
sorrow over, 34–35, 45–46, 48–50
Skjoldager, Emanuel, 33, 170 n. 14, 171 n. 22
Sløk, Johannes, 175 n. 8
Socrates, 24, 120
speculative philosophy and theology, 25, 52–53, 65, 170 n. 9
spiritual trial, 139, 148, 180 n. 19
Sponheim, Paul, 178 n. 1
Stewart, Jon, 167 n. 11, 170 n. 8, 176 n. 22
Strawser, Michael, 181 n. 23
subjectivity, Christian, 8, 165 n. 4
suffering, 8, 14, 113–48
  actual versus idealized, 134–36
  aesthetic, 115–16, 141
  alleviation of, 48–50, 129, 144–46
  Christ as paradigm for, 119–20, 122, 133, 138
  consolation for, 141–46
  earthly, ordinary, or worldly, 129, 141–42, 144–46
  ethical, 114, 117–19, 127
  human conception of, 123
  innocent versus guilty, 18, 120–21, 126, 178 n. 5
  inward versus outward, 85, 115, 118–19, 121–22, 126–27, 130–33, 137–38, 141, 180 n. 18
  occasions for joy in, 115–16, 121–23, 127–28, 138
  religious, 85, 114–16, 119, 121, 168 n. 17
  specifically Christian, 110, 113–14, 116, 120, 123, 126–27, 129–38, 141, 180 n. 18

transcendence of, 115–19, 121
voluntary, 109, 117–19, 126–27, 130,
    141, 149
sympathy, divine versus human, 44, 143, 145
Søe, N. H., 173 n. 3, 174 n. 9
Søltoft, Pia, 176 n. 22

teleological suspension, 107–8
telos, absolute versus relative, 83–84, 115,
    119
temporal, loss of the, 124–25
Taylor, Mark Lloyd, 172 n. 30
Theunissen, Michael, 167 n. 16
Thorvaldsen, Bertel, 172 n. 27
Thulstrup, Marie, 106–7, 109, 177 n. 32,
    178 nn. 2–3, 179 n. 9, 180 nn. 18, 22
Thulstrup, Niels, 172 n. 24, 180 n. 19
Tolstrup, Christian Fink, 176 n. 22, 181 n. 24
truth, the
    Christ as, 133, 179 n. 9
    knowing versus becoming, 5

understanding, human, 55–57, 59, 67–68, 76
upbuilding, the, 21, 37, 97, 137
Utterback, Sylvia Walsh, 167 n. 15

vocation, 171 n. 18
voluntary, the, 126–27

Walsh, Sylvia, 166 nn. 6–7, 11, 167 n. 15,
    168 nn. 18, 22, 171 n. 23, 172 n. 30,
    176 nn. 19–20, 22, 24, 177 n. 28, 179
    n. 13, 180 n. 16, 181 n. 4
Watkin, Julia, 172 n. 26, 177 n. 34, 179 nn.
    11–12
weakness, strength in, 28, 124
Westphal, Merold, 107–9, 168 n. 17, 177
    n. 33, 178 n. 3, 180 nn. 18, 22
will, 24, 30–31, 34, 117, 134–35, 170 nn.
    10–11, 179 n. 14
Wittgenstein, Ludwig, 173 n. 2
woman, women
    negative attitudes toward, 16, 130–31, 168
    n. 18, 172 n. 30, 177 nn. 28, 34, 179
    n. 11
    as prototype of piety, 45, 172 n. 30
working against oneself, 10–11, 26, 146,
    158, 162
worldliness, 89, 91–92, 111, 128

Printed in the United States
113621LV00003B/241-279/P

Made in the USA
Lexington, KY
06 September 2014